DEPRESSION

To Carol
—S.R.

To Kathy, Katie, and Matthew
—M.G.P.

DEPRESSION
A Primer for Practitioners

Steven Richards & Michael G. Perri
Texas Tech University   *University of Florida*

SAGE Publications
International Educational and Professional Publisher
Thousand Oaks ■ London ■ New Delhi

B S

For information:

Sage Publications, Inc.
2455 Teller Road
Thousand Oaks, California 91320
E-mail: order@sagepub.com

Sage Publications Ltd.
6 Bonhill Street
London EC2A 4PU
United Kingdom

Sage Publications India Pvt. Ltd.
M-32 Market
Greater Kailash I
New Delhi 110 048 India

Printed in the United States of America

Library of Congress Cataloging-in-Publication Data

Richards, Steven.
    Depression: A primer for practitioners / Steven Richards and Michael
G. Perri.
        p. cm.
Includes bibliographical references and index.
    ISBN 0-7619-2248-2 (p)
    1. Depression, Mental. I. Perri, Michael G. II. Title.
    RC537 .R525 2002
    616.85′27—dc21   2001006638

02   03   04   05   10   9   8   7   6   5   4   3   2   1

Acquiring Editor: Jim Brace: Thompson
Editorial Assistant: Karen Ehrman
Production Editor: Diane S. Foster
Typesetter/Designer: Siva Math Setters, Chennai, India
Cover Designer: Jane Quaney

4/29/04

Contents

Preface   vii

Acknowledgments   xiii

Part I: Depression: Symptoms and Theories About Therapies   1

  1. The Symptoms, Signs, and Diagnosis of Depression   3

  2. Theories About Therapies for Depression   19

Part II: Depression Across the Life Span   31

  3. Depression in Children   33

  4. Depression in Adolescents   51

  5. Depression in Adults   66

  6. Depression in Older Adults   85

Part III: Comorbid Conditions and Other Symptoms, Signs, and Problems Associated With Depression   99

  7. Additional Psychiatric Disorders and Severely Distressed Close Relationships Associated With Depression   101

  8. Chronic Health Problems Associated With Depression   117

  9. Suicide and Depression   137

Part IV: Treatment of Depression   157

  10. Psychotherapy   159

  11. Pharmacotherapy   180

  12. Relapse Prevention   200

Epilogue   214

References   223

Author Index   261

Subject Index   279

About the Authors   285

Preface

This book is written primarily for practitioners. We believe that a readable, scholarly, applied, and up-to-date book on depression should help the numerous practitioners who work with depressed patients. We understand that it is virtually impossible for most practitioners to keep up with the literature on depression: There have been over 60,000 empirical publications on depression since 1980 (Seligman & Csikszentmihalyi, 2000). Even ambitious depression experts find it challenging to keep up with this literature. Therefore, we wrote *Depression: A Primer for Practitioners*. One of our goals for this book is helping practitioners to stay abreast of the empirical literature on depression.

This book is organized as a primer. Therefore, we provide brief coverage of many of the topics that are central to working with depressed patients. We cannot, of course, cover all of the relevant topics. Moreover, even the topics that we do cover must be discussed briefly. We purposely and strategically include a modest amount of redundancy, particularly regarding therapy issues and clinical guidelines. We appreciate that busy practitioners will sometimes consult certain sections of the book, for context-sensitive information, when using the book as a resource for a particular patient. For example, a psychotherapist who typically works with adult patients may consult the chapter on depression in adolescence when working with an older-adolescent patient who is depressed. Thus, we include some context-sensitive information about therapy and suicide in the adolescence chapter because the practitioner may not reread the three chapters on psychotherapy, pharmacotherapy, and suicide.

The empirical literature and our own clinical experience support the merit of cooperative, interdisciplinary interventions. In addition, a wide array or practitioners work with depressed patients and clients: psychotherapists of all backgrounds and persuasions; clinical, counseling, and school psychologists; social workers; marital and family counselors; general practice physicians; psychiatrists; nurses; ambulance and emergency room staff; physical therapists; occupational therapists; pastors; crisis hotline workers; teachers; school counselors; police officers; and so on. Furthermore, significant others and family members of the depressed individual often want accessible, empirically based information regarding depression. Hence, we have written *Depression: A Primer for Practitioners* for this broad range of practitioners and significant others. For instance, our case studies, which are composites of dozens of cases with all of the identifying information changed, include many types of participants, reflecting our interdisciplinary readership.

The chapters in this book usually have the following organizational scheme within each chapter: overview, case study, discussion of the case study, symptoms, prevalence, risk factors, assessment, treatment, special topics, clinical guidelines, chapter summary, and suggested readings. In a few chapters, however, we have deviated slightly from this organizational scheme to accommodate the relevant topics and to provide more how-to examples.

This book is divided into four parts:

- Part 1: Depression: Symptoms and Theories About Therapies
- Part 2: Depression Across the Life Span
- Part 3: Comorbid Conditions and Other Symptoms, Signs, and Problems Associated With Depression
- Part 4: Treatment of Depression

Part 1, "Symptoms and Theories About Therapies," contains chapters on the symptoms, signs, and diagnosis of depression (Chapter 1) and theories about therapies for depression (Chapter 2). In Chapter 1, we focus on the most common type of serious depression, which is Major Depressive Disorder (American Psychiatric Association, 2000a). This focus dovetails with the goals of our brief volume. It would be far beyond the scope of this book to attempt a thorough discussion of all mood disorders and the many intricacies of differential diagnosis among these mood disorders; hence, we focus on the central topic of this book—depression or Major Depressive Disorder. In Chapter 2, we overview the theoretical literature regarding treatments for depression. We do not discuss the large number of theories regarding the development and course of depression, as this would be impossible in a short primer and is not central to the mission of our book. Rather, we believe that in a primer for practitioners, a discussion of theories about therapies will be the most helpful approach to theory exposition.

In Part 2, "Depression Across the Life Span," there are chapters on children (Chapter 3), adolescents (Chapter 4), adults (Chapter 5), and older adults (Chapter 6). These four chapters follow the organizational scheme within chapters that we noted previously. For example, the chapter on depression in children includes the following topics: overview, case study, discussion of the case study, prevalence, symptoms, assessment, treatment, special topics relevant to children, clinical guidelines, chapter summary, and suggested readings. All of the information in the chapter on children is context sensitive—we discuss issues in the context of depressed children. In alignment with this strategy of supplying context-sensitive information, the chapter on depression in adolescents includes both the standard topics and information on gender differences, close relationships, substance abuse, family interventions, and suicide because these topics are very germane to depressed adolescents. Similarly, the chapter on depression in adults includes both the standard topics and context-sensitive information on interview outlines, coping without professional treatment, electroconvulsive therapy, chronic depression, and a range of ethical, practical, and training issues that are relevant to depressed adults. The chapter on depression in older adults also includes both the standard topics and context-sensitive information regarding assessment, treatment, and special topics relevant to depressed older adults.

Part 3, "Comorbid Conditions and Other Symptoms, Signs, and Problems Associated With Depression," contains chapters on additional psychiatric disorders and severely distressed close relationships associated with depression (Chapter 7), chronic health problems associated with depression (Chapter 8), and suicide and depression (Chapter 9). Here again, the standard chapter organization is often followed, but some modifications are included to provide context-sensitive information, more how-to examples, special topics, and clearer chapter organization. For example, in Chapter 7, we discuss two of the additional psychiatric disorders that are frequently associated with depression: anxiety disorders and alcohol abuse. We also discuss the common association of severely distressed close relationships and depression. In Chapter 8, we discuss three of the chronic health problems that are often associated with depression: cardiovascular disease, cancer, and dementia. In addition, we provide context-sensitive clinical guidelines for each of these chronic health problems. We do not attempt to discuss all of the psychiatric disorders and chronic health problems that are associated with depression, however, because that would take us far beyond the scope of a brief primer. In Chapter 9 on suicide, we again include both the standard chapter topics and some context-sensitive topics such as risk factors, crisis intervention, and ethical issues regarding suicide.

Part 4, "Treatment," contains chapters on psychotherapy (Chapter 10), pharmacotherapy (Chapter 11), and relapse prevention (Chapter 12). The psychotherapy chapter focuses on the two psychotherapies with the most empirical support for treating depression: cognitive behavior therapy and interpersonal psychotherapy. These two psychotherapies enjoy strong empirical support from randomized controlled trials (DeRubeis & Crits-Christoph, 1998; Hollon & Shelton, 2001). Case examples are given in the context of these two treatment approaches. We also acknowledge, of course, that psychotherapists and other practitioners need thorough training in these complex treatments to use them effectively. Furthermore, no primer can come close to supplying all of the necessary information and training. Some additional psychotherapy interventions are discussed very briefly, within the confines of a primer. The pharmacotherapy chapter provides a brief overview of the major Food and Drug Administration (FDA)-approved antidepressant medications, while staying in close alignment with numerous well-regarded reviews and practice guidelines on this topic (e.g., American Psychiatric Association, 2000b; Halbreich & Montgomery, 2000). We also note that we are not physicians and that pharmacotherapy for depression should be prescribed and carefully supervised by qualified physicians. We discuss combinations of pharmacotherapy and psychotherapy, and we provide clinical guidelines for psychotherapists whose patients are receiving these combined treatments. The chapter on relapse prevention includes some of the standard chapter topics, such as a case study and discussion, along with context-sensitive discussions about risk factors, models of relapse, people coping on their own, practical issues, and booster sessions to prevent relapse. The relapse problem has been around for a long time (Richards & Perri, 1978), it is far from completely solved (e.g., Paykel et al., 1999; Reynolds et al., 1999), and it remains one of the more important challenges for practitioners working with depressed patients (e.g., Jarrett et al., 2001; Katon et al., 2001).

Our primer text concludes with a brief epilogue. This epilogue includes a case study, some highlights of the difficult therapeutic challenges for practitioners who are working with depressed patients, and an overview of the prominent clinical guidelines that pervade many of the chapters. We also discuss certain therapeutic themes that arise from these clinical guidelines. As befits an epilogue, there is a short list of suggested readings on depression, which are relatively broad in their coverage, in contrast to the more specific readings that are suggested at the end of each chapter.

At the end of this book there is a complete list of references, an index, and a brief statement about the authors.

We attempted to write a book that is a combination of "scholarly book" plus "how-to book." Our goals included writing chapters that are accessible, research-based, and practical. Moreover, our goals included writing a book with a clear style, broad coverage, extensive documentation, clinical guidelines, and up-to-date citations. We followed the format and strategy of a primer; this should be useful for practitioners who are working with depressed patients. Indeed, most mental health professionals and health care providers, along with practitioners in many other disciplines, have frequent contact with depressed patients and clients. One of our goals was to develop an up-to-date primer that would be a helpful resource for practitioners in this very diverse array of disciplines and settings. In addition, certain family members and significant others of depressed individuals may want clear, empirically based information about depression, and this brief primer may be a useful resource for some of them. First and foremost, however, this is a book for practitioners who are working with depressed patients.

Acknowledgments

In the kind of job that we have, a book gets written on weekends. Thus, our first acknowledgment goes to the Richards family and the Perri family for tolerating our frequent absences on weekends. Thanks go to Carol, Dawn, and Jill Richards, and Kathy, Katie, and Matthew Perri. Our families are wonderfully supportive, empathic, and good-natured. We love them!

Our second acknowledgment goes to university colleagues and staff members who helped us. Susan Hendrick provided thoughtful, supportive, and gracious comments on the early drafts of several of our chapters. Clyde Hendrick, James Rodrigue, and Ronald Rozensky gave us helpful advice about publication strategy. The staff members in our respective departments are always efficient in their efforts to help us. The same goes for the staff members in our respective university libraries: With the publication of over 60,000 empirical articles on depression since 1980, a book like this would be impossible to write without the resources of excellent libraries.

Our third and final acknowledgment goes to the editors, staff members, and reviewers for Sage Publications. These individuals are great to work with. The editor for this book is Jim Brace-Thompson. Jim is a marvelous source of encouragement, expertise, and tact. The staff members at Sage are consistently helpful, and we would particularly like to thank Jim's staff colleague, Karen Ehrmann, and the copy-editor for this book, Elisabeth Magnus. In addition, eight anonymous reviewers for Sage provided thoughtful comments on our book—some in the beginning and some toward the end of our writing efforts.

All of the individuals noted in this acknowledgment have helped us, and we are very grateful for their help.

Steven Richards
Texas Tech University
Lubbock, Texas

Michael G. Perri
University of Florida
Gainesville, Florida

PART I

Depression: Symptoms and Theories About Therapies

1 The Symptoms, Signs, and Diagnosis of Depression

Overview

In this chapter, we discuss the symptoms and signs of Major Depressive Disorder, as outlined in the fourth edition (text revision) of the *Diagnostic and Statistical Manual of Mental Disorders* (*DSM-IV-TR*; American Psychiatric Association, 2000a). We begin the chapter with a case study that illustrates the common symptoms and signs of Major Depressive Disorder. Next, we provide information on prevalence, demographics, symptoms, and comorbid conditions associated with depression. We discuss various assessment methods, including interviews and questionnaires, and we describe the typical course of depression. We present an interview outline for assessing depression, along with clinical guidelines for practitioners who are evaluating depressed patients. Finally, we present a summary and a list of suggested readings.

Case Study

This 28-year-old male patient is very depressed. During his second session with a psychotherapist, he gives the following description of his day.

Patient: I couldn't sleep! It took me hours to fall asleep, and then I woke up several times. I'm really frustrated. I woke up early and couldn't get back to sleep. I feel awful. I was up at 5:00 a.m., so I figured I'd do some work, but I couldn't concentrate—I couldn't think straight! I made some breakfast, but I didn't eat it. I'm never hungry. That's one of the reasons I got a physical. The doctor said that I was okay, but she noticed that I lost weight.

Therapist: One of the things that we focused on last time was your difficulty with concentration. Is this still a major concern for you?

Patient: Yes. I just can't seem to do anything right—even the simple things: I almost missed my train connection for downtown. I logged on to the mainframe incorrectly at work. Any idiot can log on to the machines correctly. Damn . . . I feel worthless now. I'm confused. It all just seems hopeless. The more I try, the more I mess up—I screwed up on some simple transfer programs today, and my boss was really angry. I've never seen him that mad. We had to redo the entire run before I took some leave time to come over here. I'll probably get fired. It's my fault first I messed up with Susan . . . she warned me again and again that we needed to work some things out, but I was too stupid or scared to listen. Now she's already dating someone else, and I feel so down. My life is falling apart, and I don't know what to do. Damn—I can't think straight!

Therapist: How do you cope when your concentration deteriorates?

Patient: Primarily by just trying again. And this has been going on for the last 2 or 3 months. It got particularly bad after Susan and I broke up. Then I started messing up at work. My brother in Kansas City used to be willing to talk with me on the phone, but now his older kid is sick with cancer and he doesn't have time for me. I can't blame him. He shouldn't have to worry about my problems. It's my fault that I'm so screwed up.

Therapist: During our last session, we talked about the cycle of self-blame that you are in. Your focusing on self-blame and guilt doesn't help. We need to get out of this pattern. And we need to understand your day-to-day coping better, so we can problem-solve together and improve some things. What was the rest of your day like?

Patient: I can't concentrate! That is probably my biggest problem. I'll be fired if I don't improve. I won't have a job or friends to rely on. My brother probably thinks that I'm pathetic—and I am.

Therapist: I hear how upset you are. Let's keep our focus so that we can problem-solve. What was the rest of your day like?

Patient: After work yesterday I went home, but I felt bad. I'm always tired, but the doctor says there's nothing wrong with me physically. I didn't eat much supper. It seems like I'm never hungry. Couldn't work. I fell asleep in front of the TV. I'm going to get fired. This whole mess seems hopeless.

Therapist: You've used the word hopeless several times today. We talked about this in our first session, but I need to be certain. Do you have any thoughts about hurting yourself or about suicide?

Patient: You already asked me about that last time. I'm not enough of a man to kill myself. I don't have the courage. I don't even know how I would do it. I'm just down in the dumps and very unhappy—seems like all of the time. I don't get any pleasure out of life, but I'm not thinking of killing myself. I'm not suicidal. I'm just miserable and disorganized. Something needs to change.

Therapist: I agree! Let's talk about what needs to change and how we can gradually do this.

As with all of the case studies in our book, this one is a composite of dozens of similar cases. Any possible identifying information has been changed. But this case is realistic (see Spitzer, Gibbon, Skodol, Williams, & First, 1994). This patient has the standard symptoms and signs of Major

Depressive Disorder as listed in the DSM-IV-TR (American Psychiatric Association, 2000a, pp. 356, 375):

1. Depressed mood, nearly every day
2. Loss of interest or pleasure in most activities
3. Significant changes in weight or appetite
4. Difficulty getting enough sleep, or sleeping too much
5. Slow talking, delayed response to others, or slow movement
6. Feeling tired, nearly every day
7. Feeling guilty and worthless
8. Difficulty concentrating, planning, and making decisions
9. Thoughts about suicide, or a plan, or a suicide attempt

For a diagnosis of Major Depressive Disorder, at least five of the previous nine symptoms must be present, most of the time, for 2 weeks. The symptoms must include either depressed mood (No. 1) or loss of pleasure (No. 2). In addition, the symptoms must be causing significant distress and disruption in day-to-day functioning (American Psychiatric Association, 2000a, pp. 356, 375).

Discussion of the Case Study

In the United States, most mental health practitioners follow the diagnostic criteria for depression from the DSM-IV-TR (American Psychiatric Association, 2000a). The patient's symptoms meet the diagnostic criteria for Major Depressive Disorder. Indeed, his symptoms exceed the minimum needed for a diagnosis of Major Depressive Disorder: He has seven of the nine symptoms; he does not have No. 5 (slow responses) or No. 9 (suicidal thoughts or attempts). His symptoms have been persistently evident for several months, far beyond the 2-week minimum required by DSM-IV-TR. Practitioners may also note the patient's lack of slow talking, his absence of suicidal thoughts, and his obvious anger; these observations may lead to additional assessment comments and treatment decisions. All of the patient's symptoms and signs have treatment implications, including therapeutic strategies to lessen the risk of relapse.

There are also some symptoms and signs that must not be present (i.e., rule-outs), such as obvious periods of mania, or a different diagnosis would be justified. For example, if in addition to the symptoms in his interview, the patient also described episodes of tremendous energy, wildly happy mood, preposterous plans for fame and fortune, and impulsive decisions that he later regretted, this behavior would justify a different diagnosis. If the patient abruptly decided to quit his job and invest his life savings in a "get-rich-quick scheme," this would illustrate the impulsive decisions and poor judgment that we are alluding to. If the patient also decided to try running in a marathon to celebrate his new career, even though he was out of shape, this would further exemplify poor judgment. Such a pattern of signs and symptoms would illustrate the kind of wild energy, inappropriately happy mood, irrational thinking, and impulsive decision making that are common in manic episodes. In this new example, if the mania and depression oscillated back and forth, the diagnosis would probably be Bipolar I Disorder (American Psychiatric Association, 2000a, pp. 388–392), which some clinicians still call Manic-Depressive Disorder. We will not focus on bipolar disorders in this book, but they are important and potentially devastating mood disorders (American Psychiatric Association, 2000b; Goodwin & Ghaemi, 1998; Jamison, 1995).

Alternatively, if the patient's symptoms were due to the physiological effects of a drug, or to the physiological effects of a general medical condition such as a malfunctioning thyroid gland, then the diagnosis of Major Depressive Disorder would not be given. Also, if the patient's symptoms appeared to be due to the death of a loved one, or to a poor adjustment following change and stress, then alternative diagnoses would be made, such as Bereavement or Adjustment Disorder With Depressed Mood (American Psychiatric Association, 2000a, pp. 740–741, 683). Making accurate psychiatric diagnoses requires training, skill, and care. Indeed, entire books have been written on this topic (e.g., Othmer & Othmer, 1994).

Prevalence, Demographics, Symptoms, and Comorbid Conditions

Major Depressive Disorder is common. Large surveys indicate that about 5% of adults in the United States and Canada are experiencing this form of depression at a given point in time. A good example of these large surveys is a study by Murphy, Laird, Monson, Sobol, and Leighton (2000). These investigators assessed depression in Canadian samples that exceeded 1,000 participants during 1952, 1970, and 1992. They found that the point prevalence for depression over a 40-year period has apparently held steady at about 5%. These findings are in alignment with the point prevalence for depression found in several other large epidemiological surveys conducted in the United States (Blazer, Kessler, McGonagle, & Swartz, 1994; Regier et al., 1988).

A 10-nation survey with a sample of 38,000 adults (Weissman et al., 1996) showed similarities—and differences—in the symptoms and rates of depression across nations. For example, in all 10 nations, including the United States, there were more depressed women than men, insomnia and fatigue were common depressive symptoms, and depression was often associated with comorbid conditions such as anxiety disorders and substance abuse. However, the annual prevalence rates of Major Depressive Disorder varied considerably from a low of 0.8% (Taiwan) to a high of 5.8% (New Zealand).

The age groups at highest risk for depression are adolescents and young adults: that is, individuals between the ages of 14 and 35 (Blazer et al., 1994; Cyranowski, Frank, Young, & Shear, 2000; Jorm, 2000; Lewinsohn, Rohde, & Seeley, 1998). More women than men experience depression during adolescence and adulthood, with a ratio of about 2 to 1; there is no gender difference in childhood (Blazer et al., 1994; Nolen-Hoeksema & Girgus, 1994). However, once depression has begun, its course is similar for men and women (Simpson, Nee, & Endicott, 1997).

There are many discussions of the finding that depression is more common in women than men (in both the United States and most other countries). Biological and psychological factors may account for this gender difference (Cyranowski et al., 2000; Frank, 2000; Nolen-Hoeksema & Girgus, 1994; Taylor, Klein, et al., 2000). For instance, Hammen (1997) has speculated that the following psychological factors partially account for depression being more common in women than men: (a) Women are more candid in reporting depression than men are; (b) women in the United States are exposed to more stress, on average, than men are, especially during adolescence; (c) in many cases, women use less effective coping strategies than men do, with women tending to rely on passive strategies like thinking obsessively about their problems, whereas men tend to rely on active strategies like increasing new activities and changing their behaviors; (d) during adolescence, females may experience stronger needs for affiliation and more vulnerability to interpersonal stress, which would increase their risk of depression compared with that of males (Cyranowski et al., 2000; Hammen & Brennan, 2001; Nolen-Hoeksema & Girgus, 1994; Shea, 1998; Taylor, Klein, et al., 2000; Weissman & Olfson, 1995).

No ethnic group, race, professional category, or economic class is immune from depression. There are some differences in the rates of depression across these groups, but we are more impressed with the similarities than the differences (Blazer et al., 1994; Regier et al., 1988; Weissman et al., 1996).

There is evidence that a high level of somatic symptoms in depression, such as problems with sleeping and eating, may be a particularly common feature of the disorder. Severe levels of somatic or "vegetative" symptoms may also predict a more challenging treatment effort for patients (Buchwald & Rudick-Davis, 1993; Dew et al., 1997; Giles Kupfer, Rush, & Roffwarg, 1998; Roberts, Shema, Kaplan, & Strawbridge, 2000).

Subthreshold depressive symptoms—that is, a depressive symptom profile not meeting the threshold for a diagnosis of Major Depressive Disorder—may still be quite disruptive for day-to-day performance and psychosocial functioning in many individuals (e.g., Flett, Vredenburg, & Krames, 1997; Lewinsohn, Solomon, Seeley, & Zeiss, 2000).

There is evidence that depression runs in families (Hammen, 1997). For example, studies indicate that there is family aggregation of adolescent depression (Klein, Lewinsohn, Seeley, & Rohde, 2001). A number of studies indicate that there is probably a moderate genetic diathesis for depression, along with the shared environmental factors that would increase family aggregation of depression (e.g., McGuffin, Katz, Watkins, & Rutherford, 1996; Weissman, Warner, Wickramaratne, Moreau, & Olfson, 1997).

Other mental disorders often occur with depression (Blazer et al., 1994; Chorpita, Albano, & Barlow, 1998). Anxiety disorders are likely to occur with depression (Mineka, Watson, & Clark, 1998; Regier, Rae, Narrow, Kaelber, & Schatzberg, 1998; Zlotnick, Warshaw, Shea, & Keller, 1997). Depression also frequently accompanies problems with substance abuse, such as alcoholism (Hammen, 1997). Furthermore, depression is often associated with eating disorders like Bulimia Nervosa (American Psychiatric Association, 2000b; Sanderson, Beck, & Beck, 1990). Additional negative symptoms may occasionally occur with depression, such as the psychological symptoms of extreme anger (Kopper & Epperson, 1996). Indeed, depression itself may represent a broad array of associated, but not identical, mental health disorders (American Psychiatric Association, 2000a; Flett et al., 1997; Kendler & Gardner, 1998; Santor & Coyne, 2001).

When depression occurs concurrently with other mental disorders, with chronic health problems, or with reduced social support, its consequences may be more serious. For instance, people in these circumstances have more trouble coping effectively with interpersonal stress (Clark, Cook, & Snow, 1998; Daley et al., 1997; Judd et al., 2000; Marx, Williams, & Claridge, 1992; Newman, Moffitt, Caspi, & Silva, 1998). Also, depression may increase the risk for developing coronary heart disease in both men and women (Ferketich, Schwartzbaum, Frid, & Moeschberger, 2000; Penninx et al., 2001), and once patients have developed coronary heart disease, chronic depression is a strong risk factor for further health problems (Frasure-Smith, Lesperance, & Talajic, 1995; Frasure-Smith et al., 2000). Moreover, reduced social support appears to increase the risk for relapse back into depression (Holahan, Moos, Holahan, & Cronkite, 2000). Finally, depression is associated with problematic relationships (Burns, Sayers, & Moras, 1994; Whisman, 2001; Whisman & Bruce, 1999).

Assessing Depression

The primary method for evaluating depression is a thorough interview. Clinicians sometimes use structured interviews, tailored after *DSM-IV-TR*. This enhances agreement between different evaluators. An example of a structured clinical interview is the Structured Clinical Interview for *DSM-IV* Axis I Disorders, Clinician Version (SCID-I; First, Gibbon, Spitzer, & Williams, 1997). This structured approach to interviewing patients about their depressive symptoms has been around for a while, and it is popular with researchers because their findings often depend on extremely accurate diagnoses and precise results (Eaton, Neufeld, Chen, & Cai, 2000; Grundy, Lunnen, Lambert, Ashton, & Tovey, 1994; Murphy, Monson, Laird, Sobol, & Leighton, 2000).

Although experienced clinicians will also find structured interview protocols such as the SCID-I to be helpful, clinicians can often arrive at an accurate diagnosis without this much structure. A careful and planned interview of the patient, for 1 to 2 hours, and a thorough coverage of the diagnostic guidelines in *DSM-IV-TR* (American Psychiatric Association, 2000a; see also Othmer & Othmer, 1994) will often suffice. This is what is typically done in clinical practice, of course, as opposed to government-funded research projects (Blazer et al., 1994; Murphy, Laird, et al., 2000; Regier et al., 1988). The clinician asks questions regarding the symptom groups outlined in *DSM-IV-TR*, observes the patient's symptoms and signs, and follows up on comments made by the patient. Two advantages of any interview, independent of the level of structure, are that (a) the clinician can see the patient, so he or she can observe some of the patient's symptoms and signs, and (b) the clinician can be flexible, so he or she can pursue new information and issues as these matters become relevant.

Questionnaires are also commonly used to screen for depression and to facilitate the assessment of depression, but they should not be used for making a diagnosis (Katz, Shaw, Vallis, & Kaiser, 1995; Kendall, Hollon, Beck, Hammen, & Ingram, 1987; Zimmerman & Coryell, 1994). Interview-based evaluations are required for making a diagnosis (American Psychiatric Association, 2000a, 2000b). Still, questionnaires can be useful; for example, they provide a quick survey of the range and severity of symptoms experienced by a patient, they provide consistent coverage of symptoms, and they are inexpensive and easy to administer. The best-known questionnaire for depression is the Beck Depression Inventory (BDI), available in a revised edition, the BDI-II (Beck, Steer, & Brown, 1996). Beck and his colleagues developed this questionnaire and conducted extensive psychometric research on it (Beck, Steer, & Garbin, 1988). This questionnaire has 21 items that ask about the cognitive, emotional, and somatic symptoms of depression experienced in the past 2 weeks. Although the BDI-II is a useful assessment tool, it should not be used alone when evaluating patients (Kendall et al., 1987). Interviews are always necessary for an accurate diagnosis of depression.

Another well-known questionnaire on depression is the Center for Epidemiologic Studies–Depression Scale (CES-D). The CES-D is a 20-item self-report scale developed by Radloff (1977) for use in survey research. It asks for self-reports on depressive symptoms that the participant has experienced during the past week. There is less emphasis on somatic symptoms than in some alternative inventories, such as the BDI-II. The CES-D has many of the same measurement strengths and weaknesses, however, as the BDI-II (Beck et al., 1988; Katz et al., 1995; Nezu, Ronan, Meadows, & McClure, 2000; Radloff & Locke, 1986; Zimmerman & Coryell, 1994).

We should also mention that interviews are very helpful for evaluating suicidal symptoms and signs, which are sometimes associated with depression. Notice that this was done in our case study, and notice that the patient denied any suicidal thoughts, plans, or attempts. Even very brief screening interviews may assist busy practitioners to screen for suicidal patients and to then pursue more extensive evaluations with the high-risk patients (Cooper-Patrick, Crum, & Ford, 1994). In the following example, the patient is obviously evidencing high suicidal risk.

Patient: It just seems hopeless. Totally hopeless! It always hurts. The pain never stops. . . . I don't mean physical pain, but . . . I don't know . . . some kind of emotional pain. Know what I mean?

Therapist: I'm not sure. Please tell me more.

Patient: I just can't stand it anymore. I'm thinking of getting out. I'm just totally out of gas. I might as well give up. Maybe it's too bad that I just stared at my gun for hours last night. Maybe I should have used it! What a mess! I just need to end it all. I should probably use my gun.

Some questionnaires may not accurately reflect this patient's obvious risk for suicide, but an interview with a skilled practitioner will. The CES-D does not even have a suicide risk question, and the one direct suicide question (Item 9) on the BDI-II may not be answered accurately by some depressed patients—it is easier to "fool" a questionnaire than a skilled interviewer. Unfortunately, some practitioners are insensitive to suicidal risks in their patients and clients. For example, Mike Wallace, famous for his work on the CBS program *60 Minutes,* indicated that when he was very suicidal his physician was skeptical and did not pursue the issue ("Special," 1998). Fortunately, Mike Wallace's wife did understand the seriousness of his suicidal symptoms and did get him help. We discuss these assessment issues further in Chapter 9 on suicide.

Course of Depression

For adults, the typical episode of depression lasts from 12 to 20 weeks (Eaton et al., 1997; Solomon et al., 1997). About 80% of all depressed individuals will move outside of the diagnostic range for Major Depressive Disorder, and thus "recover," within a year (American Psychiatric Association, 2000a; Coryell et al., 1994). (Dysthymic Disorder, a low-level but chronic form of depression lasting at least 2 years, is discussed in Chapter 5 on adults.)

However, about 80% of formerly depressed individuals will have several relapses back into serious depression during their lifetime (Judd et al., 2000; Kessing, Andersen, Mortensen, & Bolwig, 1998; Mueller et al., 1999; Solomon et al., 2000). Therefore, relapse is a challenging treatment issue regarding depression: We can usually treat depression effectively, but most patients will eventually relapse. We need to develop better relapse prevention strategies. This topic is discussed further in our chapter on relapse prevention (Chapter 12).

Some experts make a distinction between *relapse* and *recurrence*. They refer to a worsening of depression after a partial improvement as a relapse. They refer to a new episode of depression after complete recovery from the previous episode as a recurrence (American Psychiatric Association, 2000a; Beckham & Leber, 1995; Hammen, 1997). By complete recovery, we mean that the patient no longer meets diagnostic criteria for Major Depressive Disorder in *DSM-IV-TR* (American Psychiatric Association, 2000a) and that few depressive symptoms and signs are evident. However, the research literature does not offer compelling evidence to support a reliable distinction between relapse and recurrence (American Psychiatric Association, 2000b). Hence, for the sake of simplicity, we will use the term relapse to cover both types of deterioration.

Interview Outline for Assessing Depression

The following interview outline may be used with patients of all ages, except preadolescent children. We present an interview outline specifically for adults in Chapter 5.

- Establish rapport with your patient and then screen for symptoms.
- Collect thorough information about your patient's current life situation, and selectively seek information about relevant historical events that may have triggered depression.
- Ask about the various dimensions of depression, including the nature of your patient's symptoms, along with the durability of the symptoms, situational concomitants, and comorbid conditions (e.g., Othmer & Othmer, 1994).
- Always screen for suicidal ideation and plans.
- If your patient appears suicidal, arrange for immediate and emergency care for him or her.
- Consider rule-outs for a diagnosis of Major Depressive Disorder, including mania, psychotic disorders, drug effects, physiologic effects of a general medical condition, dysthymia (low-level but chronic depression for at least 2 years), and short-term bereavement

(less than 2 months) (American Psychiatric Association, 2000a). For instance, you should assess for manic episodes because these episodes have important diagnostic and treatment implications.

- Assess for comorbid conditions, particularly anxiety disorders and substance abuse.
- Before concluding that the appropriate diagnosis is Major Depressive Disorder, double-check that your patient has persistently experienced at least five of the nine *DSM-IV-TR* symptoms, including depressed mood or loss of interest and pleasure, for 2 weeks (American Psychiatric Association, 2000a).
- Do some follow-up on your preliminary observations and impressions.
- Develop a tentative diagnosis and discuss this with your patient.
- Talk about prognosis, treatment options, and long-term consequences with your patient.
- Your patient should also get a physical exam by a qualified health care professional if he or she has not had such an exam recently.

Clinical Guidelines

In all of our chapters, except Chapter 2 on theories about therapies, we present a brief list of clinical guidelines for practitioners. These clinical guidelines are derived from the empirical literature, treatment manuals, practice guidelines, reviews, and our own psychotherapy experience. The following clinical guidelines include general suggestions for assessing depressed patients that may be added to the previous interview outline.

- Always conduct a cautious and thorough interview.
- Use an interdisciplinary effort. Seek appropriate input from physicians, health care providers, and mental health professionals to get a thorough and accurate assessment of your patient. It is helpful to have a physician or an advanced nurse practitioner to consult with on a regular basis.
- Take the developmental level and health status of your patient into account, as well as the quality of close relationships in your patient's life.

- Expect your assessment effort to take some time—at least 1 to 2 hours. Depressed patients are typically upset, confused, and inefficient. You may need to split the interview into two sessions, thereby reducing patient fatigue and distress.
- Build in relapse prevention strategies from the beginning to the end of your intervention. For example, work collaboratively with your patient to anticipate future situations that will pose a high risk for relapse, and include booster sessions in your treatment program.
- Be empathic.
- Keep abreast of clinical research on the assessment and treatment of depression. Pursue continuing education on a regular basis.

Chapter Summary

About 5% of adults are seriously depressed at a given point in time. The symptoms and signs of Major Depressive Disorder include the following: depressed mood, loss of pleasure, changes in appetite, sleep difficulties, slow responding, fatigue, guilt, concentration problems, and suicidal thoughts. To meet the criteria for a diagnosis of Major Depressive Disorder, at least five of these symptoms, including depressed mood or loss of pleasure, must be present for 2 weeks; the symptoms must also be causing problems with day-to-day functioning.

The risk for depression is highest among adolescents and young adults (ages 14–35). Depression is more common among adult women than men. Depression often occurs with other mental disorders, including anxiety disorders, substance abuse, and eating disorders; it is also frequently associated with chronic health problems, such as cancer and heart disease. The typical episode of depression lasts from 12 to 20 weeks. Most depressed people recover within a year, but most of these people will relapse back to serious depression on several occasions during their lifetime. Thus, prevention of relapse is a major treatment challenge facing depressed patients and their therapists.

Clinical guidelines for the assessment of depressed patients were presented, including recommendations to always conduct a thorough interview and to never omit an assessment of the potential for suicide.

Suggested Readings

At the end of each chapter, we present a few suggested readings. This will be helpful for practitioners who wish to pursue a few of the most important and recent readings regarding the topics in that chapter.

Discussions

Diagnosis

- *DSM-IV-TR* (American Psychiatric Association, 2000a) is used by most mental health professionals in the United States. The *DSM-IV* was initially published in 1994 (American Psychiatric Association, 1994). A newer edition with revised text—but identical diagnostic criteria—was published in 2000 (American Psychiatric Association, 2000a). Although the diagnostic criteria remain the same in the 2000 edition, its text discussions of matters such as prevalence, associated features, and course of depression have been updated. This reference is indispensable for practitioners who frequently work with depressed patients.

Comorbid Conditions

- Mineka et al. (1998) reviewed the association between depression and anxiety disorders. These comorbid conditions are common, and this scholarly review is interesting and helpful.

Case Studies

- The *DSM-IV Casebook* (Spitzer et al., 1994) is a collection of case studies that put some clinical flesh on the diagnostic bones of the *DSM-IV*.

Studies

- Blazer et al. (1994) conducted an interview study with 8,098 participants (ages 15–54) from the 48 states in the continental United States. They found a point prevalence of approximately 5% for Major Depressive Disorder.

- Lewinsohn, Allen, Seeley, and Gotlib (1999) conducted a longitudinal study involving 1,709 adolescent participants. Their findings indicated that stress was a strong predictor of first episodes, whereas depressive symptoms and dysfunctional thinking were strong predictors of relapse episodes.
- Murphy, Laird, et al. (2000) conducted an interview study with three Canadian samples that were assessed over a 40-year period. Their findings indicated that the point prevalence for depression is probably holding steady at about 5%.
- Newman et al. (1998) conducted a longitudinal investigation with 961 participants, who were repeatedly evaluated from ages 3 to 21. Their findings suggested that comorbid conditions yielded difficulties for treatment planning, delivery, and adherence.
- Solomon et al. (2000) conducted a longitudinal study with 318 treated depressed patients. Their findings indicated that two thirds of the patients suffered a serious relapse.
- Weissman et al. (1996) conducted a cross-national investigation of 38,000 participants in 10 nations. Their interview findings indicated that depression was more prevalent among adult women than men in all 10 of the national samples.

2 Theories About Therapies for Depression

Overview

In this chapter, we emphasize theories about therapies for depression. Because this book is a primer for practitioners, we believe that an emphasis on theories about therapies will be the most helpful approach to theory exposition. There are also many theories regarding the development and course of depression, but this vast literature is far beyond the scope of our brief primer. We focus on the two most investigated psychotherapies for depression, namely cognitive behavior therapy and interpersonal psychotherapy. We also briefly mention theories on behavior therapy and pharmacotherapy. Clinical guidelines for practitioners regarding the use of cognitive behavior therapy, interpersonal psychotherapy, behavior therapy, and pharmacotherapy are provided in Chapters 10 and 11. We conclude this chapter with a summary and a list of suggested readings.

Cognitive Behavior Therapy

Cognitive behavior therapy is based on the theory that dysfunctional thinking styles—and the consequent maladaptive behaviors—exacerbate and maintain depression in people who have a vulnerability toward this disorder. The vulnerability may be a complex array of genetic, biological, psychosocial, and environmental risk factors. The dysfunctional thinking styles may also increase the risk for relapse into further episodes of depression. Thus, the therapeutic focus in this approach is on helping patients to change their thinking and behavior to more functional and adaptive styles. This, of course, is easier said than done, which is part of the reason that a skilled psychotherapist can be so helpful here.

The central thesis of this theory is that depression is made worse and maintained, in part, by a bias toward negative interpretations. This bias is combined with tendencies to pursue reinforcement and handle social interactions in an ineffective manner. Examples of the bias toward dysfunctional thinking include unrealistically negative interpretations of the self, world, and future. This is called the "negative triad" (Beck, Rush, Shaw, & Emery, 1979; Clark & Beck, 1999). Even when these negative interpretations are relatively accurate rather than obviously distorted, the dysfunctional thinking style entails a relentless focus on negative aspects and an equally relentless avoidance of positive aspects, which presumably worsens and maintains the depressed mood, along with increasing the risk for relapse. Moreover, there is substantial evidence that dysfunctional thinking does play a role in exacerbating and maintaining depression (e.g., Clark & Beck, 1999; Ingram, Miranda, & Segal, 1998; Zuroff, Blatt, Sanislow, Bondi, & Pilkonis, 1999), especially recurrent depression (e.g., Clark, 2001; Gemar, Segal, Sagrati, & Kennedy, 2001; Lewinsohn et al., 1999, Lewinsohn et al., 2001). We should caution, however, that mediation, specificity, and comorbidity issues regarding these dysfunctional thinking styles have yet to be fully explicated (e.g., Burns & Spangler, 2001; Dozois & Dobson, 2001).

Specific examples of dysfunctional thinking styles that are relevant to depression include *overgeneralization, selective abstraction, arbitrary inference,* and *magnification/minimization.* Overgeneralization entails drawing broad negative conclusions based on limited data. For instance, a depressed man may conclude, "I'm worthless because I did a poor job at work today," even though he usually does an effective job at work. *Selective abstraction* entails a negative bias to selectively attend to only part of the data. For instance, a depressed woman may conclude, "I'm a lousy parent because my oldest child flunked out of college, and I feel guilty about this," even though all four of her children have usually done well in school and the academic difficulties of this child were due to many factors beyond her control. *Arbitrary inference* entails reaching a conclusion without sufficient evidence. For instance, a depressed adolescent girl may conclude, "I'm pathetic and worthless because none of my teachers like me," even though there is no evidence for this–her teachers are actually friendly to her and she is doing well in school. *Magnification/minimization* entails exaggerating the negative and belittling the positive–particularly regarding personal evaluations. For instance, a depressed elderly man may conclude, "I'm a hopeless wreck who is a drag on everyone because of my health problems and limitations," despite numerous contributions as a volunteer that he is minimizing and infrequent illnesses that he is maximizing.

Changing dysfunctional thinking is not enough, however. Depressed individuals need to change their behavior too (e.g., Hayes & Strauss, 1998). Indeed, cognitive behavior therapists draw heavily on interventions for enhancing reinforcement, social skill, communication style, stress management, and problem solving (e.g., Beck et al., 1979; D'Zurilla & Nezu, 1999; Gilbert, 2000; Goldfried & Davison, 1994; Hammen, 1997; Persons, 1989). Although the theoretical literature on cognitive behavior therapy for depression is somewhat inconsistent in presenting a balanced focus on both thinking and behavior, the outcome literature is clear: Both thinking and behavior need to change (American Psychiatric Association, 2000b; Hollon & Shelton, 2001).

Nonspecific factors also play a role, of course, in cognitive behavior therapy (Ilardi & Craighead, 1994). For example, cognitive behavior therapy for depression is more likely to be efficacious when the following nonspecific factors are present: The therapist is able to effectively structure the treatment and present a clear treatment rationale (Ilardi & Craighead, 1994; Shaw et al., 1999); the therapist is highly empathic (Burns & Nolen-Hoeksema, 1992); there is a strong therapeutic alliance between the therapist and the patient (Gilbert, 2000; Safran, 1998; Safran & Segal, 1990; Zuroff et al., 2000); and the patient complies with homework assignments (Burns & Spangler, 2000; Ilardi & Craighead, 1994; Nezu, Nezu, & Perri, 1989).

There is a sizable literature supporting cognitive behavioral theory as a model for treating depression (Clark, 2001; Clark & Beck, 1999).

Nevertheless, investigators have found it challenging to identify reliable features of treatment specificity in cognitive behavior therapy for depression that correlate with outcome (DeRubeis & Crits-Christoph, 1998; Gortner, Gollan, Dobson, & Jacobson, 1998; Jacobson et al., 1996; Kazdin, 1999, 2000; Kolko, Brent, Baugher, Bridge, & Birmaher, 2000; Nathan, Stuart, & Dolan, 2000).

In summary, we know that cognitive behavior therapy is an efficacious treatment for depression (American Psychiatric Association, 2000b; Craighead, Craighead, & Ilardi, 1998; DeRubeis, Gelfand, Tang, & Simons, 1999; Hollon & Shelton, 2001). We know that the previously mentioned nonspecific factors enhance cognitive behavior therapy. However, we do not know which treatment components of cognitive behavior therapy are correlated with outcome. Finally, we should caution that efficacious treatment outcome does not logically "prove" causation: Aspirin cures a headache, but this outcome does not prove that headaches are due to a lack of aspirin.

Even a modest review of the huge empirical literature on the cognitive behavioral theory of depression is beyond the scope of this chapter. Therefore, we recommend that readers who wish to pursue a thorough review of the literature consult the Clark and Beck (1999) book, the Beck et al. (1979) treatment manual, and the Ingram et al. (1998) book.

Interpersonal Psychotherapy

There is overwhelming evidence that chronic depression is associated with severe distress in close relationships. Furthermore, the literature suggests that seriously distressed close relationships may potentially exacerbate and maintain depression (e.g., Barnett & Gotlib, 1988; Beach, 2001; Daley et al., 1997; Hendrick, 1995; Joiner & Coyne, 1999; Swindle, Heller, Pescosolido, & Kikuzawa, 2000; Whisman & Bruce, 1999). Thus, it is not surprising that psychotherapeutic approaches emphasizing interpersonal issues have been developed for treating depression. The best known of these, in terms of both the theoretical model and the specific therapy techniques, is interpersonal psychotherapy, which was developed by Gerald Klerman, Myrna Weissman, and their colleagues

(Klerman, Weissman, Rounsaville, & Chevron, 1984). Other experts have expanded and modified this approach for specific populations of depressed individuals (e.g., Markowitz, 1998, for Dysthymic Disorder patients; Markowitz et al., 1998, for depressed HIV-positive patients). Moreover, this approach has also been blended with cognitive behavioral interventions (e.g., Gilbert, 2000; Leahy & Holland, 2000). We will focus, however, on the well-known model developed by Klerman et al. (1984).

There is considerable evidence that interpersonal psychotherapy is an efficacious intervention for depression (American Psychiatric Association, 2000b; Hollon & Shelton, 2001; Spanier & Frank, 1998; Weissman & Markowitz, 1998). For example, interpersonal psychotherapy has evidenced promise with depressed adolescents (Mufson, Weissman, Moreau, & Garfinkel, 1999; Rossello & Bernal, 1999), depressed postpartum women (O'Hara, Stuart, Gorman, & Wenzel, 2000), and recurrently depressed older adults (Reynolds et al., 1999). Nevertheless, these positive outcome studies do not "prove" the theoretical premise that dysfunctional interpersonal relationships exacerbate and maintain depression. Efficacious treatment studies, by themselves, cannot prove this theory.

Numerous longitudinal and cross-sectional studies, however, indicate that dysfunctional interpersonal relationships and ineffective interpersonal skills—particularly for dealing with close relationships—are strongly associated with depression. Even a brief review of this massive literature is beyond the scope of the chapter, but we refer readers to the following studies as good examples: Davila, Hammen, Burge, Paley, and Daley (1995); Greenberger, Chen, Tally, and Dong (2000); Hammen and Brennan (2001); Hammen, Henry, and Daley (2000); Monroe, Rhode, Seeley, and Lewinsohn (1999); and Sadowski, Ugarte, Kolvin, Kaplan, and Barnes (1999).

The theory behind interpersonal psychotherapy focuses on four types of interpersonal problems: *grief, role disputes, role transitions,* and *interpersonal deficits* (Klerman et al., 1984). Grief refers to chronic levels of dysfunctional and abnormal grief, which is not resolved through existing close relationships, social support, new activities, and emotional healing. An example would be a depressed man who refuses to cope with the long-ago death of his brother. He may avoid coping attempts by not pursuing his other close relationships, exploring new social resources, or making a sincere effort to reach some emotional closure about his brother's death. Role disputes are problems with significant others, family members, colleagues, and other individuals that we have frequent interactions with; these disputes take on a dysfunctional and unrealistic pattern in important aspects of intimacy, functioning, or self-perception. An example would be a depressed adolescent girl who argues relentlessly and unrealistically with her parents about wanting total freedom and no responsibility in household matters. Role transitions overlap with role disputes, but the focus is more on the transition themes and less on the dispute themes; inaccurate perceptions, ineffective skills, and poor adaptation to change are emphasized here. An example would be a depressed mother who is reentering the work force with little success and pleasure, while desperately missing her grown child who recently moved away from home. Interpersonal deficits are deficits in skills of close relationships that are often related to depression, such as difficulties forming friendships, communication problems, and poor negotiation strategies. An example would be a depressed husband who has no friends outside his marriage, refuses to discuss important issues with his wife, and then has temper tantrums when his wife suggests compromises.

The theory behind interpersonal psychotherapy is clear. There is some empirical support for it. Moreover, the outcome literature is auspicious—particularly regarding depressed populations where interpersonal concerns are frequently obvious, such as depressed adolescents, postpartum women, and socially isolated older adults (Mufson et al., 1999; O'Hara et al., 2000; Reynolds et al., 1999; Rossello & Bernal, 1999). As with cognitive behavior therapy, however, we are not clear about the precise mechanism of action for interpersonal psychotherapy, and treatment specificity is far from certain (e.g., Rossello & Bernal, 1999).

For readers who wish to explore the theoretical (and applied) aspects of interpersonal psychotherapy in some detail, we especially recommend the book by Klerman et al. (1984), along with Markowitz's (1998) extension of this intervention to Dysthymic Disorder.

Behavior Therapy

The theory regarding behavior therapy emphasizes dysfunctional learning history, inadequate positive reinforcement, insufficient skill development, and environmental stress as variables that exacerbate and maintain depression. Therefore, behavior therapy interventions emphasize increased positive reinforcement, shaping, role playing of enhanced social and communication skills, environmental improvement, and planned behavior change. Some of the most compelling research from this theoretical perspective is with depressed children and adolescents, and the findings have often been promising (Hammen, 1997; Leahy & Holland, 2000; Lewinsohn et al., 1998; Schwartz, Gladstone, & Kaslow, 1998). The specific treatment components in behavior therapy that are most responsible for success, however, are not clear (Craighead et al., 1998; Kazdin & Weisz, 1998). Certain aspects of the theory regarding behavior therapy are sometimes blended into other skill enhancement therapy models, such as problem-solving therapy (e.g., D'Zurilla & Nezu, 1999; Nezu et al., 1989) and self-control therapy (e.g., Rehm, 1977).

Pharmacotherapy

The primary focus in this chapter is on two psychological treatment approaches–cognitive behavior therapy and interpersonal psychotherapy. Hence, we will give only very brief attention to biological theories. There is overwhelming evidence for the efficacy of pharmacotherapy treatment regarding depression, which is suggestive but not definitive support for biological theories implicating neurotransmitter uptake and transmission (American Psychiatric Association, 2000b; Halbreich & Montgomery, 2000; Nemeroff & Schatzberg, 1998; *Physicians' Desk Reference [PDR]*, 2000; Rankin, 2000; Thase & Kupfer, 1996). Norepinephrine and serotonin are the neurotransmitters most extensively studied regarding depression, but dopamine and acetylcholine have also received considerable research attention. Abnormal neurotransmitter levels and inadequate neurotransmission are two of the biological hypotheses regarding potential causes of depression. Inhibiting reuptake of these neurotransmitters and enhancing neurotransmission of postsynaptic reception are two of the theoretical mechanisms used to account for positive pharmacotherapy effects (Halbreich & Montgomery, 2000; Rankin, 2000).

The exact biological mechanisms for the etiology of depression and the efficacious pharmacotherapy of depression, however, remain less than entirely clear. Recent studies continue to explore and clarify these complicated biological processes (e.g., Lambert, Johansson, Agren, & Friberg, 2000; Mann et al., 2000; Meyer et al., 2001; Sargent et al., 2000; Yatham et al., 1999, Yatham et al., 2000). Investigations on the genetic diathesis for depression, the role of the neuroendocrine system (e.g., the hypothalamic-pituitary-adrenocortical axis and cortisol hormones), and the impact of gonadal hormones (e.g., estradiol) are also receiving considerable attention, particularly regarding depression in women (e.g., Cyranowski et al., 2000; Goodyer, Herbert, Tamplin, & Altham, 2000; Halbreich, 2000; Posener et al., 2000; Silberg et al., 1999; Young, Midgley, Carlson, & Brown, 2000).

Biological theories for the etiology of depression and for the efficacy of pharmacotherapy are complex. Many nonmedical psychotherapists are not thoroughly conversant with this literature. In any case, qualified physicians should carefully supervise pharmacotherapy regimens for depressed patients. But nonmedical psychotherapists will still find it helpful to have some familiarity with the pharmacotherapy literature regarding depression because their patients may ask them questions about such matters as the likely therapeutic mechanisms, treatment efficacy, and side effects. Thus, we recommend the pharmacotherapy references in the suggested readings at the end of this chapter.

Chapter Summary

The two most investigated psychotherapies for treating depression are cognitive behavior therapy and interpersonal psychotherapy. The theory behind cognitive behavior therapy maintains that a combination of dysfunctional thinking styles and maladaptive behaviors exacerbates and maintains depression. The efficacy of cognitive behavior therapy has been established, but this is only partial support for the theory behind it. There is considerable evidence that dysfunctional thinking plays a role in worsening and maintaining depression. Studies on treatment specificity have yielded mixed results, however, a finding that is not in alignment with the theoretical predictions for cognitive behavior therapy.

The theory behind interpersonal psychotherapy maintains that dysfunctional interpersonal relationships and ineffective interpersonal skills are variables that may exacerbate and maintain depression. There is partial support for these theoretical predictions, and there is clear support for the efficacy of interpersonal psychotherapy. We remind the reader, however, that efficacious treatment does not prove causation. There is little research on treatment specificity for interpersonal psychotherapy, and the results on specificity are less than entirely clear.

The theory regarding behavior therapy emphasizes dysfunctional learning history, inadequate positive reinforcement, insufficient skill development, and environmental stress as variables that exacerbate and maintain depression. Therefore, behavior therapy interventions emphasize increased positive reinforcement, shaping, role playing of enhanced social and communication skills, environmental improvement, and planned behavior change. Some of the most compelling research from this theoretical perspective is with depressed children and adolescents, and the findings have often been promising.

Although the efficacy of pharmacotherapy for treating depression is well established, the precise mechanisms of action remain unclear. Biological theories implicate abnormal neurotransmitter levels and inadequate neurotransmission as potential causes of depression, which pharmacotherapy presumably corrects. The exact biological mechanisms, however, are complicated and not fully understood.

Suggested Readings

Discussions

Cognitive Behavior Therapy

- Clark and Beck (1999) offered an analysis of the theory behind cognitive behavior therapy and the empirical support for this approach to treating depression. Aaron Beck and his colleagues are considered the major developers of this theoretical and treatment approach. For a recent review of the treatment outcome literature, see Hollon and Shelton (2001). For clinical guidelines and case examples, see Beck et al. (1979), Goldfried and Davison (1994), Leahy and Holland (2000), Persons (1989), Persons, Davidson, and Tompkins (2001), and Young, Beck, and Weinberger (1993).

- Ingram et al. (1998) discussed theory and research regarding cognitive vulnerability in people who experience depression. Assessing and modifying this cognitive vulnerability is a primary focus in cognitive behavior therapy of depression.

Interpersonal Psychotherapy

- Klerman et al. (1984) discussed the theoretical rationale for interpersonal psychotherapy, along with a summary of the empirical support available at that time. Gerald Klerman, Myrna Weissman, and their colleagues are considered the major developers of this theoretical and treatment approach. This book includes clinical guidelines and case examples.
- Weissman and Markowitz (1998) offered an updated summary of the theory and research on interpersonal psychotherapy (see also Markowitz, 1998; Spanier & Frank, 1998).

Interpersonal Psychotherapy and Cognitive Behavior Therapy

- Gilbert (2000) blended the theoretical principles of interpersonal psychotherapy and cognitive behavior therapy, along with a discussion of biological and evolutionary perspectives. This book includes how-to advice and case examples.

Behavior Therapy

- Lewinsohn, Rhode, and Seeley (1998) reviewed depression in adolescents from the perspective of behavior therapists. Lewinsohn and his colleagues are considered major contributors to the theory of behavior therapy, and their research group has conducted many studies with depressed adolescents.

Pharmacotherapy

- The practice guidelines of the American Psychiatric Association (2000b) include a thorough overview of pharmacotherapy for depression.
- Halbreich and Montgomery (2000) edited a series of reviews on the theories and empirical support available regarding pharmacotherapy of depression.
- Nemeroff and Schatzberg (1998) discussed the theoretical mechanisms of action for most of the antidepressant medications.
- The *Physicians' Desk Reference* (2000, updated every year) provides brief discussions of the theoretical mechanism of action for each of the antidepressant medications approved by the Food and Drug Administration. Although qualified physicians should carefully supervise pharmacotherapy regimens for depressed patients, psychotherapists without medical training will still find the *PDR* to be a useful resource because of the extensive information on side effects, contraindications, and so forth.
- Rankin (2000) edited a reader-friendly resource on psychopharmacology.

Studies

- Burns and Spangler (2001) examined the relationships between dysfunctional thinking, anxiety, and depression in a sample of 521 patients treated with cognitive behavior therapy. Rather than direct mediation of the depression by changes in dysfunctional thinking, there appeared to be an additional unknown variable that mediated the effects of psychotherapy.
- Goodyer et al. (2000) conducted a study of 246 adolescents who were at low and high risk for psychopathology. Their findings suggested that fluctuations in adrenal steroid functioning tend to occur before the first experience of Major Depressive Disorder in adolescents.
- Kolko et al. (2000) conducted a randomized controlled trial that found few areas of treatment specificity between three interventions. The interventions were cognitive behavior therapy, systemic-behavioral

family therapy, and nondirective supportive therapy. Post-treatment and 2-year follow-up assessments were completed for 92 depressed adolescents. Following acute treatment, cognitive behavior therapy was the most powerful intervention for modifying cognitive distortions. Measures of cognitive distortion and family dysfunction, however, did not mediate outcome at the 2-year follow-up.

- O'Hara et al. (2000) conducted a randomized controlled trial indicating that interpersonal psychotherapy was an efficacious intervention for women experiencing postpartum depression. Participants were randomly assigned to interpersonal psychotherapy and waiting-list control groups, with 99 participants completing the study. After 12 weeks of treatment, participants in the treatment group evidenced significant improvements in depressive symptoms and social adjustment compared with participants in the waiting-list control group.

- Rossello and Bernal (1999) conducted an efficacy study comparing cognitive behavior therapy and interpersonal psychotherapy. The participants were 71 Puerto Rican adolescents who were depressed. The results suggested that both interventions were efficacious, compared with a waiting-list control condition. Interpersonal psychotherapy, however, evidenced broader impact with this sample.

PART II

Depression Across
the Life Span

3 Depression in Children

Overview

We begin this chapter with a case study and a discussion of the signs and symptoms of depression in children. We discuss prevalence, symptoms, and assessment of depression in this age group, and we cover psychotherapy and pharmacotherapy issues as well. We highlight some of the special topics that are relevant to depression in young children. We present clinical guidelines for practitioners who work with depressed children. Finally, we present a summary and a list of suggested readings.

Case Study

Melba is a Hispanic 10-year-old girl in the fourth grade. She is seriously depressed. In a parent-teacher conference after school, Melba's teacher describes some of the symptoms and signs of childhood depression that she sees every day in Melba.

Teacher: Melba is so sad and unhappy most of the time. And she is always complaining about stomachaches and headaches, but you have already noted that her recent physical exam was okay. Apparently her physical health is good?

Mother: Yes, Dr. Smith said that Melba is physically healthy.

Teacher: That's good! But I'm still worried about her. Melba's grades have dropped the last few months: She has gone from straight As to all Cs and Ds. Melba seems to be having difficulty concentrating. Also, she gets upset very easily. She seems very irritable and anxious. Do you see this at home too?

Mother: Well, I suppose—at least for most of the things you are mentioning. Melba has been very grouchy and irritable the last few months. I agree with you: She does seem very sad and depressed. She's also been waking up in the middle of the night a lot. I don't understand these problems—we have a happy home. I don't get it.

Teacher: Children from the best of families can become depressed. At first, I wondered if this was just some temporary "phase," but Melba has been like this for several months now.

Mother: Yes, she has. I'm worried too. I just don't understand this. My husband doesn't understand it either. Our other two children are doing fine. We have a good home. We love each other. I survived my illness with breast cancer—I'm okay now. But Melba seems so unhappy . . . and angry also. She has not been eating well and complains about the stomachaches at home too—especially before she has to go to school. And she says that she is tired all of the time. The poor kid just doesn't seem to be having any fun. I guess the thing I noticed the most is that she has withdrawn from her friends. She almost never plays with them anymore. She just stays in her room or watches TV. She's become a "loner."

Teacher: That is helpful information. She has been very socially withdrawn in school also. For example, she will volunteer to do small jobs for me during the lunch period rather than sit with the other kids in the cafeteria. Until these last few months, Melba has been outgoing and assertive, but lately she is very shy and quiet. We want Melba to do well in school. We want Melba to be happy.

Mother: Me too! But . . . I don't know what to do.

Discussion of the Case Study

This case illustrates many of the age-relevant features of depression in children. The case is typical, albeit a composite of many cases. Furthermore, although *DSM-IV-TR* (American Psychiatric Association, 2000a) does not make distinctions for diagnosing Major Depressive Disorder in children versus adults, there are developmental processes at work in children that influence the symptoms and signs of depression.

Thus, for example, Melba's grades have dropped. This is often a sign of depression in an elementary school-aged child. Melba shows irritability and anger, common forms of poor emotional regulation in childhood depression. Somatic complaints, such as Melba's stomachaches and headaches, are also typical symptoms in depressed children. Comorbid conditions are frequently present in childhood depression, and Melba evidences these conditions with her anxiety symptoms and her withdrawn social behavior. Finally, good parents with good homes can have depressed children. The parents often find this bewildering, exasperating, and heartbreaking. Melba's parents may be an example. Unfortunately, some practitioners are guilty of underestimating the challenges of raising children. As Haley (1996) remarked, "I recall one child psychologist who said that after he adopted two infants, he wished he could apologize to the mothers he had advised in the past, that is, when he had no real idea what problems there were in raising children" (p. 62).

Because children's verbal and social skills do not match those of adults, early stages in the evaluation of a child's depression tend to depend heavily on the observations of others—parents, family members, and teachers—and this is what has happened with Melba. Some of the potential symptoms of childhood depression, however, such as feelings of guilt, worthlessness, and low self-esteem, are best assessed through sensitive interviewing by a clinician who is skilled at working with children. Thousands of studies in developmental psychology have established that young children do not think and talk like adults. Practitioners need to understand this, and they need to be comfortable working within the verbal and social constraints of childhood.

Prevalence, Symptoms, and Assessment

There are no huge, multisite studies regarding the prevalence of Major Depressive Disorder in *young* children (i.e., children between the ages of 4 and 12). Reviews of the available studies, however, suggest that Major Depressive Disorders in young children probably have a point prevalence that ranges between 1% and 4%, depending on the location, sampling procedures, and assessment methodology. The point prevalence of highly symptomatic children who still may not reach threshold for a diagnosis of Major Depressive Disorder probably ranges between 3% and 5% (American Psychiatric Association, 2000a; Anderson, Williams, McGee, & Silva, 1987; Birmaher, Ryan, Williamson, Brent, Kaufman, et al., 1996; Lefkowitz & Tesiny, 1985; Roberts, Attkisson, & Rosenblatt, 1998; Schwartz et al., 1998).

The course of depression in children will often include episodes that last 6 to 8 months, although short episodes of a few weeks are not uncommon. There is substantial variability in the length of depressive episodes in children and little compelling evidence of a significantly different course than for depressive episodes in adults (American Psychiatric Association, 2000a; Birmaher, Ryan, Williamson, Brent, Kaufman, et al., 1996; Kovacs, 1996; Schwartz et al., 1998).

Studies have not found gender differences in the prevalence of Major Depressive Disorder among preadolescent children (i.e., ages 4–12; American Psychiatric Association, 2000a). By middle adolescence (ages 14–18), however, the gender difference is clearly apparent, with depression twice as common among females as males (American Psychiatric Association, 2000a; Cyranowski et al., 2000; Hankin et al., 1998; Nolen-Hoeksema & Girgus, 1994; Wichstrom, 1999).

DSM-IV-TR (American Psychiatric Association, 2000a) specifies the same criteria for diagnosing depression across the life span, including young children. It is acknowledged, however, that young children may express the standard depressive symptoms and signs in a manner that reflects their developmental level. For instance, the verbal, social, and emotional regulation skills of young children may yield a depressive symptomatology in which somatic complaints, social withdrawal, irritability, and disruptions in family interactions and school performance predominate. The *DSM-IV-TR* (American Psychiatric Association, 2000a, p. 356) does allow for depressed mood in children to be either sad or irritable mood. Depressed children are less likely to evidence extensive motor retardation, hypersomnia, cognitive disorientation, and chronically disrupted appetite than are adolescent, adult, and elderly patients with depression (American Psychiatric Association, 2000a; Birmaher, Ryan, Williamson, Brent, Kaufman, et al., 1996; Cicchetti & Toth, 1998; Kovacs, 1996; Schwartz et al., 1998).

Comorbid conditions are usually a concern for depressed patients, and depressed children provide a vivid example, evidencing rates of psychiatric comorbid conditions ranging up to 83% (Angold & Costello, 1993). For instance, the association of depressive and anxiety disorders in children ranges from 30% to 75% (Angold & Costello, 1993). Depressed children frequently present intertwined symptoms of anxiety, fear, trauma, and dysphoria (Boney-McCoy & Finkelhor, 1996; Chorpita et al., 1998; Cole, Peeke, Martin, Truglio, & Seroczynski, 1998; Joiner, Catanzaro, & Laurent, 1996; Weissman et al., 1999). Moreover, aggressive and overcontrolling behaviors are common in depressed children (Block, Gjerde, & Block, 1991; Reinherz, Giaconia, Hauf, Wasserman, & Silverman, 1999; Weiss et al., 1992).

There are subtle differences in the symptoms and signs of depression for children versus adults. The similarities, however, outweigh the differences (Hammen, 1997; Kovacs, 1996). Thorough interviews are always required for a valid assessment of depression at any point in the life span (American Psychiatric Association, 2000a). With children, information from parents, family members, and teachers will also be useful in most cases. Typically, information from parents is particularly necessary and helpful. Furthermore, self-report questionnaires are never adequate by themselves, the practitioner should always interview the depressed child (Fristad, Emery, & Beck, 1997; Hammen, 1997; Speier, Sherak, Hirsch, & Cantwell, 1995).

In certain cases of childhood depression, it is less clear than it would be with most adults whether feelings of guilt and worthlessness are prominent symptoms. It is harder for a 7-year-old child to talk about "guilt" than it is for most adults. This issue reminds us that sensitive and skilled practitioners are necessary for valid interviews of depressed young children. In our opinion, this is an area of practice that lends itself well to specialization. The constraints imposed by young children's verbal, social, and emotional regulation skills, along with the vast array of developmental and maturational issues that should be considered during patient assessment, argue for practitioners who are well trained to work with this age group.

Assessment and treatment planning for depressed children raises some practical challenges. For example, short interviews are more effective than long ones, even though this may be less convenient for the practitioner. Children have short attention spans, and they tire easily. Also, more "warm-up" time may be necessary for child patients than adult patients to build the rapport and interpersonal comfort that is always part of an effective therapeutic relationship. You may have to review and summarize more than you do for adult patients. You will have to listen actively and talk simply. Your child patients will also talk simply: Your 7-year-old depressed patient may tell you, "I feel bad about my mistake" or "I don't know." For your child patients, you may have to make the interviews more fun than would be necessary for adult patients: Games, stories, role-plays, and lots of interviewer creativity will be called for. Although the symptoms and signs of Major Depressive Disorder are similar across children and adults, you need to tailor your interventions to the developmental level of your child patients.

Somatic complaints are common in depressed children, and it is often difficult to unravel the somatic complaints caused by depression from the somatic complaints caused by general medical conditions. Hence, we recommend a physical exam by a qualified health care practitioner as part of the evaluation process for depressed children. Notice that such a physical exam had already been conducted in our case study.

For child patients between the ages of infancy and 6, assessment with a parent directly participating or nearby is typically helpful—and sometimes absolutely necessary. For child patients who are in elementary school, however, a separate interview with just the child present will usually be helpful. In addition, gathering relevant information from parents, family members, and teachers is often needed for a valid assessment of childhood depression. Information from parents is parti-cularly necessary and helpful. Direct observations of depressed children in some of their natural environments—for example, while they are at school—may also be helpful, but it is rarely done because of practical limitations. As with adult depression, childhood depression is probably a heterogeneous group of mood disorders, with a diverse and complex set of causal pathways (Birmaher, Ryan, Williamson, Brent, & Kaufman, 1996; Birmaher, Ryan, Williamson, Brent, Kaufman, et al., 1996; Cicchetti & Toth, 1998; Hammen, 1997; Schwartz et al., 1998). This complexity makes assessment of the symptoms and signs of childhood depression more challenging. Moreover, a multimethod/ multisource assessment of childhood depression may be difficult to do. However, it is often worth it.

Treatment

The literature on empirically supported therapies for depressed children is less extensive than it is for adults. Randomized controlled trials (RCTs), in particular, are relatively scarce compared with the number of RCTs with depressed adults. Nevertheless, there have been some outstanding investigations of psychotherapy for depressed children. There have also been several promising studies of preventive interven-tions for children who are at risk for developing severe depression. We will briefly discuss this research.

Skill-training interventions, such as coping-skills training and cognitive behavior therapy, are the most empirically supported inter-ventions for depressed children (Birmaher, Ryan, Williamson, Brent, & Kaufman, 1996; Harrington, Whittaker, & Shoebridge, 1998; Kazdin, 1999; Kazdin & Weisz, 1998; Schwartz et al., 1998; Weisz, Weiss, Han, Granger, & Morton, 1995). These interventions reflect a rationale that depressed children need to learn more effective ways to think about their world, cope with their emotions, and problem-solve for interper-sonal challenges regarding their families and friends. These interven-tions also reflect an empirical literature that illustrates strong inverse relationships between childhood competence and depression (e.g., Seroczynski, Cole, & Maxwell, 1997). Finally, these interventions are practical, brief, and amenable to group formats, so they reflect the financial and insurance constraints of our contemporary health care environments.

The therapeutic emphases of these skill-training interventions for depressed children, or for children who are at risk for developing depression, typically include the following components (Birmaher, Ryan, Williamson, Brent, & Kaufman, 1996; Harrington, Whittaker, & Shoebridge, 1998; Kazdin & Weisz, 1998; Schwartz et al., 1998), which are often delivered in a *group* format:

- *Training to improve social interactions and interpersonal problem solving.* The following therapeutic tactics facilitate this component: therapist modeling, child role playing, social games, vivid storytelling, practice in the children's natural environment, and homework assignments.
- *Training to enhance optimistic thinking and minimize depressive thinking.* This component may be challenging for depressed children and the therapist because children have different levels of cognitive development than adults do. The therapist needs to make this training interesting and fun. The tactics that were noted for training in enhanced problem-solving skills are helpful here too. For example, role-playing games and dramatic stories about optimistic thinking will be helpful here. Modifications in the dysfunctional cognitive schemas and attribution biases that saturate depressive symptoms are challenging tasks for children.
- *Training to improve positive reinforcement.* This sounds easy— teach the depressed children to have more fun, to elicit more social contact and praise, and to earn more real-world rewards. This is harder than it sounds. Helping the child to make gradual and successive approximations toward more competence in several domains is one way to pursue this goal. For example, a gradual but structured approach toward enhanced competence in the important child domains of social acceptance, academic proficiency, emotional and behavioral regulation, athletic participation, and physical attractiveness should generate more positive reinforcement (see Seroczynski et al., 1997). Developing improved skills for selecting and pursuing

mood-enhancing activities should also be helpful. As with most psychotherapy, practitioners will encounter more success if they work from the child's strengths rather than focusing on the child's weaknesses.

- *Training to enhance coping with comorbid conditions.* A common starting point is an anxiety management intervention because anxiety and depressive disorders show such a strong association in children. Various forms of progressive relaxation training, adjusted to the physical and cognitive abilities of children, are a common component here. Furthermore, most children find that relaxation training is fun, and it helps to build some positive reinforcement directly into the therapeutic process. Another example is the enhancement of academic performance, which may require a long-term interdisciplinary effort with attention to verbal skills, study strategies, and work habits. When dealing with comorbid conditions, the therapist needs to be sensitive, creative, and engaging.

- *Training to enhance problem-solving skills that are specific to the challenges faced by particular children.* Depressed children are often under a lot of stress. For instance, they may have depressed parents, which is very stressful (Campbell, Cohn, & Meyers, 1995; Downey & Coyne, 1990; Ferro, Verdeli, Pierre, & Weissman, 2000; National Institute of Child Health and Human Development [NICHHD], 1999; Nolen-Hoeksema, Wolfson, Mumme, & Guskin, 1995; Weissman et al., 1997; Weissman et al., 2000). Thus, these depressed children may benefit from problem-solving training that is focused on interpersonal situations with their parents. Complementary therapies to the child interventions, such as marital or family therapies, may also have advantages here (Baucom, Shoham, Mueser, Daiuto, & Stickle, 1998). Sometimes the specific challenge is concrete and prosaic and arises from one of the many problems in our society. For example, if depressed children do not get a good breakfast at home, then they will be happier—and healthier—if the practitioner arranges for them to get a free breakfast at school. In addition, just getting a child to therapy sessions may be a major obstacle for parents who are economically challenged or marginally involved.

An example of the skill-training approach to treating depressed children is an RCT by Weisz, Thurber, Sweeney, Proffitt, and LaGagnoux (1997). These researchers evaluated an eight-session group treatment program for moderately depressed elementary school students. From a sample of 48 depressed children (54% male) in Grades 3 to 6, the authors randomly assigned 16 children to the group treatment and the rest to a no-treatment control group. The intervention was essentially cognitive behavior therapy, which was adjusted to the verbal and social skills of elementary school students. The results at the 9-month follow-up were promising: Children in the treatment group evidenced significant reductions in depressive symptoms, improved significantly more than children in the control group, and were more likely (65%) to have moved into the normal range of depressive symptomatology than were control group children (27%). The investigators wisely cautioned, however, that further research was needed to see if these encouraging results would generalize to interventions with severely depressed children.

Although studies of skill-training interventions for depressed children, such as the Weisz et al. (1997) investigation, are promising, RCTs for skill-training interventions with children are not as numerous as those conducted with depressed adults (Kazdin & Weisz, 1998). Furthermore, some of the available studies on skill-training interventions for depressed children and adolescents have generated rather modest patient improvements (e.g., Harrington, Kerfoot, et al., 1998). In addition, relapse is a problem here, just as it is in all other areas of depression treatment (Birmaher, Ryan, Williamson, Brent, & Kaufman, 1996; Kovacs, 1996). Therefore, caution is warranted and more research is necessary. We need a better understanding of what works and particularly of why it works (Kazdin, 1999, 2000).

Another promising approach is the use of skill-training interventions as *prevention programs* for children who are at high risk of developing severe depression. Obvious risk factors include mild to moderate depressive symptoms in the children, high stress or chaos in the children's home environments, and depressed parents. Like the treatment programs developed for children who are already depressed, these prevention programs need—and deserve—more research attention (Birmaher,

Ryan, Williamson, Brent, & Kaufman, 1996; Cicchetti & Toth, 1998; Harrington, Whittaker, & Shoebridge, 1998; Kazdin & Weisz, 1998).

Several studies, however, have generated positive outcomes regarding skill-training interventions that were used for preventing depression in high-risk children. For example, building in part on the "learned helplessness" and "learned optimism" models developed by Seligman (1975, 1991), Gillham, Reivich, Jaycox, and Seligman (1995) found positive results for a group treatment intervention. Their participants were 118 high-risk elementary school children (fifth and sixth graders, 53% male). Their intervention was an 18-hour, 12-week prevention program that was primarily based on cognitive behavior therapy and social problem solving. At the 2-year follow-up, children in the prevention group reported less depressive symptomatology than did children in a matched no-treatment control group. In addition, the prevention group children evidenced a 50% reduction in severe depressive symptoms during the follow-up. Several other research teams have also reported positive outcomes for prevention programs (e.g., Beardslee et al., 1997; Beardslee, Wright, Rothberg, Salt, & Versage, 1996). The prevention approach deserves more attention.

Pharmacotherapy is a rapidly increasing treatment for depression (Mamdani, Parikh, Austin, & Upshur, 2000; Olfson, Marcus, et al., 1998; Olfson, Marcus, & Pincus, 1999; Pincus et al., 1999; Schatzberg, 2000). It is sometimes used with young children, but this treatment approach is much more common with patients who are adolescents, adults, or elderly individuals. Furthermore, although treatment outcome studies have established pharmacotherapy as an efficacious intervention for depressed adults, the outcome literature on early adolescents is sketchy and inconsistent, and studies with young children are virtually nonexistent (Baldessarini & Tondo, 2000; Consumer Reports, 2000; De Lima, Hotoph, & Wessely, 1999; DeRubeis et al., 1999; Nemeroff & Schatzberg, 1998; Niederehe & Schneider, 1998). Indeed, pharmacotherapy outcome studies with depressed elementary school or preschool children are restricted by legislation in many jurisdictions (Graham, 1999).

Nevertheless, pharmacotherapy for depression in children and early adolescents appears to be increasing, despite the lack of research support (Nemeroff & Schatzberg, 1998). The outcome literature on antidepressive medication for children is less than auspicious, but there are occasional reports of modestly positive outcomes. For instance, Emslie et al. (1997) conducted a well-controlled investigation of fluoxetine (Prozac) with 96 depressed outpatients who were between 7 and 17 years old. They reported modestly positive results: for example, 31% of the participants in the fluoxetine group demonstrated a full remission of symptoms compared to 23% of the participants in the placebo group. This outcome from a well-controlled study does not seem very promising, yet this is one of the most positive outcomes in the literature.

In summary, pharmacotherapy with depressed adults is well supported by the research literature, but pharmacotherapy with depressed children is not. In addition, the standard pharmacotherapy concerns about adherence, side effects, and toxicity, along with negative interactions with other medications, maturation, and growth, are obviously exacerbated in young children. These concerns extend to the use of pharmacotherapy for children with common types of comorbid conditions: For example, lithium treatment of aggressive children has an array of negative side effects (Malone, Delaney, Luebbert, Cater, & Campbell, 2000).

Thus, we emphasize the need for careful supervision of pharmacotherapy by an appropriately trained physician. Given the incomplete state of research on this matter, our personal opinion is that pharmacotherapy is best reserved as a backup intervention with depressed children ages 12 or younger, and then tried only when less invasive interventions such as cognitive behavior therapy have not worked sufficiently. Nevertheless, the pharmacotherapy drummer keeps marching on: A recent investigation suggests that there has been a significant increase in the use of psychotropic medications—including antidepressants—for preschool children during the early to middle 1990s (Zito et al., 2000).

We are skeptical that this increased pharmacotherapy with depressed preschool children is supported by methodologically sophisticated treatment studies; we are not aware of any large, well-controlled studies on pharmacotherapy of depression with this preschool age group. Rather, we suspect that the forces of overwhelmed parents, upset day care workers, and insufficient treatment resources are driving this explosion in psychotropic medication for the very young. If preschool children have serious depressive symptoms, then we recommend psychological rather than pharmacological interventions.

Special Topics

Several special topics regarding depression in children have important clinical implications. For instance, depressed children often have depressed parents (Birmaher, Ryan, Williamson, Brent, Kaufman, et al., 1996; Downey & Coyne, 1990; Ferro et al., 2000; Hammen, 1997; Jones, Forehand, & Neary, 2001; Weissman et al., 1997; Weissman et al., 2000). Group prevention programs (e.g., Gillham et al., 1995) have tended to shy away from confronting this issue for an array of financial, practical, and political reasons. With individual treatment programs for children who are already severely depressed, however, it is quite feasible to explore the possibility of depression in the parents and then pursue additional treatment options accordingly.

Another special topic for depressed children is stigma (Cicchetti & Toth, 1998). Childhood depression is largely untreated or under-treated. The social stigma that unfortunately accompanies psychiatric disorders in the United States may be part of the reason. The under-treatment of severely depressed children is a tragedy—and it can lead to additional tragedies (see Jamison, 1999; Quindlen, 1999). This phenomenon of undertreatment may be further exacerbated by the "parent bashing" that appears to sometimes occur in both research literature and public media reports on childhood depression (Downey & Coyne, 1990). Parent bashing is unfair and unsupported by most research; furthermore, "bashed" parents are less likely to seek help for their children. If not successfully treated, severe depressions in young children generate a poor prognosis and a negative lifetime trajectory of numerous depressive episodes (Kovacs, 1996; Kovacs, Akiskal, Gatsonis, & Parrone, 1994; Kovacs, Devlin, Pollock, Richards, & Mukerji, 1997; Kovacs, Feinberg, Crouse-Novak, Paulauskas, & Finkelstein, 1984; Kovacs, Feinberg, Crouse-Novak, Paulauskas, Pollock, et al., 1984; Nolen-Hoeksema, Girgus, & Seligman, 1992; Reinherz et al., 1999; Weissman et al., 1999).

Although parent bashing is unfair and unproductive, we should acknowledge that some depressed children have been abused—physically, sexually, or through extreme neglect. When the practitioner is suspicious that this may be the case, the issue should be explored carefully and in accordance with the mandated reporting laws for child abuse.

Because patients who are depressed children are also minors, these cases can yield some special ethical dilemmas for the practitioner. For example, inadequately informed consent, breaches of confidentiality, inappropriate dual-role relationships, and insufficient competencies are ethical violations that are easy to fall into when working with depressed children and their parents, families, and teachers (American Psychological Association, 1992; Bersoff, 1999; Graham, 1999; Koocher & Keith-Spiegel, 1998; Pope & Vasquez, 1998). An example would be the possible breaches of confidentiality and dual-role relationships that can develop if the practitioner is not clear about who is the primary client among the children, parents, families, teachers, administrators, and social service people that the practitioner is working with. Another example is the almost inevitable dual-role relationships that will occur if the practitioner is serving as the primary therapist for both the child and the child's parents. A further example is the challenge of working with a preschool child: Although *DSM-IV-TR* (American Psychiatric Association, 2000a) does not make distinctions between young children and adults in *diagnosing* depression, it would be preposterous to deny the differences involved in *working therapeutically* with these two groups. To avoid ethical problems, we recommend that practitioners plan thoroughly, keep excellent records, and frequently consult with colleagues.

Clinical Guidelines

- Do not treat depressed children unless you have appropriate training, experience, and consultation.
- Attempt to use a multimethod/multisource approach when assessing childhood depression.

- Always include interviews with the depressed child in your assessment effort.
- Be alert to age differences in symptom expression (American Psychiatric Association, 2000a).
- Be sensitive to the developmental level of your patient's verbal, social, and emotional regulation skills.
- Assess for comorbid conditions.
- Assess for child abuse, and know the mandated reporting laws in your state.
- Tailor treatment sessions to the developmental level and ability of your patient.
- Incorporate a skill-training intervention into your treatment programs for young children.
- Make it a team effort; interdisciplinary interventions are common and desirable.
- Parents, and sometimes family and teachers, should be involved in treatment planning for depressed children.
- Avoid "parent bashing."
- Pharmacotherapy for elementary school children should be limited to a backup intervention when the psychological interventions have failed to produce satisfactory improvement.
- An appropriately trained physician should carefully supervise pharmacotherapy.
- Use psychological rather than pharmacological interventions for depressed preschool children.
- Consider marital therapy or family counseling by another therapist as complementary interventions to your child patient's individual treatment.
- Build relapse prevention procedures, such as a schedule of booster sessions, into your treatment planning.
- Consider skill-training programs for preventing depression in high-risk elementary school children.
- Use thorough planning, careful record keeping, and extensive consultation to avoid ethical problems.
- If you have expertise in this area, then be generous and do some pro bono work with children—they are our future.

Chapter Summary

Although *DSM-IV-TR* (American Psychiatric Association, 2000a) does not make distinctions for diagnosing depression in children versus adults, developmental processes at work in children will influence the symptoms and signs of depression. For example, somatic complaints, irritability (which the *DSM-IV-TR* allows for depressed mood), social withdrawal, academic problems, and disruptions in interpersonal relationships are often prominent symptoms in depressed children. Comorbid conditions are also common.

Major Depressive Disorder (American Psychiatric Association, 2000a) in young children evidences a point prevalence that ranges between 1% and 4% across studies. Depressive episodes may often last 6 to 8 months, although short episodes of a few weeks are not uncommon. There is no compelling evidence of a gender difference in the prevalence of Major Depressive Disorder among preadolescent children.

A valid assessment of a depressed child requires some adjustments for the developmental level of the child. For example, extra "warm-up" time may be necessary. Short interviews with lots of breaks will be helpful. It is beneficial to include activities that are fun for the child, such as games, stories, and role playing. The interviewer should match his or her own style to the verbal, social, and emotional regulation skills of the child. A valid assessment usually requires information from the depressed child's parents and perhaps also from family members and teachers. The complexity of evaluating depressed children argues for specialized training and frequent consultation.

Skill-training programs are the most empirically supported psychological interventions for depressed children. These interventions include coping-skills training and cognitive behavior therapy. The outcome research with moderately depressed children is promising, but more studies are needed to see if these results will generalize to severely depressed children. Prevention programs with high-risk children, which also rely on this skill-training approach, have witnessed encouraging results.

Pharmacotherapy for depressed children appears to be increasing despite the meager research support. With elementary school children, there are a few islands of modestly positive outcomes in a sea of negative results. With preschool children, well-controlled outcome studies are nonexistent. Therefore, we recommend reluctance and caution in the use of pharmacotherapy with depressed young children. Skill-training interventions appear more effective—and safer.

There are several special topics regarding the treatment of depressed children. For instance, depressed children often have depressed parents. Social stigma frequently accompanies depression in children, and many severely depressed children go untreated. Common ethical dilemmas in the treatment of depressed children include inadequate informed consent, breaches of confidentiality, inappropriate dual-role relationships, and insufficient competencies.

Suggested Readings

Discussions

General Reviews

- Birmaher and his colleagues (Birmaher, Ryan, Williamson, Brent, & Kaufman, 1996; Birmaher, Ryan, Williamson, Brent, Kaufman, et al., 1996) have discussed recent research on child depression. These reviews are thorough and scholarly.
- Schwartz et al. (1998) discussed the assessment and treatment of childhood depression and provided clinical suggestions.

Cognitive Behavior Therapy

- Harrington, Whittaker, and Shoebridge (1998) provided a review of the empirical literature. They concluded that cognitive behavior therapy is an effective treatment for childhood depression.

Coping-Skills Training

- Kazdin and Weisz (1998) discussed the empirical literature and concluded that interventions based on coping-skills training are promising, but not conclusively supported, therapies for depressed children.

Studies

- Caspi, Moffitt, Newman, and Silva (1996) conducted a longitudinal study of 1,037 children. Their findings indicated that children who were inhibited at age 3 were at increased risk for exhibiting Major Depressive Disorder at age 21.
- Ferro et al. (2000) studied 117 mothers who were seeking assessment or treatment of depression for their children. Findings indicated that 14% of the mothers were depressed themselves, a figure considerably above the population point prevalence of 5% for adult depression.
- Gillham et al. (1995) used a matched-control design to investigate a group treatment for preventing depression in children. They found promising results for an 18-hour, 12-week intervention that was primarily based on cognitive behavior therapy and social problem solving.
- NICHHD (1999) supported a multisite, longitudinal study of 1,215 mothers and their infants. Findings indicated that, when interacting with their children, chronically depressed mothers were less sensitive than were nondepressed mothers.
- Weisz et al. (1997) conducted a randomized controlled trial to evaluate an eight-session group treatment for moderately depressed elementary school students. The intervention was cognitive behavior therapy, and the results were promising.
- Zito et al. (2000) studied over 200,000 participants in several Medicaid and HMO programs. Their findings indicated that there was a substantial increase in the use of psychotropic medications, including antidepressants, for preschool children during the early to middle 1990s.

4 Depression in Adolescents

Overview

We begin this chapter with a case study of adolescent depression and a discussion of the case study. Next we discuss prevalence, including gender differences in the prevalence of adolescent depression. Then we give an overview of the symptoms, signs, and assessment of adolescent depression. We follow this with a discussion of close relationships, treatment, and prevention. We also have a brief section regarding concerns about suicide in adolescents. Finally, we cover certain special topics and present clinical guidelines, a chapter summary, and some suggested readings.

Case Study

Kim is sending e-mail to her best friend, Liz, who has recently moved 1,300 miles away. Kim is 16 years old, in the 10th grade, and physically healthy. However, she seems to be depressed.

Hi Liz,
How are you?
I'm not doing so hot. I feel humiliated, worthless, and dumb. But the worst part is that I'm lonely.

I really miss you!

Things are bad:

I didn't want to have sex with Dennis. But he kept bugging me. I finally gave in and we had sex. Then he goes off and cheats on me—with Karen of all people! And then he stopped telling me he "loves me." And then he disappeared. I hate Dennis!

Things at home are bad: Dad is rarely here. He is still a lot nicer to my brothers than to me. He still fights with Mom a lot. Who cares?

And Mom is no angel. All she talks about is "our money problems."

Give it a rest! We do have money problems. I'm surprised that Mom and Dad let me buy the nice clothes I do. But I pay for my nice clothes. So what can they say? Mom worries that I work too many hours bagging groceries: "Oh, honey, wouldn't it be better if you cut down on your store hours and studied more? Besides, you're only making minimum wage at the store." Give me a break! What does she think she is making in that lousy secretary job? Minimum wage! And then she has the nerve to give me grief! She's just mad at me because I'm getting lousy grades at school. Who cares?

It's late, but Mom and Dad are both still at work. I wish I didn't feel so horrible.

I better go now. Dad will be home soon and he'll want to talk about his long day at the store. Big deal. He'll talk and laugh with my brothers. And Dad will ask ME to fix him some dinner because he's tired. I don't care. No wonder Mom and Dad aren't wild about me—I'm "mean and nasty Kim."

Liz, I miss you! I feel awful. Sometimes things seem hopeless. Please send me some e-mail.

Kim

Discussion of the Case Study

Kim's case includes many of the risk factors for depression in any age group, along with some stressors that are especially relevant for adolescents. For instance, money problems and failure with important tasks such as school (or work) are risk factors in any age group. It is stressful to have numerous economic challenges. Indeed, economic adversity is a major risk for dying prematurely, even after unhealthy behaviors such as smoking, heavy alcohol consumption, excessive eating, and insufficient exercising are factored out of the analysis (Lantz et al., 1998). But the obsessive self-consciousness, low self-esteem, and ruminative coping styles present in Kim's case are particularly relevant to *adolescent* depression (Lewinsohn, Gotlib, & Seeley, 1997; Lewinsohn et al., 1998). Moreover, the extreme loneliness is common in depressed adolescents too. Finally, the sense of hopelessness that is evident in Kim's e-mail is a reminder that suicidal risk is a very important concern regarding depressed adolescents. A face-to-face interview with an appropriately trained practitioner would be needed, of course, to establish whether Kim meets the diagnostic criteria for Major Depressive Disorder (American Psychiatric Association, 2000a).

Prevalence and Gender Differences

About 5% of all adolescents are seriously depressed at a given point in time, and about 20% of all adolescents experience serious depression sometime between the ages of 12 and 19 (Blazer et al., 1994; Cicchetti & Toth, 1998; Kessler et al., 1994). Thus, adolescent depression is common and disruptive. It is clear that practitioners should carefully attend to how they assess, treat, and prevent adolescent depression (Birmaher, Ryan, Williamson, Brent, & Kaufman, 1996, Birmaher, Ryan, Williamson, Brent, Kaufman, et al., 1996).

Equivalent numbers of males and females are depressed as children. But in adolescence, depressed females outnumber depressed males by two to one (American Psychiatric Association, 2000a; Cicchetti & Toth, 1998; Compas, Ey, & Grant, 1993; Nolen-Hoeksema & Girgus, 1994). A dramatic empirical demonstration of this gender difference is the study of Hankin et al. (1998). They conducted a longitudinal evaluation of 653 males and females as the participants developed from ages 11 to 21. The investigators found that most of the gender differences in depression occur between the ages of 15 and 18. Wichstrom's (1999) investigation of 12,000 adolescents found parallel results, although the gender difference accelerated at age 14 rather than age 15.

Hence, we know that depression is twice as common among adolescent females as males. Experts seem to converge on several possible— but not conclusively proven—theories for this gender difference:

- On average, adolescent females may be more candid in admitting their depression (Compas et al., 1997; Hammen, 1997; Kendall, Cantwell, & Kazdin, 1989; Nolen-Hoeksema, 1987).
- On average, adolescent females may be exposed to more interpersonal stress (Compas et al., 1993; Cyranowski et al., 2000; Davis, Matthews, & Twamley, 1999; Frank, 2000; Hammen, 1997; Reisberg, 2000; Weissman & Olfson, 1995).
- On average, adolescent females may be more likely to rely on passive coping strategies, such as rumination. Active coping strategies, such as problem solving and distraction through new activities, are probably more effective methods for decreasing depressive symptoms (Cicchetti & Toth, 1998; Nolen-Hoeksema, 1987; Nolen-Hoeksema & Girgus, 1994; Shea, 1998).
- Adolescent females may experience biological changes that put them at more risk for depression (Bierut et al., 1999; Cyranowski et al., 2000; Frank, 2000; Silberg et al., 1999; Taylor, Klein, et al., 2000; Young et al., 2000; cf. Piccinelli & Wilkinson, 2000).

Symptoms, Signs, and Assessment

As with any particular age group, there are assessment, diagnostic, and interpretive considerations that apply specifically to depressed adolescents (American Psychiatric Association, 2000a; Compas et al., 1993; Kendall et al., 1989; Nolen-Hoeksema & Girgus, 1994). For instance, the environmental and social circumstances of adolescents should be taken into account. Pre-college-age adolescents typically do not live alone; they live with one or more parents or guardians, and often they also live with siblings. Thus, it is often helpful to assess the adolescent patient's family environment. Adolescents frequently have strong connections to a peer group, and if they do not have these connections this tends to be an important source of concern. Thus, it is often helpful to ask adolescent patients about their friends and peers. Adolescents are usually in school; their school performance and their relationships through school tend to be an important part of their world. Thus, it is often helpful to evaluate adolescent patients' academic achievement and social rewards.

In addition, the symptoms of serious depression often play out in a particular way for *each age group*, including adolescents (American Psychiatric Association, 2000a). For example, depressed *adolescents* are likely to evidence the following symptoms and signs:

- Anger and aggression, especially if they are male (Block et al., 1991)
- Low self-esteem, high self-criticism, and extreme pessimism, especially if they are female (Lewinsohn et al., 1997; Lewinsohn et al., 2000; Tram & Cole, 2000)
- Anxiety (Chorpita et al., 1998; Hinden, Compas, Howell, & Achenbach, 1997)
- Confused and dysfunctional thinking (Lewinsohn et al., 1999; Lewinsohn, Joiner, & Rohde, 2001; Orbach, Mikulincer, Stein, & Cohen, 1998)
- High self-consciousness (Lewinsohn et al., 1997, 1998)
- Irritable mood (Compas et al., 1993). Regarding adolescents, the *DSM-IV-TR* (American Psychiatric Association, 2000a, p. 356) allows for irritable mood to substitute for depressed mood and sadness in the diagnostic criteria.
- Reduced activities due to physical illness or injury (Lewinsohn, Rohde, & Seeley, 1996; Lewinsohn et al., 1997; Lewinsohn et al., 1998; Reinherz et al., 1999)
- Poor interpersonal problem solving and high stress from close relationships (Davila et al., 1995; Hammen & Brennan, 2001; Klein et al., 2001; Monroe et al., 1999; Nolen-Hoeksema & Girgus, 1994)
- Antisocial behavior, particularly in males (O'Connor, McGuire, Reiss, Hetherington, & Plomin, 1998)
- Sleep difficulties and weight loss or gain (Compas et al., 1993)

- Difficulty coping effectively with interpersonal stress, family chaos, or depressed parents (Daley et al., 1997; Ferro et al., 2000; Hammen & Brennan, 2001; Reinherz et al., 1999; Rueter, Scaramella, Wallace, & Conger, 1999; Summers, Forehand, Armistead, & Tannenbaum, 1998; Weissman et al., 1997)
- Additional psychiatric problems or comorbid conditions (American Psychiatric Association, 2000a, 2000b; Compas et al., 1993; Compas et al., 1997; Gose, 2000b; Johnson et al., 1999; Weissman et al., 1999). Comorbid conditions that are frequently associated with adolescent depression include anxiety disorders, substance use disorders, eating disorders, and attention-deficit/disruptive-behavior disorders.
- Suicidal risk factors (Lewinsohn et al., 1996; Westefeld et al., 2000).

Many empirical studies and discussion articles address these assessment issues in more detail than space allows us to here (e.g., American Psychiatric Association, 2000b; Hurry & Storey, 2000; Roberts et al., 1998; Schwartz et al., 1998). Practitioners will find it helpful to pursue this literature. Indeed, concerns about the prevalence of depression in adolescents, and about evaluating and treating depression effectively in this age group, are even appearing regularly in the mass media (e.g., Estrada, 1998).

Close Relationships

Family and friends are very important to adolescents. If these close relationships go poorly, then, as you would expect, the adolescent is more likely to become depressed. However, the details are complex— exactly why, when, and how depression develops in the context of poor close relationships is still being investigated. We will mention a few examples.

Hammen and her colleagues have conducted a broad array of studies looking at the interactions between adolescent depression, difficult close relationships, and interpersonal problem solving (Daley et al., 1997; Daley, Hammen, Davila, & Burge, 1998; Davila et al., 1995; Hammen, 1997; Hammen & Brennan, 2001). Not surprisingly, they found that a depressed adolescent creates some of his or her own interpersonal stress—especially if he or she has several psychiatric problems. They find that poor problem solving is a risk factor for depression and that depression is a risk factor for poor problem solving.

The research of Weissman and her colleagues (Weissman et al., 1997; Weissman et al., 2000) on the large risk imposed by having a close relationship with a depressed parent is another example of important research in this area. These researchers longitudinally evaluated a sample of participants for 10 years and found that the child of a depressed parent experiences a large increase in the risk for depression when compared with the child of nondepressed parents (Weissman et al., 1997).

Depression is a social phenomenon: Depressed people can cause stress for the people with whom they are close, and vice versa. Thus, even if one factored out the influences of genetics and shared environments, it would not be surprising that depression runs in families (Hammen, 1997; Joiner & Coyne, 1999; Jones et al., 2001; Kovacs et al., 1997).

Treatment and Prevention

Coping-skills training and cognitive behavior therapy appear to be the most efficacious psychotherapies for depressed adolescents (Harrington, Whittaker, & Shoebridge, 1998; Hollon & Shelton, 2001; Kazdin & Weisz, 1998; Lewinsohn et al., 1996, 1998; Reinecke, Ryan, & DuBois, 1998; see also Kolko et al., 2000). Treatment programs aimed at improving the coping skills of depressed adolescents typically target several skill areas:

- How to assess and change depressive thinking styles
- How to improve interpersonal skills
- How to facilitate effective problem solving in social situations
- How to reduce anxiety, which helps to improve problem solving and to enhance enjoyment—particularly in social situations
- How to get more rewards and pleasures out of life, in a reasonable and responsible way

In essence, coping-skills interventions focus on what depressed adolescents think and do in the context of issues that are important to depression. (Cognitive behavior therapy for depression has a similar focus, though with more emphasis on dysfunctional thinking and less emphasis on interpersonal skills.) The style of therapy is often educational and conducted in groups—like a small, informal class—with attention to peer or therapist examples, brief presentations by the therapist, discussion, role playing by the participants, and homework assignments. Of course, this intervention can be done in one-to-one sessions or small-group meetings. The group format has the advantages of peer support, group social interactions, and economy; but the group format has the disadvantage of being more intimidating to certain adolescent patients and more challenging to some therapists. In addition, concerns about confidentiality may become heightened with group interventions.

An interesting example of coping-skills training for depressed adolescents is the work of Birmaher et al. (2000; see also Kolko et al., 2000). They found that coping-skills training interventions were an effective therapy for depressed adolescents. They also found that family therapy and supportive therapy were equivalently effective at the 2-year follow-up evaluation. Furthermore, they found that although most participants recovered from their depression, adolescents with severe depression or self-reported parent–child conflict were at a stronger risk for relapses and recurrences.

Lewinsohn and his colleagues (Clarke et al., 1992; Lewinsohn et al., 1996, 1998) have also found promising results for a psychoeducational intervention to reduce depressive symptoms in adolescents. Moreover, there are indications that mild depressive symptoms in adolescents may be successfully treated via reading materials (i.e., "bibliotherapy"), which can offer guidance on modifying dysfunctional thinking and on improving coping skills (Ackerson, Scogin, McKendree-Smith, & Lyman, 1998).

Interpersonal psychotherapy is another example of a skill-oriented brief psychotherapy for depressed adolescents for which encouraging results have been reported (Mufson & Moreau, 1998; Mufson et al., 1999; Rossello & Bernal, 1999). However, this intervention has not yet been investigated with depressed adolescents to the extent that cognitive behavior therapy and coping-skills training have.

Moreover, we still do not have clear answers to the following questions: Why do these psychoeducational interventions work with depressed adolescents? Are all of the skill components necessary? How practical and user-friendly will these skill-oriented psycho-therapies be on a large scale? Why do the additions of parent training or family therapy seem to be less effective here than with some other age groups (Kazdin, 1999, 2000; Kazdin & Weisz, 1998; Lewinsohn et al., 1996, 1998)?

Of course, pharmacotherapy is also sometimes used for treating depressed adolescents, although less so than for treating adult and elderly depressed patients (American Psychiatric Association, 2000b; Halbreich & Montgomery, 2000; Nemeroff & Schatzberg, 1998; Niederehe & Schneider, 1998; Schatzberg, 2000; Thase & Kupfer, 1996). In alignment with these practice differences, the controlled outcome research on pharmacotherapy with adolescents is much less extensive than it is with adults. A few studies suggest modestly positive effects for pharmacotherapy-focused interventions with depressed adolescents, but complete and lasting recovery is quite rare (e.g., Emslie et al., 1997).

Finally, it would be optimal to prevent adolescent depression before it gets started—or at least before it has fully developed and generated considerable disruption in the adolescent's life. There are some impressive studies on this issue (Lewinsohn et al., 1998) that use a coping-skills emphasis, but much more prevention research is needed. With the huge increase in depressive episodes during middle to late adolescence (ages 14–18; Hankin et al., 1998; Wichstrom, 1999), effective prevention programs for adolescents would have obvious advantages. Clearly, it is better to prevent severe depression than to treat it after it has fully developed (Beardslee et al., 1997; Birmaher, Ryan, Williamson, Brent, & Kaufman, 1996; Birmaher, Ryan, Williamson, Brent, Kaufman et al., 1996; Cicchetti & Toth, 1998; Gillham et al., 1995; Quindlen, 1999). Furthermore, we know that adolescent depression is a risk factor for experiencing multiple depressive episodes as an adult (Pine, Cohen, Cohen, & Brook, 1999). Thus, prevention efforts deserve more attention.

Suicide

Depressed adolescents are at a serious risk for suicide (Harrington, Kerfoot et al., 1998; Jamison, 1999; Jobes, Berman, & Martin, 2000; Rotheram-Borus, Piacentini, Cantwell, Belin, & Song, 2000). For example, some experts (Lewinsohn et al., 1996) estimate that 40% of the depressed adolescents seen in their treatment programs have made a suicide attempt. We will leave most of our discussion about suicide to our chapter on this topic (Chapter 9). However, in this chapter we will mention the strongest risk factors for adolescent suicide attempts (Lewinsohn et al., 1996): current depression, history of several chronic depressions, current suicidal thoughts, past suicide attempts, depressive thinking styles, low self-esteem, poor coping skills, appetite problems, having been born to a teenage mother, hopelessness, suicide attempt by a friend, and difficulty functioning because of an illness or injury. Chronic substance abuse is another important risk factor for suicide in depressed adolescents (Jacobs, 1999; Maris, Berman, & Silverman, 2000; Westefeld et al., 2000).

Suicide attempts are distressingly common in depressed adolescents (Jamison, 1999). No matter who we are and what we do, most of us will encounter at least one suicidal adolescent during our lifetime. Most health care practitioners and mental health professionals will encounter *many* suicidal adolescents. Therefore, it is useful to know the risk factors for adolescent suicide attempts.

Special Topics

Comorbid conditions are frequently associated with Major Depressive Disorder in adolescents (American Psychiatric Association, 2000a). For example, anxiety disorders are frequently associated with depression in this age group (Mineka et al., 1998), and practitioners will find it helpful to be aware of practice guidelines for treating anxiety disorders (e.g., American Psychiatric Association, 2000b; Craske & Zucker, 2001). In addition, depressed adolescents often have the comorbid conditions of substance use disorders, eating disorders, and the diverse group of attention-deficit/disruptive-behavior disorders (American Psychiatric

Association, 2000a). Thus, practitioners should assess for these conditions and then thoroughly treat these comorbid conditions if they are present (e.g., American Psychiatric Association, 2000b; McCrady & Ziedonis, 2001; Wilson & Agras, 2001).

Family therapy interventions may be an attractive treatment option for depressed adolescents because some of their conflict and dysphoria is often intertwined with their family relationships. In our opinion, family therapy may be particularly helpful as a complementary intervention to individual therapy for depressed adolescent patients. Individual therapy affords obvious advantages such as personal focus, security, and confidentiality for the adolescent patient. Family therapy affords obvious advantages such as communication enhancement and interpersonal problem solving for the family system. We recommend, however, that practitioners avoid dual-role relationship problems by arranging for different therapists to conduct the individual and family interventions (Koocher & Keith-Spiegel, 1998; Pope & Vasquez, 1998). The literature on family therapy includes some promising outcome studies (e.g., Birmaher et al., 2000; Kolko et al., 2000) and some thorough reviews of the empirical research (e.g., Baucom et al., 1998; Beach, 2001).

Clinical Guidelines

- Always include a thorough interview in your assessment effort.
- Confidentiality should be carefully discussed with your depressed adolescent patients, and the limits of confidentiality should be explicitly covered.
- Include some evaluation of suicidal risk factors.
- Assess for comorbid conditions. If comorbid conditions are present, then provide thorough treatment interventions for them.
- Evaluate your patient's social support, peer relationships, family system, and interpersonal skills.
- Calibrate for puberty changes during adolescence when counseling your patients.
- Evidence sensitivity regarding the social stigma related to depression.

- Include a brief, skill-oriented psychotherapy as part of your treatment package.
- Emphasize training in problem solving and active coping skills, particularly with female patients, given the findings regarding adolescent gender differences in depression.
- Consider the merits of family therapy as a complementary treatment to individual therapy. Avoid dual-role relationships by having different therapists conduct these two interventions.
- If you have expertise in this area, then consider the merits of doing some pro bono work.
- If possible, add booster sessions to your treatment protocol because relapse is a problem.
- Empathy is crucial here—adolescence is often a challenging developmental period.

Chapter Summary

About 5% of adolescents are depressed at a given point in time, and about 20% of adolescents experience depression between the ages of 12 and 19. In middle to later adolescence, from ages 14 to 18, depression is twice as common in females as males. Assessment of adolescent depression should include an interview, along with an evaluation of the adolescent's family, peer, and school situations. The symptoms and signs of adolescent depression will often include some of the following thoughts, emotions, and behaviors: anger and aggression, low self-esteem and high self-criticism, anxiety, confused and dysfunctional thinking, high self-consciousness, irritable mood, reduced activities because of illness or injury, poor interpersonal problem solving, antisocial behavior, sleep difficulties and weight loss or gain, difficulty coping effectively with close peer relationships or family chaos or depressed parents, suicidal risk factors, and additional psychiatric problems (e.g., chronic substance abuse).

Depressed adolescents typically cope poorly with interpersonal stress, and they often cause some of their own social stress. A close relationship with a depressed parent is an important risk factor for adolescent depression.

Coping-skills training and cognitive behavior therapy appear to be the most efficacious psychotherapies for adolescent depression. The goals of these psychoeducational interventions include modifying depressive thinking styles, improving interpersonal skills, facilitating social problem solving, reducing anxiety, and increasing pleasurable activities. Interpersonal psychotherapy has also evidenced promise in this area. Pharmacotherapy for depressed adolescents may sometimes be helpful, but pharmacotherapy-alone interventions rarely yield complete or durable recoveries in severely depressed adolescents. We recommend that brief, skill-oriented psychotherapy be part of the treatment package. Family therapy may also be helpful as a complementary intervention to individual treatment. There is some promising prevention research, but we need more.

Depressed adolescents are at a serious risk for suicide. The strongest risk factors for *adolescent* suicide attempts are the following: current depression, chronic depressions, suicidal thoughts, past attempts, depressive thinking styles, low self-esteem, poor coping skills, appetite problems, having been born to a teenage mother, hopelessness, suicide attempt by a friend, difficulty functioning because of an illness or injury, and chronic substance abuse.

Suggested Readings

Discussions

Gender Differences

- Cyranowski et al. (2000) discussed the increase in stressors, affiliation needs, and interpersonal challenges that are faced by many adolescent females. This review integrates much of the literature on the gender differences in prevalence and course of adolescent depression.

Research on Psychotherapy

- Kazdin (2000) discussed a broad array of research issues regarding psychotherapy for adolescents, including the need for more attention to the mechanisms of efficacious psychotherapy. Kazdin made a compelling argument for more programmatic research on why psychotherapy works.

Psychological Interventions

- Kazdin and Weisz (1998) concluded that training in coping skills is a promising treatment for adolescent depression. This review of the empirical treatment literature also raises some interesting methodological and practical issues.

General Review

- Lewinsohn et al. (1998) discussed symptoms, risk factors, assessment, treatment, and clinical issues regarding depressed adolescents.

Studies

- Birmaher et al. (2000) conducted a randomized controlled trial and found no differences, at the 2-year follow-up, between cognitive behavior therapy, family therapy, and supportive therapy for depressed adolescents (see also Kolko et al., 2000). Most (80%) of the 107 participants recovered, and participants in the three psychotherapy conditions evidenced similar improvements.
- Hankin et al. (1998) conducted a longitudinal study that evaluated 653 males and females as they developed from ages 11 to 21. This study indicated that the gender difference in depression, with more females than males experiencing depression, develops primarily between the ages of 15 and 18 (see also Wichstrom, 1999).
- Pine et al. (1999) conducted a longitudinal study with 776 adolescent participants. Their findings suggested that symptoms of depression during adolescence yield a strong risk factor for depression during adulthood.

- Rotheram-Borus et al. (2000) used a quasi-experimental design to evaluate an intervention for 140 female adolescents who had attempted suicide. The investigators' findings suggested that a brief emergency room intervention to enhance adherence for outpatient therapy yielded some positive effects, especially for participants with the most severe psychiatric symptoms.

5 Depression in Adults

Overview

We begin this chapter with a case study. Then we briefly discuss research on the prevalence of adult depression. We cover some of the issues for assessment, including how well the depressive signs and symptoms illustrated in the case study mesh with the American Psychiatric Association's *DSM-IV-TR* (2000a) diagnostic criteria for Major Depressive Disorder. In addition, we provide an interview outline for evaluating adult depression. We review some treatment issues. We discuss the reality that most depressed adults cope without professional treatment. We discuss a low-level but chronic depression, Dysthymic Disorder, which lasts at least 2 years. We mention a few special topics regarding depression in adults. Finally, we present clinical guidelines, a chapter summary, and some suggested readings.

Case Study

Staci, age 33, is apparently depressed, and she has been this way for at least 3 months. She is having coffee with her best friend, Pam.

Staci: Oh . . . I just feel low and worthless. I'm miserable. It is probably hopeless for Todd and me. We just can't get our marriage together. He's a decent person, but all we do is fight and then pout and then avoid each other. I sometimes wonder if he's having an affair on the side. Maybe I'm paranoid in addition to being depressed? Everything we do together seems to have a negative tone to it. And Todd seems distant and aloof. Oh, Pam, I'm a mess—I can't even sleep and eat right.

Pam: Can you arrange for more help on evenings and weekends? You know, to handle errands and housework? And also, to take care of Nicki for a few hours here and there, so you have more time to relax and exercise and just enjoy the good things in life? And I wonder if ... well, if it might be helpful for you to get some therapy? Maybe a therapist could help you to understand your situation and feel better.

Staci: I don't know about the baby-sitting help. I feel guilty about the little time that I spend with Nicki. I'm so depressed and anxious that I can't get out of this rut. Nothing is fun anymore. I had a physical exam that was normal, but I'm tired all of the time. I'm a lousy mother, and now things are falling apart at work too. I can't think worth a damn. Yesterday, I got in a stupid argument with my boss. Pam, I'm falling apart!

Pam: Please stop this "I can't think worth a damn" stuff. Come on Staci, you're only 33 years old and already the associate managing editor for a major newspaper. This is a big deal! And I don't want to hear you saying you're a "bad mother." I've seen you and Nicki together a hundred times, and she loves you a lot! Please think about hiring some more help around the house. And you've avoided discussing my suggestion about getting therapy. Might this help?

Staci: It might. But I feel awkward about this issue. I've never had any therapy. It's scary for me. And I don't think I could handle marital counseling right now, even though Todd and I have big problems. The therapy thing seems like such a big step. I don't know.

Pam: I think that you would benefit from some therapy. I want to help you, but I don't know how. Look Staci, we need to get you some expert help. And we also need to get you some more help at home—you're overwhelmed with work and totally exhausted!

Staci: I feel hopeless and inadequate. You want to help me—this is really nice of you, Pam. But I don't know. I just feel miserable. I'm sorry. I'm a mess.

Pam: Let's make some calls about getting you help!

Discussion of the Case Study

This case study illustrates many of the symptoms and signs regarding the common type of depression that we are focusing on in this book: Major Depressive Disorder (American Psychiatric Association, 2000a). The persistent depressed mood and loss of pleasure are obvious. The disruptions in sleep, appetite, and concentration are clearly evident. Staci is experiencing fatigue without a general medical condition, and she is feeling very guilty. She reports considerable disruption in her daily functioning for several months. She is also experiencing some problems in her personal life, but not because she is inept with social situations; after all, she is associate managing editor for a major newspaper, which implies a high level of social skills. Finally, she does not appear to have the *DSM-IV-TR* (American Psychiatric Association, 2000a) depressive sign of psychomotor retardation or the symptom of suicidal ideation. An interview with a practitioner, of course, would be necessary to establish whether Staci meets the diagnostic criteria for Major Depressive Disorder.

This case illustrates that caring and well-meaning people may still be overwhelmed by severe depression in their friends. Pam is patiently trying to help. Reminding Staci, however, that she is professionally successful will probably not be enough to cure her depression. As Pam understands, some skillful psychotherapy from an appropriately trained practitioner is probably needed here. Furthermore, it is likely that additional treatment beyond individual psychotherapy, such as marital counseling or pharmacotherapy, may be helpful here; but a thorough assessment will be needed to evaluate the merits of these treatment options.

Prevalence

Approximately 5% of the adults in the United States and Canada are depressed and meeting the diagnostic criteria for Major Depressive Disorder at a given point in time (American Psychiatric Association, 2000a; Blazer et al., 1994; Murphy, Laird, et al., 2000). This figure indicates that about 14 million adults in the United States are currently experiencing Major Depressive Disorder and that they would meet the diagnostic criteria for Major Depressive Disorder (American Psychiatric Association, 2000a).

The prevalence of Major Depressive Disorder in U.S. adults does not have a strong relationship to race, education, salary, or marital status (American Psychiatric Association, 2000a). Nevertheless, there is some evidence that higher rates of depression, and health problems in general, are present in the economically disadvantaged (e.g., Lantz et al., 1998). Approximately twice as many adult women are depressed as men (Kessler et al., 1994). Once depressed, however, adult men and women show a similar course of depression (Simpson et al., 1997). There is some evidence that the first experience of depression is occurring at earlier ages—for instance, during adolescence (Weissman & Olfson, 1995). Why the onset of depression is happening at younger ages is unclear. However, cultural changes involving less social support and more social stress–particularly for *females* during adolescence—are possible explanations (Cyranowski et al., 2000; Frank, 2000; Nolen-Hoeksema & Girgus, 1994; Taylor, Klein, et al., 2000). In addition, the prevalence of depression in the United States may be slowly increasing (Weissman et al., 1996).

Other mental disorders often occur with adult depression (Kessler et al., 1994). Examples of comorbid conditions with depression include anxiety disorders (Zlotnick et al., 1997), substance abuse (American Psychiatric Association, 2000b), eating disorders (Sanderson et al., 1990), and extreme, unmanageable anger (Kopper & Epperson, 1996). Furthermore, depression itself may reflect a broad array of related mental health disorders (American Psychiatric Association, 2000a; Kendler & Gardner, 1998; Lewinsohn et al., 2000).

For adults, the typical episode of depression lasts from 12 to 20 weeks (Eaton et al., 1997). Approximately 80% of depressed adults will recover within a year (Coryell et al., 1994). Unfortunately, about 80% of formerly depressed individuals will have at least three relapses back into Major Depressive Disorder during their lifetime (Judd, 1997; Judd et al., 2000; Solomon et al., 2000). Thus, the prevention of relapse is a major treatment challenge, and then a lifelong coping challenge, for depressed patients (e.g., Jarrett et al., 1998; Jarrett et al., 2001; Paykel et al., 1999; Richards, 1999; Teasdale et al., 2000).

Assessment

In some respects, adults are the easiest age group to assess regarding depression. But in other ways, they are the hardest. They are the easiest because their language skills tend to be advanced. Depression is complex, and it is partially cognitive: It involves complex thought processes and feelings such as guilt. It is much easier to discuss "guilt" with an adult than with a child. In addition, most adult patients are voluntary—they are seeking evaluation and treatment of their own accord. Thus, they are likely to be motivated, cooperative, and conscientious in providing information and in pursuing treatment recommendations. Finally, adult patients typically have control of the information about their lives, so they can easily provide relevant information to their practitioners and therapists.

In some respects, however, adults are very challenging to assess accurately. Adults lead complex lives. Witness our case study with Staci: Her life is extremely complicated and multifaceted. Hence, an accurate assessment of Staci's depression, and of the circumstances related to it, will be challenging.

From the information presented in the case study, it does appear that Staci probably meets the criteria for a diagnosis of Major Depressive Disorder (American Psychiatric Association, 2000a). Careful interviewing will be required to see if her mood disorder is more accurately described with an alternative diagnosis or course specifier. For instance, her symptoms may meet the criteria for the course specifier of Recurrent. A diagnosis of "Major Depressive Disorder, Recurrent" requires that at least two Major Depressive Episodes be separated by at least 2 consecutive months during which criteria were not met for a Major Depressive Episode (p. 376). Moreover, her symptoms may meet the criteria for Dysthymic Disorder (less extensive depressive symptoms and signs than above but depressed mood for most of the day, for a majority of days, and for at least 2 years; pp. 380–381). It is also possible that Staci meets the criteria for "double depression," which means that she has superimposed episodes of Dysthymic Disorder and Major Depressive Disorder, after an initial 2 years of Dysthymic Disorder, so that both diagnoses may be given.

Staci clearly seems to have the *DSM-IV-TR* (American Psychiatric Association, 2000a, p. 356) symptoms of persistently depressed mood that are required for a diagnosis of Major Depressive Disorder. These symptoms must be persistent and present for at least 2 weeks, a criterion that she easily meets. In addition, Staci evidences the symptoms of persistent loss of interest or pleasure in most activities, which is one of the nine symptom-and-sign clusters for Major Depressive Disorder.

As noted previously, Staci also appears to have at least five additional symptoms of Major Depressive Disorder, which have been persistently evident for at least 2 weeks. Four additional symptoms and signs (beyond depressed mood or loss of interest/pleasure) are required for a diagnosis of Major Depressive Disorder. (If both depressed mood and loss of interest/pleasure are established, then only three additional symptoms are required.) Diagnostic rule-out decisions regarding whether Staci is experiencing symptoms of mania, whether her symptoms are due to substance use or general medical conditions, and whether her symptoms are causing significant distress or impairment in functioning will also need to be established via the interview process. Additional diagnostic rule-outs, such as not having Schizoaffective Disorder, seem likely in Staci's case because she does not evidence psychotic thinking (e.g., delusions or hallucinations).

To be valid, the assessment process must include an *interview* by an appropriately trained practitioner (American Psychiatric Association, 2000b). The practitioner must observe the patient's signs and discuss the patient's symptoms and then be able to flexibly pursue additional issues as these become relevant. For instance, while the clinician is interviewing Staci, it may become apparent that she also coped with depression as an adolescent and that her mother was seriously depressed. This is information that is very relevant to Staci's risk for recurrent depression (Pine, Cohen, Gurley, Brook, & Ma, 1998; Pine et al., 1999). The interview should cover a wide range of relevant issues, including depression history, social matters, health status, economic stability, substance use, additional psychiatric disorders, and other stressors. More-over, the interview is important for noting objective signs of depression, such as psychomotor retardation.

If questionnaires are used, they should *supplement* the interview. Examples of relevant questionnaires include the Center for Epidemiol-ogic Studies-Depression Scale (CES-D; Radloff, 1977), a 20-item screen-ing questionnaire. The well-known Beck Depression Inventory-II (BDI-II; Beck et al., 1996) is a 21-item questionnaire. The results of these questionnaires, however, do not correspond closely to the diag-noses of depression that are determined by interviews (Zimmerman & Coryell, 1994). A four-item screening questionnaire for suicidal risk in general medical patients, developed by Cooper-Patrick et al. (1994), may be a useful screening device, but you should follow it with an inter-view for patients who have high-risk scores.

Interview Outline for Adults

- *Use an organized interview system.* For example, the "five phases of the interview" system proposed by Othmer and Othmer (1994, p. 273) provides a sensible framework, which we summarize here: (a) Allow for some warm-up and then interview about symptoms; (b) do some follow-up on your preliminary observations; (c) collect infor-mation about your patient's history and current circumstances; (d) establish a diagnosis (American Psychiatric Association, 2000a) and discuss this diagnosis with your patient; and (e) discuss prognosis and treatment options with your patient.

- *Do not rely only on paper-and-pencil tests* (Meier & Davis, 1997). For instance, due to a response bias such as trying to portray herself favorably, Staci might score 8 on the BDI-II. A score of 8 is not con-sidered in the diagnosable range for depression (Beck et al., 1996). But during the interview, Staci might explain that "I hate question-naires that tell everyone how inadequate I am, so I decided to put a 0 for almost every statement, regardless of how I really feel."

- *When you suspect that a mood disorder is central to the patient's symptoms, you should ask about this directly.* For example, Othmer and Othmer (1994) recommended the following question: "Have there ever been times when you felt unusually depressed, empty, sad, or hopeless for several days or weeks at a time?" (p. 222).

- *Depression has several dimensions that you should ask about, such as length, severity, and disruptions in daily living* (American Psychiatric Association, 2000a, 2000b).
- *Use an outline for the DSM-IV-TR (2000a) symptoms of a Major Depressive Episode.* For example, here is a brief outline of the *DSM-IV-TR* (2000a) criteria for a Major Depressive Episode: The patient has at least five symptoms from the nine possible symptom clusters, including (a) or (b): (a) depression, (b) interest, (c) appetite, (d) sleep, (e) psychomotor, (f) fatigue, (g) guilt, (h) concentration, and (i) suicide. Symptom duration for at least 2 weeks. Distress or impaired functioning. Rule-outs include the following: mania, psychotic disorders, drug effects, physiological effects from a general medical condition, dysthymia, and short-term bereavement. During the interview, you should carefully inquire about each of these symptom-and-sign clusters, and the associated diagnostic criteria.
- *Be cautious.* "*Do not assume that you know clients' feelings, thoughts, and behaviors*" (Meier & Davis, 1997, p. 37).
- *Get information about your patient's history and current circumstances.* Moreover, give your patient plenty of time to talk. You should inquire about social support, marital and family issues, health problems and recent physical exams, employment situation, economic stability, substance use, comorbid conditions, and other stressors.

Treatment

There is a consensus among most experts that three psychotherapies for adult depression enjoy the strongest empirical support. These psychotherapies are behavior therapy, cognitive behavior therapy, and interpersonal psychotherapy. Behavior therapy emphasizes learning, skill enhancement, increased reinforcement, and the modification of observable behavior in more adaptive directions (see Lewinsohn et al., 1998). Cognitive behavior therapy includes these goals from behavior therapy but adds an effort to modify dysfunctional cognitions and emotions (Beck et al., 1979; Clark & Beck, 1999). Interpersonal psychotherapy focuses on improving interpersonal skills and resolving problems in close relationships (Klerman et al., 1984; Markowitz, 1998). These psychotherapies are typically conducted in a time-limited fashion—often 20 or fewer therapy sessions. In addition, these psychotherapies have compatible goals: They teach more adaptive skills and more effective coping to depressed patients.

Craighead et al. (1998) and DeRubeis and Crits-Christoph (1998) provided reviews of this topic. They summarized the *compelling* research support for behavior therapy, cognitive behavior therapy, and interpersonal psychotherapy. These psychological interventions for depressed adults, particularly the latter two, are supported by numerous well-controlled studies with depressed patients. Cognitive behavior therapy and interpersonal psychotherapy may also have some protective features in terms of lowering relapse rates (Hollon & Shelton, 2001).

DeRubeis and Crits-Christoph (1998) also noted that there is empirical support for a problem-solving therapy of depression. This approach includes a focus on five steps in effective problem solving: problem orientation, definition, alternatives, decision, and implementation (Arean et al., 1993; D'Zurilla & Nezu, 1999; Nezu et al., 1989).

Some experts have estimated that approximately 60,000 empirical publications on depression have appeared since 1980 (Seligman & Csikszentmihalyi, 2000). It would be easy for the busy practitioner to become overwhelmed by this huge and diverse literature. Therefore, we will mention only a few of the most crucial issues below.

Although efficacious psychotherapies for adult depression have been developed, these psychotherapies will work better under favorable conditions. For instance, interpersonal psychotherapy works better if it is delivered under standardized conditions, including the use of treatment manuals, planned therapy guidelines, and organized therapy sessions (Lave, Frank, Schulberg, & Kamlet, 1998). It costs more to do this way, but the extra cost is apparently worthwhile (Nathan, 1998; Rost, Zhang, Fortney, Smith, & Smith, 1998).

Another important treatment issue regards the *combination* of psychotherapy and pharmacotherapy. For particularly severe and chronic depression, this may be the most efficacious approach (American Psychiatric Association, 2000b; Hollon & Shelton, 2001). For example, Keller et al. (2000) found a combined approach to be the most efficacious with 681 chronically depressed adults. Thase et al. (1997) reached similar conclusions with an evaluation of 595 depressed patients.

Whether or not psychotherapy is provided, there has been a large increase during the last 15 years in the use of medication to treat depression. This trend in significantly greater use of pharmacotherapy to treat depression is clearly illustrated by the research of Olfson, Marcus, et al. (1998). Experts are less certain, however, that pharmacotherapy is necessary for *mild* cases of depression, and this matter should be carefully evaluated by the practitioner (American Psychiatric Association, 2000b; DeRubeis et al., 1999; Halbreich & Montgomery, 2000; Hollon & Shelton, 2001; Rankin, 2000).

In addition, some investigations have suggested that psychotherapy without pharmacotherapy may yield successful outcomes for severely depressed individuals (e.g., DeRubeis et al., 1999; Jarrett et al., 1999). For example, Rudd et al. (1996) have provided evidence that a psychological intervention for suicidal young adults may achieve favorable results without pharmacotherapy. Their intervention focused on improved problem-solving and interpersonal skills, and it yielded more positive results than a comparison intervention of hospitalization plus pharmacotherapy plus counseling. Nevertheless, the standard intervention for adults who are quite severely and chronically depressed, imminently suicidal, or depressed and psychotic is a *combination* of brief hospitalization (day and night), pharmacotherapy, and psychotherapy.

The empirical literature suggests that electro-convulsive therapy (ECT) is a potentially helpful therapy for severely depressed adult patients who have failed to respond to any of the front-line therapies (American Psychiatric Association, 2000b; Fava & Rosenbaum, 1995; Hammen, 1997). Nevertheless, there are many concerns about ECT, including problems with toleration, memory, and durability. For example, relapse is common following the completion of ECT. Illustrating this concern, a large randomized controlled trial by Sackeim et al. (2001) indicated that "without active treatment [maintenance pharmacotherapy], virtually all remitted patients relapse within 6 months of stopping ECT" (p. 1299). Even in the most effective of the maintenance pharmacotherapy conditions, the relapse rate was 39% for the 6 months following ECT completion.

Another important treatment issue is the presence of *comorbid conditions and problems associated with depression:* Depression is often associated with other disorders and problems. For example, Kessler et al. (1994) interviewed a representative sample of 8,098 Americans between the ages of 15 and 54. Approximately 17% of this sample had a history of three or more disorders, and these multiple disorders occurred together. Comorbid conditions that were often associated with depression included anxiety disorders, eating disorders, personality disorders, and substance abuse.

A specific example of comorbid conditions comes from the association of depression and anxiety disorders: "Comorbid anxiety-depressive disorders have a poor outcome compared with single anxiety and depressive disorders" (Emmanuel, Simmonds, & Tyrer, 1998, p. 35). The most severe cases usually include comorbid conditions. Moreover, the comorbid conditions of depression and anxiety are common. For instance, interviews of a representative sample of 20,291 adults in the United States indicated that 47% of those who had experienced Major Depressive Disorder had also experienced a serious anxiety disorder, which occurred together with the depression (Regier et al., 1998).

The association of depression with chronic health problems, such as cardiovascular disease, also dovetails with our theme. "Clinical depression appears to be an independent risk factor for incident coronary artery disease for several decades after the onset of the clinical depression" (Ford et al., 1998, p. 1422; see also Ferketich, Schwartzbaum, Frid, & Moeschberger, 2000; Penninx et al., 2001).

In addition, the association of depression with severely distressed close relationships is thoroughly established (Beach, 2001; Butzlaff & Hooley, 1998; Joiner & Coyne, 1999). Recent examples include a study by Gottman, Coan, Carrere, and Swanson (1998), which illustrated the association of depression and divorce. An investigation by Moos, Cronkite, and Moos (1998) demonstrated the relationship of meager social resources to relapse in depression. Furthermore, a study by Keitner et al. (1995) showed that hostile family relationships correlate with relapse back into depression (see also Butzlaff & Hooley, 1998).

Practitioners should carefully assess for comorbid conditions and problems that are frequently associated with depression. Then they should aggressively treat these conditions if the conditions are present.

Relapse back into depression is a major problem with no easy solutions (Fava, 1999; Richards, 1999). Coping effectively with severe depression may require a lifelong effort, and preventing relapse may require at least 6 to 12 months of occasional booster sessions. This appears to be the implication of several large outcome studies on using booster sessions to reduce depressive relapse (e.g., Fava, Rafanelli, Grandi, Conti, & Belluardo, 1998; Jarrett et al., 1998; Jarrett et al., 2001; Katon et al., 2001; Paykel et al., 1999; Reynolds et al., 1999). Even providing pharmacotherapy for 5 years after initial treatment does not eliminate relapse (e.g., Kupfer et al., 1992). In addition, this latter approach could raise concerns about the side effects of the medications, which may become problematic following many years of use (American Psychiatric Association, 2000b; Halbreich & Montgomery, 2000; Nemeroff & Schatzberg, 1998; Rankin, 2000; Thase & Kupfer, 1996).

With particularly high-risk patients, a form of continuous care may be necessary during the remainder of the patient's life to prevent or minimize relapses. This "continuous-care model" of maintaining treatment effects has also been suggested for other domains of psychological and physical health, such as obesity (e.g., Perri, 1998). Providing brief counseling opportunities and monitored pharmacotherapy throughout the life span will pose practical, evaluative, and financial challenges. Nevertheless, coping with these challenges is preferable to coping with a relentless series of relapses (Jamison, 1999; U.S. Surgeon General, 1999). Thus, providing adequate treatments and support systems will entail significant financial commitments, but we believe that these commitments are worth it (see Quindlen, 1999, 2001).

An investment on the research side of this issue is already paying off. For instance, we are seeing some progress on dealing with the relapse problem. Thus, for example, a study by Fava et al. (1998) suggested that booster sessions of cognitive behavior therapy may dramatically reduce the percentage of patients who relapse during a 2-year period after treatment; relapse was reduced from 80% to 25%. This result is particularly impressive because the patients in the Fava et al. (1998) study were at a high risk for relapse due to numerous previous relapses. In summary, booster sessions may cost more money, but they appear to have some merit for reducing relapse in depressed patients (e.g., Jarrett et al., 1998; Jarrett et al., 2001; Katon et al., 2001; Paykel et al., 1999; Reynolds et al., 1999; see also Richards, 1999). Long-term pharmacotherapy is also a well-established relapse prevention strategy (American Psychiatric Association, 2000b; Rankin, 2000).

Coping Without Treatment

Most depressed individuals do not receive any professional help for their depression. They cope on their own. A convincing demonstration of this phenomenon is the research of Kessler et al. (1994): "The majority of people with psychiatric disorders fail to obtain professional treatment" (p. 8). In this large study of 8,098 adults, the investigators found that less than 40% of the individuals with a psychiatric disorder ever received some kind of professional treatment for their disorder. Thus, most depressed people cope on their own, without pharmacotherapy or psychotherapy or even a brief discussion of the matter with their primary care physician (Olfson, Kessler, Berglund, & Lin, 1998).

When individuals cope with depression on their own, without professional help, they are more likely to be successful if their coping efforts are active rather than passive. It also is beneficial if they make positive changes in their social environment and if they emphasize the positive aspects of their lives. Further, it helps if they plan and problem-solve. Finally, improvement is more likely if they avoid alcohol abuse and ruminating about anger, negative experiences, and records of failure. We also discuss this issue in the chapter on relapse prevention (Chapter 12; see also Doerfler & Richards, 1981, 1983).

Chronic Depression

Some adults experience a low-level but chronic depression, diagnosed as Dysthymic Disorder, which lasts for 2 years or longer (American Psychiatric Association, 2000a). The research literature documents the very serious consequences of low-level but chronic depression (Klein et al., 1998). Being depressed for a long time, even if it is not extremely severe depression, can be particularly debilitating. Moreover, it can have negative impact across a broad array of issues in daily living. For example, there is evidence that Dysthymic Disorder is quite disruptive to close relationships (Burns et al., 1994; Whisman & Bruce, 1999). These themes are evident in our case study of Staci. Low-level but chronic depression is a problem for many Americans; about 3% of the adult U.S. population have the symptoms of Dysthymic Disorder (Kessler et al., 1994).

Fortunately, Dysthymic Disorder can be treated efficaciously. Long-term pharmacotherapy evidences promise for treating Dysthymic Disorder (e.g., Keller et al., 2000; Kocsis et al., 1996; see also Markowitz, 1998). Another approach is psychotherapy that is geared to the realities of chronic depression. Within the psychotherapy approaches, we find interpersonal psychotherapy very attractive for treating Dysthymic Disorder because it focuses on enhancing interpersonal skills and resolving problems in close relationships. We know that Dysthymic Disorder may be quite disruptive for close relationships. Markowitz (1998) provided an overview of the research on interpersonal psychotherapy for Dysthymic Disorder and a treatment manual.

Not surprisingly, cognitive behavior therapy also shows promise for treating Dysthymic Disorder (DeRubeis & Crits-Christoph, 1998; DeRubeis et al., 1999; Hollon & Shelton, 2001; Keller et al., 2000). Both interpersonal psychotherapy and cognitive behavior therapy address specific depressive symptoms and consequences, which are highlighted in chronic depression. Both of these psychological interventions are time limited and amenable to group treatment formats. Most important, both of these psychotherapies enjoy strong empirical support (Craighead et al., 1998). We should caution, however, that a more comprehensive treatment may sometimes be required with Dysthymic

Disorder than with Major Depressive Disorder (Keller et al., 2000; Markowitz, 1998). For example, *combined* treatments of cognitive behavior therapy and long-term pharmacotherapy may be particularly helpful interventions for patients with Dysthymic Disorder (Keller et al., 2000). Finally, practitioners should always be alert for the risk factors regarding depressive relapse and recurrence.

Special Topics

For the practitioner, ethical and practical challenges include the goal of arranging for your patient to receive the best possible care (American Psychiatric Association, 2000b; Appelbaum, Grisso, Frank, O'Donnell, & Kupfer, 1999). At the same time, practitioners must be realistic about the treatment limitations implied by economics, resources, and patient motivations. Even when finances are not a problem, depressed individuals are often reluctant to pursue treatment. For example, Olfson, Kessler, et al. (1998) found that the percentage of depressed adults seeking treatment in Canada, which has universal medical coverage, was not markedly different than in the Unied States, where many adults are uninsured. In both Canada and the United States, only about one third of all depressed adults seek treatment within the first year of their depressive episode.

It is difficult to imagine a mental health or health care practitioner who will not see depressed patients. Obviously, these professionals should pursue training and continuing education regarding depression. In addition, some depressed patients will be very challenging for the practitioner. This area of psychotherapy can be difficult: "Therapy can be a grim business, and a sense of humor helps us survive" (Haley, 1996, p. 36). We provide a discussion of difficult therapeutic challenges in the epilogue to this book.

Perhaps the most daunting research and practice goal is to develop more effective maintenance strategies following initial treatment. Relapse prevention not only is difficult but often requires a significant amount of effort, time, and money. The practical constraints of the real world do not always afford us these resources. In addition, even with all of the effort imaginable, we are still not sure *how* to effectively accomplish relapse prevention. Thus, we need more research on this issue.

Clinical Guidelines

- Conduct a thorough assessment. An interdisciplinary effort, involving relevant health care, human service, and mental health practitioners, will give you the most thorough and accurate assessment.
- Always include a face-to-face interview in your assessment process.
- Assess for suicidal risk factors, and then intervene as necessary.
- Evaluate your depressed patients for comorbid conditions.
- Issues involving social support and close relationships should be assessed with your depressed patients.
- For severe cases of depression, arrange for immediate treatment of your patient.
- For severe cases of depression, a *combination* of pharmacotherapy and psychotherapy is often considered the most efficacious treatment; and you should consider the merits of this combined approach.
- For mild cases of depression, consider the merits of psychotherapy as a stand-alone treatment, but carefully monitor the progress that your patient makes.
- Include a type of psychotherapy in your treatment program that enjoys strong empirical support. The three most supported psychotherapies for adult depression are behavior therapy, cognitive behavior therapy, and interpersonal psychotherapy.
- Pharmacotherapy as a stand-alone treatment option under physician monitoring is common and widely accepted, but we recommend also including brief psychotherapy in your treatment programs.
- Consider the merits of *combined* psychotherapy and pharmacotherapy for your patients with Dysthymic Disorder.
- Maintenance procedures should be built into your treatment programs. These relapse prevention strategies could include booster psychotherapy sessions, phone and mail follow-up contacts, and long-term pharmacotherapy.
- You should help your patients who have experienced numerous relapses to adopt the following perspective: Coping with depression is a lifelong process.

- Develop a solid knowledge base for this topic, and then regularly pursue continuing education.

Chapter Summary

About 5% of the adults in the United States are depressed (i.e., they meet diagnostic criteria for Major Depressive Disorder) at a given point in time. Approximately twice as many adult women are depressed as men, but the course of depression is similar for adult women and men. A typical episode of depression lasts from 12 to 20 weeks. About 80% of formerly depressed individuals will have at least three relapses back into depression during their lifetime.

The psychotherapies for adult depression with the strongest empirical support are behavior therapy, cognitive behavior therapy, and interpersonal psychotherapy. The latter two interventions, in particular, enjoy clear empirical support from numerous randomized controlled trials with depressed adult patients. These psychological interventions can often be completed within 20 therapy sessions. The focus of these psychotherapies is on teaching enhanced skills and effective coping.

For extremely severe and chronic cases of depression, the most efficacious intervention may be a combination of pharmacotherapy and psychotherapy. Pharmacotherapy also enjoys strong empirical support as a stand-alone intervention. We believe that it is preferable, however, that pharmacotherapy not be used in isolation; rather, brief psychotherapy should also be a part of the treatment package. For mild cases of depression, psychotherapy as a stand-alone treatment frequently yields successful outcomes.

Even following successful treatment, most depressed adults relapse. Booster sessions of psychotherapy and/or contact with well-trained practitioners evidences promise for preventing relapse. Long-term follow-ups, however, suggest that booster sessions and other post- treatment interventions are not always sufficient to prevent relapse. Coping effectively with severe depression may require a lifelong effort and a continuous-care model of treatment. Multiyear interventions with pharma- cotherapy have also shown promise for reducing depressive relapse, although this relapse prevention strategy raises concerns about the side effects of long-term antidepressant use.

Suggested Readings

Discussions

Reviews of Psychotherapy Research and Practice Guidelines

- Craighead et al. (1998) concluded that there is considerable empirical support regarding three psychological treatments for adult depression: behavior therapy, cognitive behavior therapy, and interpersonal psychotherapy. This review is thorough and readable.
- DeRubeis et al. (1999) concluded that cognitive behavior therapy has demonstrated clear efficacy for the treatment of depression, which is equivalent to the efficacy demonstrated by pharmacotherapy. This interesting review documents the impressive efficacy of cognitive behavior therapy for treating adult depression.
- Hollon and Shelton (2001) discussed the empirical literature on psychotherapy for depression, particularly cognitive behavior therapy and interpersonal psychotherapy, which enjoy the strongest empirical support among the various psychotherapies for adult depression. This review includes extensive commentary on the practice guidelines for treating Major Depressive Disorder that were developed by the American Psychiatric Association (2000b).

Cognitive Behavior Therapy

- Persons (1989) provided examples and clinical guidelines regarding cognitive behavior therapy. This is a helpful "how-to" book (see also Beck et al., 1979).

Interpersonal Psychotherapy

- Markowitz (1998) offered literature reviews, how-to examples, and recommendations for treating chronic depression through interpersonal psychotherapy. This is a useful "how-to" book (see also Klerman et al., 1984).

Practice Guidelines for Pharmacotherapy

- The American Psychiatric Association's (2000b) practice guidelines regarding pharmacotherapy of depression are quite helpful. A panel of experts representing the American Psychiatric Association developed these practice guidelines.

Studies

- Katon et al. (2001) conducted a randomized controlled trial with 386 depressed participants who were receiving long-term pharmacotherapy through their primary care physicians. Booster sessions entailed follow-up visits to the clinic, phone calls, and personalized mailings over a 1-year period. Results suggested that these booster sessions enhanced adherence to antidepressant medications and reduced depressive symptom profiles. The booster sessions were implemented by three "depression prevention specialists" (p. 243): a psychologist, a nurse practitioner, and a social worker.
- Keller et al. (2000) conducted a randomized controlled trial. The findings indicated that combined psychotherapy (cognitive behavior therapy) and pharmacotherapy (nefazodone) was more efficacious than either therapy alone in the treatment of 681 adults with chronic depression.
- Moos et al. (1998) conducted a longitudinal study with 313 depressed patients who had received treatment. The investigators' findings indicated that relapse was less likely for patients who had extensive and stable social relationships.
- Shaw et al. (1999) analyzed data from the National Institute of Mental Health (NIMH) Treatment of Depression Collaborative Research Program, which is a large randomized trial. Their findings suggested that to be most efficacious, psychotherapists using cognitive behavior therapy need to translate their treatment plans into a coherent therapy experience for the patient (e.g., the therapy is highly structured).
- Whisman and Bruce (1999) conducted a prospective investigation. Their results indicated that the development of depression was three times more likely in dissatisfied spouses than satisfied ones.

6 Depression in Older Adults

Overview

We begin this chapter with a case study. We review the symptoms, prevalence, and assessment of depression in older adults. Then we provide an overview of pharmacological, psychological, and complementary treatment approaches. We follow this with a discussion of four topics that are particularly relevant to depression in older adults: religious beliefs and response to treatment, the association of chronic health problems and depression, social isolation, and nursing homes. We conclude with clinical guidelines, a chapter summary, and some suggested readings.

Case Study

Juan is 75 years old. His wife, Mary, died a year ago. Juan is recovering from prostate cancer and he is apparently depressed. The following discussion is between Juan and his home health care nurse, Bonnie.

Juan: I'm always sick and tired from my illness. And these medications bother me sometimes. Maybe the medications make me depressed? But I know I have to take them. I'm often in pain. But I have to deal with it. I just wish I wasn't always so sad and nervous. It seems hopeless. I miss Mary so much! I never thought that she'd be the first to go.

Bonnie: Yes, I know how much you miss Mary. We need to keep coping with this as best we can. Did your friend Jesse come over here this week?

Juan: No. He's been busy with his chemotherapy. That chemo they use for bladder cancer is nasty stuff. He's pretty sick. But I wish he would come over more. I like Jesse. I wish I could get out and walk more! But with this bad leg I'm a cripple. I hope to see Jesse soon—I like him.

Bonnie: I like him too! He is a very nice person. And he likes you.

Juan: Yeah. We like each other. We're both "under the weather" right now. But Jesse has a good attitude—he doesn't get depressed. He lost his wife 2 years ago. He's always in some pain from his chemo and his arthritis. Like me, he's always broke—we don't have good health insurance for the medications we take. Jesse and I are in the same boat—we lost our wives, we have lots of health problems, we don't have much money, and it seems we don't have any fun.

Bonnie: Juan, maybe we can figure out a way to get you and Jesse together more often—this would be good for both of you! Can your friends from church help?

Juan: I don't know. I hate to bother them. But they are nice people. They do offer to drive me places. I don't know. I'm so tired. I can't sleep right. I just hurt all of the time.

Bonnie: I understand. I bet your friends from church would be very happy to drive you over to Jesse's apartment. Maybe we can call them now and set up a ride? I'll bet that Jesse would be thrilled to see you! What do you think?

Juan: Okay—let's call them. But I hope they don't see this ride as an imposition.

Discussion of the Case Study

Juan's case highlights many of the symptoms and signs that older adults evidence when they are seriously depressed. In this age group, physical illness and pain are frequently associated with depression. Numerous studies have demonstrated that the lack of contact with friends and a low level of social support are risk factors for depression in older adults. Death of a spouse, of course, is a major risk factor. However, severe bereavement and depression lasting *more than 2 months* after the loss, and disrupting day-to-day functioning, are not considered a normal grief response to such a common event (American Psychiatric Association, 2000a). In addition to the diagnostic criterion of more than 2 months' duration since the loss, other symptoms and signs that typically distinguish normal bereavement from Major Depressive Disorder are pervasive guilt, persistent suicidal ideation, preoccupied sense of worthlessness, obvious psychomotor retardation, and severe functional impairment (pp. 740–741). Juan has not come to terms or coped effectively with the loss of his wife, who died a year ago. In the United States, the average life expectancy for women is close to 80, whereas it is in the low 70s for men. Thus, husbands do not usually expect to outlive their wives, and husbands may be less skilled at self-care following the loss of a spouse (Allumbaugh & Hoyt, 1999; National Institutes of Health [NIH], 1992).

Understandably, Juan's physical handicaps limit his opportunities to get out of his apartment, see people, and have fun; but the nurse correctly realizes that this is a crucial issue, which Juan must cope with as effectively as possible. Moreover, stresses from financial difficulties, inadequate health insurance for prescription medications, and sleep disruption are frequent shadows in the lives of depressed older adults. Juan is challenged by these problems. Furthermore, some medications have depressive side effects, a possibility that Juan has developed insight about (e.g., his question "Maybe the medications make me depressed?"). Finally, depressed men over the age of 69—with or without the stress of chronic health problems—are at an increased risk for suicide (Hirschfeld & Russell, 1997; Richards & Perri, 2001). Juan, however, is not evidencing clear suicidal symptoms. We discuss suicide and depression more in Chapter 9.

Symptoms, Prevalence, and Assessment

The symptoms of severely depressed mood, diminished interest and pleasure, sleep disruption, fatigue, and suicidal thinking are often prominent in depressed older adults (Alexopoulos, Bruce, Hull, Sirey, & Kakuma, 1999; Futterman, Thompson, Gallagher-Thompson, & Ferris, 1995; Roberts et al., 2000). Concentration problems, and associated cognitive difficulties such as disorientation and memory loss, are also frequently prominent in depressed geriatric patients (American Psychiatric Association, 2000a; Alexopoulos et al., 2000). In contrast, dramatic changes in appetite, severely agitated or retarded movement, and extreme feelings of guilt tend to be less obvious in depressed older adults than in depressed young adults (American Psychiatric Association, 2000a). These symptoms, however, may be prominent in some cases among the very old (Berger, Small, Forsell, Winblad, & Backman, 1998; Copeland et al., 1999). In addition, depression may have a more chronic course in older adults than in young adults (Achat, Kawachi, Spiro, DeMolles, & Sparrow, 2000; American Psychiatric Association, 2000b; Berger et al., 1998; Cole, Bellavance, & Mansour, 1999; Steffens et al., 2000). Moreover, depression and anxiety are often associated as comorbid conditions in geriatric patients (Chen, Bierhals, et al., 1999; Jorm, 2000; Mineka et al., 1998).

Depression in older adults frequently occurs with chronic health problems. Indeed, depression may be a risk factor for the development of some chronic health problems, such as cardiovascular disease (e.g., Ferketich et al., 2000). Examples of chronic health problems that are often associated with depression in older adults include the following physical illnesses: cardiovascular disease, cancer, dementia, arthritis, lung disease, diabetes, cerebrovascular disease, physical disability via a handicap, and chronic pain (Alexopoulos et al., 2000; Lyness, Duberstein, King, Cox, & Caine, 1998; NIH, 1992; Prince, Harwood, Thomas, & Mann, 1998; Richards & Perri, 1999, 2000). Somatic complaints are commonly woven among the symptoms and signs of depression in older adults (Futterman et al., 1995). Certain depressions in older adults are primarily due to a "general medical condition" or to the side effects of a medication. This has numerous assessment and treatment implications, some of which are discussed in the *DSM-IV-TR* (American Psychiatric Association, 2000a) and associated practice guidelines (American Psychiatric Association, 2000b).

Depression in older adults is sometimes associated with irreversible cognitive decline or dementia (NIH, 1992). Geriatric patients who have experienced a series of depressive episodes seem to be at a particularly high risk for cognitive impairment (Kessing, 1998). Depression, however, does not appear to cause this cognitive decline; rather, depression is a concomitant of it (Bassuk, Berkman, & Wypij, 1998). An abrupt and *inconsistent* cognitive decline that was preceded by normal cognitive functioning is likely to reflect depression rather than dementia. This is because dementia typically has a gradual and irreversible course, whereas depressive symptoms often have a sudden onset and then fluctuate (American Psychiatric Association, 2000a; American Psychological Association, 1998; Small et al., 1997). We should also note, however, that an abrupt and *consistent* cognitive decline may be the result of a stroke. In addition, following a stroke, some patients develop severe depressive symptoms, partially as a result of this negative health experience (NIH, 1992). Practitioners should be especially cautious and thorough with their assessment efforts when both depression and dementia are suspected regarding their geriatric patients because there is considerable overlap in the symptoms and signs for these disorders.

(The prevalence of depression in the geriatric population depends on how depression is assessed. Between 2% and 4% of community older adults meet the diagnostic criteria for Major Depressive Disorder (American Psychiatric Association, 2000a; Futterman et al., 1995; NIH, 1992). The prevalence climbs to at least 6% for older adults whose chronic health problems can be treated on an outpatient basis, and it climbs to approximately 12% for older adults whose chronic health problems must be treated on an inpatient basis (Katon & Sullivan, 1990). Furthermore, the prevalence rates may climb to 25% in some nursing homes (Katz & Parmelee, 1997; NIH, 1992).)

If prevalence is assessed by a procedure that asks older adults if they experience "depressive symptoms," then the prevalence rates jump dramatically. For instance, several studies have indicated that the prevalence of clear depressive symptomatology in geriatric community residents ranges from 15% to 20% (Futterman et al., 1995; NIH, 1992).

Most experts suggest that depression in older adults is underrecognized, underdiagnosed, and undertreated (Jeste et al., 1999; Koenig & Kuchibhatla, 1998). Family members, close friends, and primary health care providers are the major "gatekeepers" for recognizing depression in older adults and for assisting depressed older adults to get treatment (Schulberg, Katon, Simon, & Rush, 1998). Thus, more effective campaigns of public and professional education may be helpful here.

More research to develop practical screening systems should also be helpful. For example, Cooper-Patrick et al. (1994) developed a four-question interview that effectively screens for suicidal thinking in general medical patients. Older adults are often general medical patients. Moreover, some depressed older adults—especially white males—are at considerably increased risk for suicide (Hirschfeld & Russell, 1997; Jacobs, 1999). Therefore, practical and effective screening procedures are very important in this situation.

As always, the hallmark for a careful assessment of depression is a thorough interview. Questionnaires that are tailored to assessing depression in geriatric patients may also be helpful here, but these questionnaires should supplement the interview, not replace it (American Psychiatric Association, 2000b; American Psychological Association, 1992, 1998; Futterman et al., 1995; NIH, 1992; Small et al., 1997). With geriatric patients, an extensive medical evaluation of the patient's health status and a thorough psychological evaluation of the patient's cognitive functioning are also frequently helpful.

Treatment

The most thoroughly evaluated treatment for depression in older adults is pharmacotherapy (De Lima et al., 1999; Halbreich & Montgomery, 2000; Nemeroff & Schatzberg, 1998; Niederehe & Schneider, 1998; Schatzberg, 2000; Thase & Kupfer, 1996). In geriatric patients who are depressed but who otherwise evidence a healthy profile, these medications work approximately as well as they do for young adults. If depressed older adults are also burdened with chronic health problems, however, then the antidepressants are typically less efficacious than they are with healthy comparison groups. Relevant health problems include cardiovascular disease, cancer, persistent sleep disruption, dementia, psychosis, or histories of substance abuse (Dew et al., 1997; Musselman, Evans, & Nemeroff, 1998; Stevens, Merikangas, & Merikangas, 1995). We should also note that the effectiveness of antidepressants with the "oldest old" (often defined by experts as being over 85 years of age) has not been extensively investigated (Futterman et al., 1995; Rankin, 2000; Reynolds, Miller, Mulsant, Dew, & Pollock, 2000).

Although pharmacotherapy is the most investigated treatment for depressed older adults and is often efficacious, it is not an effective remedy in all cases. For instance, some geriatric patients will refuse to take antidepressants, and many older adults will not take them consistently. Poor treatment adherence is a problem in the pharmacotherapy of depressed older adults: "It has been estimated that 70% of patients fail to take 25% to 50% of their medication" (NIH, 1992, p. 1020). In addition, side effects are a problem. Particularly for geriatric patients with cardiovascular disease, side effects may be quite serious, and pharmacotherapy should be accompanied by regular and extensive medical monitoring. Some of the newer antidepressants, such as the selective serotonin reuptake inhibitors (SSRIs; e.g., fluoxetine/Prozac), apparently offer hope of milder side effects with geriatric heart disease patients, but this issue needs more research (Mamdani et al., 2000; Reynolds et al., 2000; Roose et al., 1998; Schatzberg, 2000). Moreover, potentially inappropriate prescriptions of antidepressants frequently occur with older adults (Mort & Aparasu, 2000). Finally, even when the antidepressants do help, there is still the crucial issue of learning more effective coping strategies; taking a pill does not teach the patient how to cope with stress, but successful psychotherapy does (Hollon & Shelton, 2001; Morin, Colecchi, Stone, Sood, & Brink, 1999; Scogin & McElreath, 1994).

If the standard treatments for depression—pharmacotherapy and psychotherapy—fail with a severely depressed geriatric patient, then electro-convulsive therapy (ECT) is sometimes considered as a backup treatment option. In such cases, ECT is frequently helpful in the short run, although relapse rates are high over the long run (Fava & Rosenbaum, 1995; NIH, 1992). For instance, a randomized controlled trial that was conducted recently suggested that most adult depressed patients (average age was 57) relapse within 6 months of ECT completion

(Sackeim et al., 2001). The biological mechanisms responsible for a positive treatment effect from ECT are not well understood. Side effects, such as post-ECT confusion, may be a concern. Substantial memory loss may occur in a small percentage of the patients that are treated with ECT (NIH, 1992). Older adults who are seriously ill or in delicate health pose a complex monitoring challenge for the physician who is considering ECT as a treatment option (American Psychiatric Association, 2000b; Niederehe & Schneider, 1998). Of course, brief hospitalization (day and night) is also sometimes considered as a treatment option for depressed geriatric patients (NIH, 1992).

Brief psychotherapies offer considerable promise for treating depression in older adults. Furthermore, some kind of psychosocial intervention is almost inevitably going to be helpful, regardless of the medical and complementary therapies that are being implemented (American Psychiatric Association, 2000b; Lebowitz, 1997; NIH, 1992).

The psychotherapy for depressed older adults that has been investigated most thoroughly is cognitive behavior therapy. Particularly in nursing home residents and medically ill participants, cognitive behavior therapy is the most empirically supported psychotherapy (Niederehe & Schneider, 1998). This therapeutic approach focuses on teaching patients more effective coping skills and more adaptive ways to think about themselves and their world. This approach is practical: It can be pursued in a time-limited fashion, it works in a group format, and it is easily taught to health care providers.

A number of studies have demonstrated promise for several other brief psychotherapies, such as problem-solving therapy, interpersonal psychotherapy, short-term psychodynamic therapy, educational support groups, and caregiver problem-solving groups (e.g., Arean et al., 1993; D'Zurilla & Nezu, 1999; Niederehe & Schneider, 1998; NIH, 1992; Reynolds et al., 1999). For example, there is support for problem-solving therapy (Arean et al., 1993), cognitive behavior therapy or brief psychodynamic therapy for the depressed caregivers of elderly relatives (Gallagher-Thompson & Steffen, 1994), combined interpersonal psychotherapy and pharmacotherapy (Little et al., 1998; Reynolds et al., 1999), and "befriending" (Harris, Brown, & Robinson, 1999).

Unfortunately, most depressed older adults do not receive treatment: "Only about 10% of the elderly who are in need of psychiatric treatment ever receive this service" (NIH, 1992, p. 1020). Furthermore, even when they do receive treatment, relapse prevention is a major challenge with depressed geriatric patients: "The central issue in treatment is the prevention of recurrence" (NIH, 1992, p. 1021). A positive finding, however, is that psychotherapy enhances the maintenance of treatment gains for depressed older adults (Niederehe & Schneider, 1998; Reynolds et al., 1999). We should have more public education about these issues because effective coping strategies and adaptive thinking styles for dealing with geriatric depression can be learned (Schulberg et al., 1998).

Complementary treatments for geriatric depression include moderate exercise, herbal therapy, acupuncture, relaxation training, and massage therapy. These complementary treatments are frequently used by young adults and older adults: A national survey, with 2,055 participants, suggested that two thirds of the depressed patients who were seen by a conventional provider also used complementary treatments (Kessler et al., 2001). Some of these treatments have evidenced promising support in controlled research trials, whereas the evidence for others is shaky (Ernst, Rand, & Stevinson, 1998; Field, 1998; Wong, Smith, & Boon, 1998). Perhaps the most supported complementary treatment for depression is moderate exercise (Ernst et al., 1998). Moderate exercise is also good for general health. In serious cases of geriatric depression, these complementary therapies may be a *supplement* to the standard treatments of psychotherapy and pharmacotherapy. To our knowledge, there is no group of experts on geriatric depression who would recommend these complementary therapies as the front-line or only treatments for severe depression in older adults (Niederehe & Schneider, 1998; NIH, 1992).

Finally, we need more research on how to effectively extend treatments developed for younger adults to older adults. We also need research on developing empirically based decision trees for when to use single therapies versus combinations of therapies with depressed geriatric patients.

Special Topics

We will briefly discuss four topics that are particularly relevant to depression in older adults: religious beliefs and response to treatment, the association of chronic health problems and depression, social isolation, and nursing homes.

Religious beliefs may be relevant to how quickly depressed geriatric patients respond to treatment. For instance, Koenig, George, and Peterson (1998) studied 87 medically ill patients who were at least 60 years old. Most of these participants were also seriously depressed at the beginning of the study. The investigators found that highly religious patients were more likely to experience a quick recovery from their depression. Patients who were low on religious beliefs were more likely to evidence a slow improvement in their depressive symptoms. It is possible, for example, that the "meaning and purpose of life" concepts that are inherent in many religious beliefs facilitate coping and self-care. The Koenig et al. (1998) study should be replicated, however, with larger samples (see Larson, Swyers, & McCullough, 1998; Sloan, Bagiella, & Powell, 1999; Walters & Bennett, 2000). Moreover, the patient's preferences and religious inclinations should always be given respect in psychotherapy and health care (American Psychological Association, 1992; McCullough, 1999; Sloan et al., 1999).

For older adults, depression and chronic health problems are often associated with each other (Richards & Perri, 1999, 2000). In addition, chronic health problems are very common in older adults. Moreover, depression is a major risk factor for poor health and dying in older adults (Boes & McDermott, 2000; NIH, 1992; Penninx et al., 1999). Our case study of Juan is a reminder of these issues. An empirical study of this issue was conducted by Prince et al. (1998). This investigation of 889 elderly individuals found that physical disablement, such as a handicap from a chronic health problem, was the most important predictor for the onset of depression. Virtually all experts agree that medical illness burden—especially when it is chronic—is an important risk factor for depression in older adults (e.g., Alexopoulos, 2001; Glassman & Shapiro, 1998; Lyness et al., 1998; Ormel, Oldehinkel, & Brilman, 2001; Small et al., 1997; Stevens et al., 1995). On the other hand, unusually good physical health appears to be a strong protective factor against depression in late life (e.g., Vaillant, 1998; Vaillant & Mukamal, 2001).

Many older adults are socially isolated; they rarely see the people that they are fond of. This represents a major risk for depression, particularly for the possibility of long-term depression and associated comorbid conditions (see Allumbaugh & Hoyt, 1999; Frasure-Smith et al., 2000; Penninx et al., 1998; Prince et al., 1998; Turvey, Carney, Arndt, Wallace, & Herzog, 1999). Concerns about social isolation were evident in our case study of Juan. The home health care nurse was gentle but determined in her effort to help Juan cope with this problem. When social support is very limited, the risk of a depressive relapse increases substantially (e.g., Holahan, Moos, Holahan, & Cronkite, 2000).

Depression is a frequent challenge for older adults who are living in nursing homes (Lebowitz, 1997). Implementing depression treatment programs is a frequent challenge for health care providers who are working in nursing homes. This topic deserves more attention from researchers and practitioners.

Clinical Guidelines

- Conduct a thorough interview of your geriatric patient.
- During the assessment effort, include an evaluation of your patient's losses.
- Assess for suicidal risk factors, and intervene as necessary.
- Evaluate your patient's social support system and potential strategies for enhanced social contact.
- Assess your patient's situation for lack of transportation and physical mobility.
- Help your patient to get the best medical and physical care available.
- Pursue a cooperative, interdisciplinary effort.
- Build at least one of the following interventions into your treatment program: cognitive behavior therapy, problem-solving therapy, interpersonal psychotherapy, enhanced social support, caregiver support, and general health education.
- Consider the merits of group interventions.

- Consider the benefits of moderate exercise as a complementary treatment that might *supplement* the standard interventions for geriatric depression.
- Ensure thorough physician assessment and supervision when your depressed older patient is receiving antidepressants.
- Consider the merits of *combined* pharmacotherapy and psychotherapy for severe cases of geriatric depression.
- Consider the potential benefits of ECT as a backup treatment option if standard treatments have failed and the depression is quite debilitating. Thorough physician assessment and supervision are required for ECT.
- Put in a determined effort with your nursing home patients—they may be harder to treat efficaciously.
- Consider the advantages of an illness support group for the caregivers of your geriatric patients.
- Include booster sessions in your treatment program.

Chapter Summary

Depression is a concern for many older adults, with 4% to 12% meeting criteria for Major Depressive Disorder in community populations and up to 25% meeting criteria in nursing homes. The symptoms and signs of depression in geriatric patients overlap with those in young adults. In older adults, however, the symptoms are more likely to evidence extended chronicity and to be associated with health problems and cognitive decline. Depression in older adults is underrecognized, underdiagnosed, and undertreated.

Assessment should include an interview, along with an evaluation of the patient's health status, social circumstances, and cognitive functioning. The standard treatments for depression in older adults are psychotherapy and pharmacotherapy. Experts typically recommend that some version of brief counseling should always be part of the treatment package. The psychotherapy with the most empirical validation for treating geriatric depression is cognitive behavior therapy. Unfortunately, only about 10% of all depressed older adults receive any kind of treatment for their depression.

Depressed geriatric patients who are highly religious may get well faster than do patients who are low in religious beliefs. Depression is often associated with chronic health problems in geriatric patients. In older adults, social isolation is a major risk factor for depression. Compared with older adults living in the community, nursing home residents are more likely to become depressed, have more comorbid conditions, be harder to treat, relapse more often, and require modifications in their treatment programs.

Suggested Readings

Discussions

Complementary Therapies

- Ernst et al. (1998) discussed complementary therapies for depression, including moderate exercise, herbal therapy, and relaxation training. This is an excellent review of a diverse literature.

Geriatric Mental Health

- Jeste et al. (1999) prepared a "consensus statement" indicating that the number of older adults (older than 65) with psychiatric disorders will increase to 15 million people in the United States by 2030. This is a sobering review of the large treatment challenge facing practitioners who are working with older adults.

Nursing Homes

- Lebowitz (1997) discussed the challenges for nursing home residents who are depressed. This review is thoughtful and passionate.

Treatments for Geriatric Depression

- Niederehe and Schneider (1998) concluded that numerous studies support the efficacy of antidepressant medications and cognitive behavior therapy for treating depression in older adults. This review is thorough and readable.

Studies

- Arean et al. (1993) conducted a randomized controlled trial. The findings indicated that problem-solving therapy was more effective than reminiscence therapy for treating depression in older adults.
- Morin et al. (1999) conducted a randomized controlled trial. The results suggested that sleep improvements for patients with late-life insomnia were maintained better with cognitive behavior therapy than with pharmacological treatment.
- Prince et al. (1998) conducted a prospective study with 889 older adults. The findings suggested that physical illness and disablement were important predictors of depression.
- Roberts et al. (2000) conducted a prospective investigation of 2,370 older adults. The results indicated that sleep problems were moderately strong predictors of future depression.
- Vaillant and Mukamal (2001) reported on a longitudinal study that followed a sample of 569 adolescent males for 60 years or until death. The results suggested that depression was a significant predictor variable affecting the quality of life for older adults. In addition, the results suggested that many variables under some "personal control" (p. 839)—for example, exercise, alcohol abuse, smoking, and coping mechanisms—are also significant predictor variables of the quality of life for older adults.

PART III

Comorbid Conditions and Other Symptoms, Signs, and Problems Associated With Depression

7 Additional Psychiatric Disorders and Severely Distressed Close Relationships Associated With Depression

Overview

In this chapter, we focus on two examples of "psychiatric comorbid conditions" that are frequently associated with depression. These examples are the association of anxiety disorders and alcohol abuse with depression. Many additional psychiatric disorders are often associated with depression, but a discussion of all of them would be far beyond the scope of this book. We also discuss the association of severe problems in close relationships with depression. *DSM-IV-TR* (American Psychiatric Association, 2000a) Axis I psychiatric disorders do not include "severe problems with close relationships," but this is an important problem area that is frequently associated with depression. We thought that a brief presentation of recent research on this area justified inclusion in this book but *not* an entire chapter, so we discuss it here. We provide short case studies for each of these three areas of association with depression, and we discuss relevant assessment and treatment issues. We conclude with clinical guidelines, a chapter summary, and suggested readings.

Anxiety Disorders

In this case study, the patient is experiencing both depression and anxiety.

Patient: I don't want to talk about my depression right now—I can deal with that. It is this feeling of always being stressed out and nervous that is making me miserable. And I had another anxiety attack today. It seemed like it came from nowhere—like a time bomb going off. I suddenly felt like I was going to die. It was an awful experience! I'm always living in fear of the next anxiety attack.

Therapist: I can appreciate that these panic episodes are very unpleasant for you. I think that the cognitive behavior therapy approach we talked about will help with both your depression and your panic attacks, but I continue to wonder if some medication might be beneficial here also. Did you set up an appointment with the psychiatrist that I recommended, for a medication consultation?

Patient: Yes. But I'm nervous about that too. I'm nervous about everything!

Across the life span from childhood to old age, almost 50% of all seriously depressed patients have also experienced an anxiety disorder (Beekman et al., 2000; Lewinsohn et al., 1998; Mineka et al., 1998; Regier et al., 1998; Weissman et al., 1993; Zlotnick et al., 1997). The patient's anxiety disorder is typically present with or in close proximity to his or her depressive disorder. Therefore, practitioners should evaluate their depressed patients for the possibility of anxiety disorders.

Several reviews of epidemiological research indicate that the comorbid conditions of depression and anxiety disorders are common. For instance, Angold and Costello (1993) reviewed epidemiological studies with child and adolescent participants and found that association between depressive and anxiety disorders ranged from 30% to 75%. In the Epidemiologic Catchment Area Study with 20,291 adult participants, Regier et al. (1998) found that 47% of the participants evidenced comorbid conditions of depressive and anxiety disorders. In alignment with these results, Weissman et al. (1993) used a family study methodology to investigate the comorbid conditions of Major Depressive Disorder and Panic Disorder. Their study of 193 probands and 1,047 of the probands' adult relatives demonstrated the substantial association of these disorders, with the risk for the second disorder increasing several times if the first disorder was present. Furthermore, Beekman et al. (2000) found that approximately half (47%) of the 3,056 older adults with depression in their sample were also experiencing anxiety disorders.

Recent reports from the practice sector further highlight the association of depressive and anxiety disorders. For example, Pincus et al. (1999) found that a principal diagnosis of a mood disorder is much more common in psychiatric practices than a principal diagnosis of an anxiety disorder (54% vs. 9%). They also reported, however, that 55% of the patients evidenced at least one additional Axis I diagnosis and thus experienced psychiatric comorbid conditions.

Although depressive and anxiety disorders are often comorbid conditions, the reasons for this association are not clear. Many theoretical possibilities are still being explored—for example, the possibility that depression and anxiety share a common biological diathesis (Barlow, 2000; Burns & Eidelson, 1998; Clark, 2001; Clark & Beck, 1999; Mineka et al., 1998; Piccinelli, Rucci, Ustun, & Simon, 1999; Watson et al., 1995). There is also suggestive evidence that principal diagnoses of depressive and anxiety disorders, and associations among them, may gradually decrease during older adulthood (Christensen et al., 1999; Jorm, 2000; Steffens et al., 2000). Nevertheless, a personality trait of negative or unstable emotionality—which is often labeled "neuroticism" (Funder, 2001)—appears to be a risk factor for depressive and anxiety disorders throughout the adult life span (Jorm et al., 2000).

The risk for comorbid conditions also appears to vary depending on the specific depressive and anxiety disorders, and on which one comes first. For instance, Kessler et al. (1998) found that primary depression was a strong risk factor for secondary panic attacks but that primary panic attacks were not a strong risk factor for secondary depression. In contrast, Regier et al. (1998) found that onset of social phobias in adolescence increases the vulnerability to depressive disorders in early adulthood. Furthermore, Zlotnick et al. (1997) reported that patients with a history of trauma, and comorbid conditions of depressive and anxiety disorders, were more likely to experience chronic or recurrent depression than were similar patients without a trauma history. The relationships among various depressive and anxiety disorders are very complex, and practitioners should always look for comorbid conditions.

Patients who evidence comorbid conditions of depressive and anxiety disorders are *more challenging to treat effectively* than are patients who just have a single disorder (American Psychiatric Association, 2000b; Craske & Zucker, 2001; Dew et al., 1997; Emmanuel et al., 1998; Foa et al., 1999; Hollon & Shelton, 2001; Newman et al., 1998; Zlotnick et al., 1997). This conclusion also typically holds for other types of comorbid conditions and associated problems, as when depression is associated with substance abuse, severely distressed close relationships, chronic health problems, suicidal symptoms, and Axis II personality disorders (American Psychiatric Association, 2000a, 2000b). A few studies (e.g., McLean, Woody, Taylor, & Koch, 1998) indicate that an empirically validated treatment for depression, such as cognitive behavior therapy, will work as well with patients exhibiting comorbid conditions with the depression. These studies, however, are the exception rather than the rule. A reasonable conclusion is that *patients with comorbid conditions will be harder to treat effectively than single-disorder patients.*

In addition, the percentage of depressed individuals, with or without comorbid conditions, who are receiving treatment remains discouragingly low. Even depressed older adults (ages 65–100), who have had most of their life to pursue some treatment for their depression, usually do not get counseling (e.g., 76% did not in Steffens et al., 2000). Moreover, they often do not get pharmacotherapy either (e.g., 52% did not in Steffens et al., 2000; see also Olfson, Kessler, et al., 1998). We focus on the treatment of depression in Chapters 10 through 12. In the context of comorbid conditions with anxiety disorders, we will only note a few matters regarding treatment.

Cognitive behavior therapy and related exposure psychotherapies have been thoroughly investigated with adults suffering from anxiety disorders (Barlow, Esler, & Vitali, 1998; Craske & Zucker, 2001; DeRubeis & Crits-Christoph, 1998; Franklin & Foa, 1998; Keane, 1998). These interventions are often efficacious. Relaxation training and stress management therapy for adults have also received considerable research attention, but their effectiveness appears to be less certain and more dependent on the specific anxiety disorder. The research with older adults is much more limited, and treatment recommendations are often extrapolated from research with younger adults (Niederehe & Schneider, 1998). Social skills training may possibly be helpful for patients with Social Phobia, but cognitive behavior therapy and exposure therapy are better supported interventions for patients with this anxiety disorder (Barlow et al., 1998; DeRubeis & Crits-Christoph, 1998). Cognitive behavior therapy is empirically established as an effective intervention for Panic Disorder (Craske & Zucker, 2001). Exercise and relaxation interventions have shown promising results as complementary therapies for depressed patients, and these interventions may possibly be helpful for depressed patients who also have anxiety disorders (Ernst et al., 1998). In summary, the most empirically supported psychotherapies for anxiety disorders are cognitive behavior therapy and exposure therapy.

There is a large research literature supporting the efficacy of pharmacotherapy for anxiety disorders (e.g., Halbreich & Montgomery, 2000; Lydiard, Brawman-Mintzer, & Ballenger, 1996; Rankin, 2000; Rauch & Jenike, 1998; Roy-Byrne & Cowley, 1998; Yehuda, Marshall, & Giller, 1998). For instance, examples of common medications for Panic Disorder are the benzodiazepines (e.g., alprazolam or Xanax). These medications have been extensively studied. Moreover, they are often efficacious, but some experts recommend a very cautious approach to long-term pharmacotherapy for anxious patients, given the addictive properties of the benzodiazepines. Potentially negative interactions between the benzodiazepines and other medications, certain foods, and alcoholic beverages need to be carefully monitored and avoided (American Psychiatric Association, 2000b). This is a reminder that pharmacotherapy for depressed patients—including patients with comorbid conditions—should be carefully monitored by a qualified physician. Even references available in most public libraries, such as the *Merck Manual* (Berkow, Beers, & Fletcher, 1997) and the *Consumer Reports Complete Drug Reference* (Consumer Reports, 2000), raise these pharmacotherapy cautions. These references recommend careful medical evaluation, thorough patient education regarding proper use of the medication, and frequent physician reassessment of the patient.

We should also note that some of the antidepressant medications (e.g., some SSRIs, such as Paxil, Prozac, and Zoloft) have well-documented anxiolytic or anxiety-reducing effects (American Psychiatric Association, 2000b; Craske & Zucker, 2001; Halbreich & Montgomery, 2000; Rankin, 2000).

Alcohol Abuse

In this case study, the patient is disclosing some of his motives and emotions regarding his abuse of alcohol.

Patient: I feel better after a few drinks. And then I just keep on drinking. It may not be the smartest thing to do. But it helps me cope with doing poorly in my college courses, being lonely a lot of the time, and not knowing what I'm doing at this damn college in the first place.

Therapist: I think I understand most of what you are saying. It sounds like this is a very unhappy time for you and your drinking seems to help reduce the stress in your life.

Patient: Yes! Plus the few friends I have drink a lot—one of them even drinks more than I do. I don't want to give up the few friends that I have at this lousy college.

Therapist: So part of our challenge is to find other ways to reduce your stress and enhance your social life, besides heavy drinking almost every day?

Patient: I suppose. I probably need to cut back on the heavy drinking. . . . But it won't be easy!

Depression and chronic alcohol abuse often go together (American Psychiatric Association, 2000a; Birmaher, Ryan, Williamson, Brent, &

Kaufman, 1996; Birmaher, Ryan, Williamson, Brent, Kaufman et al., 1996; Blazer et al., 1994; Hammen, 1997; Lewinsohn et al., 1998; Sanderson et al., 1990). Their combination, of course, implies a more serious symptom pattern and a more challenging treatment effort. For instance, Henriksson et al. (1993) found that 59% of their sample of suicide victims evidenced depressive disorders and that 43% also evidenced alcohol abuse or dependence. In alignment with these results, the San Diego Suicide Study (Fowler, Rich, & Young, 1986) found that 53% of the suicide victims among their sample of adolescents and young adults met the criteria for a *DSM* diagnosis of substance abuse.

Moreover, an investigation of 6,091 clinic-referred participants (Fombonne, 1998) suggested that the comorbid conditions of suicidal symptoms, depression, and alcohol abuse may be particularly important for adolescent males. These results are strong enough to implicate alcohol abuse as a causal variable in suicidal behaviors among male adolescents. Furthermore, with a nationally representative sample of 4,609 undergraduate college students, Brener, Hassan, and Barrios (1999) found that students who had seriously considered suicide were more likely to be abusing alcohol and illegal drugs. Finally, the hopelessness and unemployment problems that often accompany chronic alcohol abuse and depression were found to be significant independent risk factors for suicide in a sample of 6,891 adult psychiatric outpatients (Brown, Beck, Steer, & Grisham, 2000).

Unfortunately, the prevalence of alcohol abuse and dependence appears to be increasing dramatically among adolescents and young adults, including those on college campuses (e.g., Gose, 2000b; Nelson, Heath, & Kessler, 1998; Nicklin, 2000).

The comorbidity of depression and alcohol abuse has long-term implications. For example, the children of depressed parents are at increased risk for experiencing depression and alcohol abuse during adolescence and for having this symptomatology carry into early adulthood (Weissman et al., 1997). The children of alcoholic parents are also at increased risk for evidencing alcohol abuse and depression as they pass from adolescence to young adulthood (Chassin, Pitts, DeLucia, & Todd, 1999).

Numerous studies have found that the comorbid conditions of depression and alcohol abuse tend to persist over time (e.g., Peirce, Frone, Russell, Cooper, & Mudar, 2000; Schutte, Hearst, & Moos, 1997; Vaillant & Mukamal, 2001). In addition, the combination of depression and alcohol abuse at treatment entry does not predict an auspicious future for long-term improvement (Greenfield et al., 1998). Indeed, patients with more comorbid conditions may be good candidates for inpatient treatment because initial treatment in these inpatient settings may afford better outcomes (Finney & Moos, 1998). The most efficacious treatments are likely to be *comprehensive*, with careful attention to biological, cognitive, emotional, behavioral, and social features of patients who are depressed substance abusers (Leshner, 1999; McCrady & Ziedonis, 2001).

Relapse is a major problem with depressed alcohol abusers. Interventions that include cognitive behavior therapy and teaching patients enhanced problem-solving skills show promise here (e.g., Brown, Evans, Miller, Burgess, & Mueller, 1997; Irvin, Bowers, Dunn, & Wang, 1999). Lifelong intervention models, such as 12-step programs (e.g., Alcoholics Anonymous [AA]), have also demonstrated promise (Finney & Moos, 1998). Low-intensity, long-duration treatments may be helpful in this context (Finney & Moos, 1998). For example, spacing the same number of treatments out over twice the time period may be more effective. Finally, the use of booster sessions always represents an advisable treatment strategy for depressed patients. The threat of relapse is ever present in the lives of depressed alcohol abusers.

Severely Distressed Close Relationships

DSM-IV-TR (American Psychiatric Association, 2000a) Axis I psychiatric disorders do not include "severe problems with close relationships," but this is an important problem area that is frequently associated with depression, so we discuss it in this chapter. In this case study, the patient is complaining about her depression, social isolation, role transition, and lack of support from her husband since the birth of their child.

Patient:	I feel like I've fallen off of a social cliff. I used to have so much fun and social contact at work. Now I never see my friends—it's just me at home, taking care of Annette. I love Annette—she is such a wonderful baby—but I sure wish that my husband would get off his butt and help me out around the house! I know I should be thrilled with the birth of a healthy, beautiful child, but I'm depressed most of the time. I need to interact with adults, I need help, and I need Jeff to help out and do something. Plus he could take me out once in a while. Damn!
Therapist:	I hear both your depression and your anger. I can appreciate how unhappy you are right now. This has been a big transition for you, and it is clearly generating some conflict with Jeff. Should we talk about this conflict?
Patient:	I suppose. I'm not good at talking about my hurt with Jeff. I'm not good at explaining how I feel betrayed because he won't help more with our child. Part of this is my fault because I just brood and avoid the subject with Jeff. But I'm tired—I need some help!

Depression is often associated with severely troubled close relationships. Moreover, serious problems with close relationships often include depression. The literature on close relationships is so massive that it has generated numerous books that review this literature (e.g., Beach, 2001; Hendrick & Hendrick, 2000; Joiner & Coyne, 1999). There are also many focused review articles on this topic in journals (e.g., Barnett & Gotlib, 1988; Baucom et al., 1998; Butzlaff & Hooley, 1998; Cyranowski et al., 2000; Davis et al., 1999; Hendrick, 1995; Mazure, 1998). Some theoretical approaches reflect the common association of depression and distressed close relationships (e.g., Anderson, Beach, & Kaslow, 1999; Cummings & Davies, 1999; Cyranowski et al., 2000; Hammen, 1997; Harkness, Monroe, Simons, & Thase, 1999). For instance, Coyne and his colleagues have conducted several studies and developed a theoretical model of the strong association between depression and severe interpersonal problems (see Coyne, 1999; Joiner, Coyne, & Blalock, 1999). Furthermore, one of the most empirically supported psychotherapies for depression, interpersonal psychotherapy, relies heavily on the assumption that depression and problematic close relationships frequently go together (e.g., Frank et al., 1990; Mufson et al., 1999; O'Hara et al., 2000; Reynolds et al., 1999; Rossello & Bernal, 1999; Shea et al., 1992).

Epidemiological investigations indicate that marital dissatisfaction and depression are strongly associated (e.g., Kurpius, Nicpon, & Maresh, 2001; Whisman, 1999, 2001; Whisman & Bruce, 1999; Whisman, Sheldon, & Goering, 2000). For example, dissatisfied spouses are three times more likely to develop depression during the following year than are satisfied spouses (Whisman & Bruce, 1999). Even low-level depression, if it is chronic (e.g., Dysthymic Disorder, *DSM-IV-TR*, 2000a), has a strong association with disruptions in close relationships (Burns et al., 1994). Furthermore, there is compelling evidence that depressed individuals tend to *generate* ineffective problem-solving methods and stressful interpersonal conditions for themselves (e.g., Daley et al., 1997; Davila et al., 1995; Gilbert, 2000; Hammen, 1997; Hammen & Brennan, 2001; Harkness et al., 1999).

A clinically interesting way to look at this issue is to focus on what depressed spouses actually experience and do. For instance, Johnson and Jacob (2000) conducted a study suggesting that depression is particularly disruptive to effective problem solving in husbands and that it leads to more negative and less positive communications from their nondepressed wives. This communication pattern is important: Several studies of marital satisfaction and stability have supported the ratio of positive-to-negative communications as a strong predictor of marital happiness (e.g., Gottman et al., 1998).

In alignment with marital research, investigations of social interactions across an array of close relationships suggest that depressed individuals find these interactions less enjoyable and intimate (e.g., Nezlek, Hamptom, & Shean, 2000). In addition, an erosion of interpersonal resources or an explosion of interpersonal difficulties are risk factors for several depressive phenomena: first episodes of depression, incomplete recovery from depression, and relapse back into depression (Holahan et al., 2000; Monroe et al., 1999; Moos et al., 1998). Suicidal risk is also increased by serious problems with close relationships

(Foster, Gillespie, McClelland, & Patterson, 1999). Furthermore, the specter of depression may show itself in close relationships later in life: For example, depression in adolescence appears to have negative implications for marriage in adulthood (Gotlib, Lewinsohn, & Seeley, 1998).

Practitioners need to be keenly sensitive to the *social* context of depression (Beach, 2001; Jamison, 1995, 1999; Joiner & Coyne, 1999; Quindlen, 2001). Part of the assessment process should include a careful evaluation of your patient's social resources and problems. The treatment process should often include a thorough intervention that addresses your patient's interpersonal problem-solving skills and social support network. Cognitive behavior therapy and interpersonal psychotherapy have shown promise for treating distressed married couples who are depressed. These treatment approaches, however, need more research evaluation for various kinds of close relationships (Baucom et al., 1998; O'Hara et al., 2000; Rossello & Bernal, 1999; Whisman, 2001).

In summary, practitioners should remember that their depressed patients are often coping with severely distressed close relationships (Barnett & Gotlib, 1988; Cyranowski et al., 2000; Gilbert, 2000; Markowitz, 1998; O'Hara et al., 2000; Sanders & McFarland, 2000). Moreover, patients in distressed close relationships are often coping with depression (Anderson et al., 1999; Baucom et al., 1998; Beach, 2001; Coyne, 1999; Hendrick, 1995; Joiner & Coyne, 1999). Depression has many social implications!

Clinical Guidelines

- Be very empathic because depressed patients with comorbid conditions are facing *extremely* difficult challenges.
- Always assess for comorbid conditions because they are common in depression.
- If you suspect comorbid conditions following an initial screening, then a particularly thorough interview (or series of interviews) may be required because depression with a comorbid condition is more complicated than depression by itself.
- Evaluate your patients for severely distressed close relationships.

- Assess for chronic health problems and suicidal risks, which are often associated with depression. We discuss these issues in Chapters 8 and 9.
- When your patient evidences a comorbid condition with his or her depression, a more *comprehensive* treatment program is often required.
- Pursue interdisciplinary evaluations and interventions for your depressed patients with comorbid conditions.
- Consider the merits of the following interventions, which have *strong empirical support* for depressed patients with comorbid conditions: cognitive behavior therapy, interpersonal psychotherapy, problem-solving therapy, pharmacotherapy, inpatient treatment for chronic substance abusers, and marital or family therapy for patients in severely distressed relationships.
- Consider the advantages of empirically supported psychotherapies for anxiety disorders, which include cognitive behavior therapy and exposure therapy.
- Consider the benefits of pharmacotherapy, carefully supervised by a physician, for your depressed patients with anxiety disorders.
- Pursue continuing education and frequent consultation regarding treatments for the comorbid conditions. For example, if your depressed patient is experiencing Panic Disorder, then consult with practice guidelines and experts on the treatment of Panic Disorder (e.g., American Psychiatric Association, 2000b; Craske & Zucker, 2001).
- Be flexible in your treatment programs regarding depressed patients with numerous comorbid conditions.
- Consider the merits of booster sessions because relapse is a major problem for depressed patients with comorbid conditions, including depressed substance abusers.
- Get expert legal advice when your depressed patients with chronic alcohol abuse or dysfunctional marriages get tangled in legal complications.
- If at all possible, follow the standard policy that initial correspondence with an outside attorney should occur through your own institutional attorney.

- Relentlessly monitor confidentiality issues in cases with legal complications.
- Pursue expert consultation with your colleagues because comorbid conditions can be very complex.

Chapter Summary

Comorbid conditions are common in depressed patients. Practitioners should always assess for this. We discussed two examples of psychiatric comorbid conditions: anxiety disorders and alcohol abuse. We also discussed the frequent association of depression and severely distressed close relationships. In addition, we presented clinical guidelines regarding these three areas of association with depression.

Approximately 50% of the adult patients who evidence Major Depressive Disorder will also evidence comorbid conditions with an anxiety disorder. Patients with both depression and anxiety disorders are typically *harder to treat efficaciously* than are patients with only one disorder. Cognitive behavior therapy and related exposure therapies are the most empirically validated psychotherapies for anxiety disorders. Pharmacotherapy is well researched and thoroughly established as an effective intervention for anxiety disorders. Careful physician assessment and monitoring are required for pharmacotherapy. Long-term pharmacotherapy raises concerns about the side effects and addictive properties of some anxiety-reducing medications.

Depression and alcohol abuse often go together. Suicidal risk appears to increase substantially for adolescent and young adult males with these comorbid conditions. There are implications for family members: The children of depressed and alcoholic parents are at increased risk for developing these disorders during adolescence and young adulthood. The most effective treatments for depressed alcohol abusers are likely to be comprehensive. For patients with more severe symptoms of alcohol abuse or more limited social resources, initial treatment on an inpatient basis may be most efficacious. The threat of relapse is ever present in the lives of depressed alcohol abusers. The relapse problem justifies early attention during the intervention, booster sessions after the initial intervention, and then a lifelong coping effort.

Depressed people are often in severely troubled relationships. For example, dissatisfied spouses are three times more likely to develop depression during the following year than are satisfied spouses. Chronic low-level depression is also associated with disruptions in close relationships. Moreover, depressed people often generate ineffective problem-solving methods and stressful interpersonal circumstances for themselves. Suicidal risk is increased by serious problems with close relationships. Adolescent depression appears to have negative implications for marriage in adulthood. Thus, practitioners should be sensitive to the social context of depression. Cognitive behavior therapy, interpersonal psychotherapy, and marital/family therapy may be helpful in this social context.

Suggested Readings

Discussions

Marital and Family Therapy

- Baucom et al. (1998) discussed research on empirically supported psychotherapies for distressed married couples and families. This review is thorough and interesting.

Treating Anxiety Disorders

- Emmanuel et al. (1998) concluded that patients with the comorbid conditions of depression and anxiety are more difficult to treat effectively than are patients with only one of these disorders. This review provides a sobering reminder of the treatment challenges regarding comorbid conditions (see also American Psychiatric Association, 2000b; Craske & Zucker, 2001).

Close Relationships

- Hendrick and Hendrick (2000) edited a series of reviews on most areas of research regarding close relationships. This is an excellent collection of reviews on a complicated research literature (see also Barnett & Gotlib, 1988; Beach, 2001; Joiner & Coyne, 1999).

Relapse Prevention for Alcohol Abuse

- Irvin et al. (1999) suggested that relapse prevention strategies that are focused on cognitive behavior therapy and enhanced problem-solving skills show promise for patients with alcohol abuse problems. This is an interesting analysis of a very difficult problem—preventing relapse for alcohol abusers (see also American Psychiatric Association, 2000b; McCrady & Ziedonis, 2001).

Young Versus Older Adults

- Jorm (2000) concluded that susceptibility to depression and anxiety gradually decreases from early to late adulthood. This review of the research literature challenges some stereotypes regarding aging.

Research on Comorbid Anxiety Disorders

- Mineka et al. (1998) offered a review on the comorbid conditions of depression and anxiety disorders. This review is scholarly, thorough, and insightful (see also Barlow, 2000).

Studies

- Beekman et al. (2000) conducted an epidemiological survey with 3,056 older adults. Their findings indicated that 47% of the participants with Major Depressive Disorder also evidenced comorbid conditions with an anxiety disorder.
- Johnson and Jacob (2000) conducted an observational study of problem-solving interactions among 140 married couples. Their results suggested that depression in the husbands was more disruptive to effective problem solving than depression in the wives (see also Kurpius et al., 2001; Whisman, 2001; Whisman et al., 2000).
- Kessler et al. (1998) conducted an epidemiological survey with 8,098 participants from the National Comorbidity Survey. The findings suggested that primary depression is a strong risk factor for secondary panic attacks.
- McLean et al. (1998) conducted a treatment outcome study with cognitive behavior therapy. Their findings indicated that cognitive

behavior therapy yielded similar effectiveness for patients with the comorbid conditions of depression and panic disorder, compared with patients who were experiencing only panic disorder.

- Peirce et al. (2000) conducted a longitudinal study with 1,192 adult participants. Their findings indicated that increased alcohol use leads to reduced social support, which leads to increased depression.
- Regier et al. (1998) conducted an epidemiological survey with 20,291 participants from the Epidemiologic Catchment Area Study. The investigators' findings suggested that 47% of the participants who met diagnostic criteria for Major Depressive Disorder also met diagnostic criteria for an anxiety disorder.

8 Chronic Health Problems Associated With Depression

Overview

Chronic health problems are frequently associated with depression. We focus on three examples: the association of cardiovascular disease, cancer, and dementia with depression. We do not attempt to discuss all of the chronic health problems that are associated with depression, however, for that would take us far beyond the scope of this brief volume. We begin with a case study regarding the association of cardiovascular disease and depression, and we discuss some relevant assessment issues. Then we present discussions regarding cardiovascular disease, cancer, and dementia. We also provide clinical guidelines that are sensitive to the context of each of these three chronic health problems. We conclude with a chapter summary and a list of suggested readings.

Case Study

The patient is a 49-year-old mathematics professor, married, and the father of three children. He just had his second myocardial infarction (i.e., heart attack). The patient is eager to get out of the hospital. He is extremely hostile. Moreover, he appears to be very depressed.

Patient: I think if I stay in the hospital any longer, then I'm wasting my time here. Let me go home! I can't get any work done around here. No wonder I'm so depressed. And don't ask me to discuss those symptoms of depression again. I have the symptoms—over and over again. Just leave it alone.

Nurse: I'm sorry that you are so upset. We want to help. Your doctor will be by soon to review your current medical status and to talk with you about possible discharge and follow-up care.

Patient: It's about time! While I stay here in the hospital, my competitors are working hard on a math theorem that I'm trying to solve. Damn! I'm miserable! My oldest son is sick, but I can't see him. My math work is at a standstill, but they won't let me out of this stupid hospital. I can't eat, I can't sleep, I can't concentrate, I can't function, I'm racked with guilt about not getting any of my math research done, and I can't do what I want. My wife, Jean, understands—she has been very supportive. It's because of her that I'm still here. I was ready to bolt last night, but she convinced me to stay and hear what the doctors have to say.

Nurse: I understand. Your doctor is very effective—she will give you a thorough summary of your current medical status, and she'll answer your medical questions. We're concerned about your depression because it is an important risk factor for people with heart problems. We want to discuss treatment options for you. Have you thought about the possibility of medication or counseling for depression?

Patient: Not really. You did a good job of summarizing that stuff yesterday. I'm resigned to having to take antidepressant medications, and I know that you want me to participate in that stress management group for a while. I'm willing to try almost anything to get out of this hospital! But I'm still frustrated—do you realize how difficult it is to work for years and fail? You people have no idea how hard it is to publish in the best math journals in the world. I don't think that you can appreciate why I'm so frustrated, worried, and depressed!

Nurse: I understand how upset you feel right now, but I want you to know that I am concerned about you. I'll be one of the staff working with you during follow-up, and I want to help you. The stress management groups are interesting and helpful—and they are fun! Please work with us on this!

Patient: Okay, I'm trying to. But I'm so upset that it is hard to think straight. If I can get out of this hospital, then I'll feel better. I'm asking you to help me get out of here. Then I can see more of my family and my sick son. Then I can get my math work done. We need to talk with my doctor to get me out of here!

Discussion of the Case Study

This patient has life-threatening health problems. He also appears to be seriously depressed. In addition, his personality style is saturated with concerns about time, competition, and professional accomplishment, and he is very hostile. This personality style is called the "Type A Personality." The extreme hostility, which appears to be the toxic component of Type A Personality for cardiovascular disease patients, may possibly increase his risk for developing and exacerbating cardiovascular problems. The severe depression, if it continues for at least 6 months, is very likely to increase his risk for having further cardiovascular problems. For instance, severe and chronic depressive symptoms after the myocardial infarction are associated with an increased risk for another myocardial infarction, which is more likely to be lethal.

Assessment

The patient in our case study has just had a myocardial infarction. It is understandable that he is depressed (Mazure, 1998). In such circumstances, *many* patients might be temporarily depressed, anxious, and angry. Drawing the line, however, between the natural psychological consequences of a chronic illness and a morbid—and very dysfunctional—preoccupation with negative emotions is one of the challenges facing clinicians (American Psychiatric Association, 2000b; American Psychological Association, 1998; Massie & Popkin, 1998; Musselman et al., 1998; Nicassio & Smith, 1995).

The diagnosis that experts would probably make in our case study is that the patient's depression is not just a temporary reaction to his medical problems. Rather, his depressive style is chronic, it is dysfunctional, and, if not changed for the better, it will be an important risk factor for further cardiovascular problems. For his own health and survival, this patient should cope more effectively with his depression.

The symptoms of chronic health problems and depression overlap. Hence, clinicians must evaluate whether the symptoms are a natural and temporary reaction to a health concern or a serious case of depression that is superimposed on a health problem. The physical symptoms of depression, such as fatigue, loss of appetite, slow movement, and sleep disruption, are also common symptoms in some chronic diseases. In addition, the cognitive symptoms of depression, such as sad mood, loss of pleasure, and concentration difficulties, need to be evaluated in the context of experiencing a chronic disease: It is sad, disruptive, scary, and painful. When a seriously ill patient is facing the possibility of death, the practitioner must assess for the difference between a normal grief reaction and a distorted depressive reaction. There are also treatment implications regarding whether the depression preceded or followed the myocardial infarction. For example, chronic depression preceding the myocardial infarction implies that the treatment program may need to address more attention to dysfunctional thinking styles and relapse prevention strategies.

Screening measures may prove useful and practical in this situation. For instance, it is possible to screen efficiently for suicidal thinking in general health care settings. An example of a screening effort with general medical patients, which we have noted previously, is the four-item questionnaire developed by Cooper-Patrick et al. (1994). We have also noted before, however, that a valid assessment of depressive symptoms and signs requires a thorough interview (Eaton et al., 2000; Murphy, Monson, et al., 2000).

In summary, when the patient is confronted with a chronic health problem, the assessment, diagnosis, and evaluation of depression can be quite complex. The overlap of symptoms may lead to errors—either underdiagnosing or overdiagnosing depression. The matter is further complicated by various bureaucratic, economic, political, emotional, and insurance factors, which may also yield errors (see Bach, Cramer, Warren, & Begg, 1999; Eist, 1998; Mort & Aparasu, 2000; Simon et al., 2001).

Cardiovascular Disease

Issues Regarding Depressed Patients

Cardiovascular disease is the most frequent cause of death for U.S. adults. Myocardial infarctions are the most common consequence of cardiovascular disease. Moreover, if severe and chronic depression accompanies a myocardial infarction, then the risk of another myocardial infarction increases considerably (e.g., Frasure-Smith et al., 1995). There is a large research literature supporting the conclusion that chronic depressive symptoms are associated with numerous cardiovascular difficulties (Glassman & Shapiro, 1998; Musselman et al., 1998; Wulsin, Vaillant, & Wells, 1999). Furthermore, depression and cardiovascular disease are often associated with each other. For instance, whereas the population point prevalence for depression in adults remains stable at 5% (Blazer et al., 1994; Murphy, Laird, et al., 2000), the average point prevalence for depression in patients who have myocardial infarctions is 20% (range = 5–45% across 11 studies; Stevens et al., 1995). Thus, for example, Frasure-Smith et al. (1995) found a point prevalence of 18% for Major Depressive Disorder following myocardial infarctions.

Severe hopelessness, which is a symptom related to depression, is associated with a threefold increase in the risk of another myocardial infarction (see Everson et al., 1996). In addition, the risk of a myocardial infarction is doubled for those who have experienced a depressive episode, even when the first depression was 10 years earlier (Ferketich et al., 2000; Ford et al., 1998). Finally, primary care patients with depression evidence a broad array of problems with cognitive, emotional, and social functioning (Wells & Sherbourne, 1999).

One of the better-known examples of implications from the association of depression and coronary heart disease is the research of Frasure-Smith et al. (1995). The investigators evaluated patients for 18 months after the patients' myocardial infarction. The researchers found that if patients *continue* to evidence strong depressive symptomatology for a considerable period of time after their myocardial infarction, then the risk of additional cardiovascular problems goes up considerably.

Even strong depressive symptomatology that was experienced a long time ago—well before the coronary heart disease—may be a risk factor. For instance, Ford et al. (1998) found that men who had a depressive episode 10 years before they had developed coronary heart disease were at twice the standard risk for myocardial infarctions. In alignment with Ford et al. (1998), Ferketich et al. (2000) found parallel results regarding initial cardiovascular disease, with depression serving as a risk factor for both men and women (see also Penninx et al., 2001).

Numerous research teams are conducting psychological treatment studies with cardiovascular disease patients. For example, Blumenthal et al. (1997) evaluated 107 patients who received stress management training or exercise enhancement training. All of these patients were given standard medical care. There was also a comparison group that only received standard medical care. The follow-up period averaged 38 months. The results indicated that stress management training offers additional benefit beyond standard medical care. The patients in the stress management group evidenced about one fourth of the risk for heart pain and further cardiovascular problems as the comparison group (which received only standard medical care). Exercise training was also a helpful addition to standard medical care, but it was less effective than the stress management training. Dusseldorp, Elderen, Maes, Meulman, and Kraaij (1999), in a meta-analysis of 37 studies, concluded that health education and stress management programs are associated with a 34% reduction in deaths for patients with coronary heart disease (see also Rozanski, Blumenthal, & Kaplan, 1999).

A multisite randomized controlled trial, with approximately 3,000 participants, is evaluating the efficacy of cognitive behavior therapy as a supplemental intervention for patients with cardiovascular disease, most of whom are also experiencing depressive symptomatology (Taylor, Carney, et al., 2000). All patients are receiving standard medical care, and 50% of the patients are also receiving the psychosocial intervention. The study plan includes a protocol of follow-up assessments for approximately 5 years, with a target completion date of 2005.

Significant others and caregivers of patients with coronary heart disease would also benefit from using more effective coping strategies. For example, a study by Dew et al. (1998) indicated that caregivers of heart transplant recipients were negatively affected by weak coping styles.

Not all of the psychosocial treatment news is strongly positive. For example, well-intentioned efforts to develop very short and practical counseling methods for patients with coronary heart disease have sometimes yielded modest or no effects (Frasure-Smith et al., 1997; Jones & West, 1996). Depression and lifestyle are difficult to change. We may have to accept the possibility that only *intensive and lifelong* models of care will work well here (Perri, 1998). We should also note that some of these brief interventions were never intended to be interventions for chronic and severe depression.

Pharmacotherapy for depression will also be beneficial for some patients with cardiovascular and cerebrovascular diseases (Halbreich & Montgomery, 2000; Nelson et al., 1999; Robinson et al., 2000; Roose et al., 1998; Schatzberg, 2000). A very cautious medical approach and careful monitoring should be undertaken, however, to make sure that the antidepressant does not have side effects that might be harmful to the patient (Nemeroff & Schatzberg, 1998; Thase & Kupfer, 1996). The selective serotonin reuptake inhibitors (SSRIs; e.g., fluoxetine/Prozac, paroxetine/Paxil, and sertraline/Zoloft) appear to produce less harmful side effects—and better compliance—for patients with cardiovascular disease than some of the alternative medications for depression (e.g., the tricyclic nortriptyline/Aventyl; Nelson et al., 1999; Roose et al., 1998; Schatzberg, 2000).

Nevertheless, we should not forget that *behavior change* is also needed here. Some of patients' behaviors may be worsening their depression. In addition, patients recovering from myocardial infarctions need to behave differently—eat differently, exercise more, smoke less, and avoid stress more. Psychological interventions that focus on learning to think, feel, and behave in more adaptive ways will help the patient to improve these health-promoting behaviors (Niederehe & Schneider, 1998).

An additional psychosocial issue is close relationships, which can help patients to reduce stress and to cope better with the stress that remains. A good example of this is a study by Williams et al. (1992): The 5-year survival rate among patients with coronary heart disease increased from 50% to 82% if they had strong social support. Organized social support is another possible intervention, rather than just relying on the natural support system of the patient (Harris et al., 1999).

Finally, with cardiovascular disease patients, it is appropriate to emphasize the need for thorough, state-of-the-art, and long-term medical care. Comprehensive, high-quality, and sustained medical interventions will reduce mortality and increase quality-of-life outcomes, including those for heart disease patients who are also depressed (e.g., Druss, Bradford, Rosenheck, Radford, & Krumholz, 2001).

Clinical Guidelines

The following guidelines regarding patients with depression and cardiovascular disease reflect reviews of the psychological-educational treatment literature in this area (e.g., Dusseldorp et al., 1999; Glassman & Shapiro, 1998; Musselman et al., 1998; Richards & Perri, 1999, 2000; Rosen, 2000; Rozanski et al., 1999; Wing, Voorhees, & Hill, 2000).

- Make your intervention an interdisciplinary effort, working cooperatively with the various medical and health care providers that are treating your patient.
- Work tirelessly to ensure that your depressed patient with cardiovascular disease is receiving medical care that is comprehensive, state of the art, and long term.
- Always conduct thorough interviews of your patient during the assessment process. These interviews should include multiple questions about depression and chronic health problems, along with

simple and clear styles of inquiry. Determining whether the depression preceded or followed the myocardial infarction has implications for treatment and follow-up. For example, if a chronic depression preceded the myocardial infarction, then substantial therapeutic attention to dysfunctional thinking styles may be called for.

- Executive dysfunctions in cognitive processing (e.g., abnormal initiation and perseveration responses), but not memory impairment, are associated with increased risk for relapse in depressed geriatric patients, including those with cardiovascular disease. Carefully assess for these dysfunctions.

- Empathize with your patient's perspectives and preferences. For example, most depressed patients with cardiovascular disease prefer a psychotherapist who is sympathetic and collaborative, rather than judgmental and autocratic.

- Depression should be aggressively treated in your patients with cardiovascular disease. Comprehensive interventions are preferable.

- Consider the merits of empirically supported psychological interventions, which include stress management, cognitive behavior therapy, problem-solving therapy, and general health education programs.

- Consider the advantages of pharmacotherapy for depression and anxiety disorders, but very careful supervision by physicians is necessary because of concerns regarding side effects and negative interactions with other medications.

- Anticipate that cardiovascular disease and severe depression may adversely affect your patient's close relationships.

- Your patient's caregivers may need their own education and support groups.

- Build in maintenance strategies, such as booster sessions of psychotherapy, long-term pharmacotherapy under close physician supervision, thorough health education, and enhanced social support.

- Some of your cardiovascular disease patients will die. Be prepared to grieve, cope, and get your own help.

Cancer

Issues Regarding Depressed Patients

Cancer is the second most frequent cause of death for U.S. adults. Cancer patients are confronted with incredibly high levels of stress. Moreover, whereas the population point prevalence for depression in adults continues to be stable at 5% (Blazer et al., 1994; Murphy, Laird, et al., 2000), the average point prevalence for depression in cancer patients is 18% (range = 5–85% across 21 studies; Stevens et al., 1995). Thus, treatments for depression can make a big difference for many cancer patients (Compas, Haaga, Keefe, Leitenberg, & Williams, 1998; Davison, Pennebaker, & Dickerson, 2000; Holland, 1998; Nezu, Nezu, Friedman, Faddis, & Houts, 1998; Richards & Perri, 1999, 2000).

One of the most common psychological interventions is a cancer support group, which typically meets at a hospital. These groups usually meet on a regular basis, and there is almost always a health care professional who serves as the group leader. When observing these groups, it is obvious that the cancer patients have to cope with large amounts of stress: physical symptoms, emotional reactions, concerns of family and friends, social stigmas, relentless medical tests and treatments, body image and pain issues following surgery, and unpleasant side effects of the medications (Davison et al., 2000). Finally, many cancer patients are "looking death in the face"—and it is painful emotionally and physically. Thus, patients may benefit from therapeutic support and discussion about the difficult issue of facing death. Fortunately, the depression that may accompany cancer can typically be treated through psychological interventions.

Pharmacotherapy for depression is also efficacious here. We will give a few brief examples of psychological interventions for cancer patients. We will focus on *group* interventions, in part because these are common and practical and in part because we discuss individual psychotherapy in Chapter 10. We should note that the psychological-educational group interventions typically target a broad array of goals—for example, medication adherence, health promotion, good nutrition, moderate exercise, stress reduction, and enhanced quality of life—rather than just targeting reduced depressive symptomatology.

Before we discuss these psychological interventions, however, we should note that the primary purpose of these psychosocial treatments is to improve psychological functioning and day-to-day adjustment. Whether or not these psychological interventions can also have positive impact on medical outcomes and immune functioning remains a controversial issue (e.g., Miller & Cohen, 2001). Therefore, these psychological interventions are intended to *supplement* standard medical interventions.

Fawzy et al. (1993) reported encouraging results from a study of psychological treatment for cancer patients. The participants had a serious form of skin cancer. All participants received state-of-the-art medical treatments. The investigators found that a psychological group program that enhanced effective coping and reduced emotional distress appeared to improve the psychological and physical health of their participants. At the 6-year follow-up, only 9% of the "medical intervention *plus* psychological group treatment" patients had died, whereas 29% of the "medical intervention *only*" patients had died.

Spiegel, Bloom, Kraemer, and Gottheil (1989) reported a promising study with metastatic breast cancer patients. As they expected, the patients in the psychological group therapy condition evidenced lower levels of depression, anxiety, and pain than the patients in the standard care condition. Spiegel et al. were surprised, however, to also find that patients in the psychological group therapy condition survived about twice as long as patients in the standard care condition. (All patients received routine medical treatments and thorough medical care.) Thus, group therapy appeared to enhance the quality of the patients' lives and extend the length of the patients' survival. The survival results are controversial and merit several replications (see also Holland, 1998; McKenna, Zevon, Corn, & Rounds, 1999; Miller & Cohen, 2001).

Fortunately, some replications are published or in progress, including a randomized control trial by Classen et al. (2001). The investigators' results suggested that, compared to an educational control condition, weekly supportive-expressive group psychotherapy sessions, conducted for 1 year, significantly reduced depressive and traumatic stress symptoms for metastatic breast cancer patients (125 female patients participated in the study). Thus, this ambitious study yielded promising results, although some experts might question the feasibility of numerous cancer patients participating in weekly psychotherapy for an entire year.

One of the largest investigations of educational and peer support interventions for cancer patients has been done by Helgeson, Cohen, Schulz, and Yasko (1999). This randomized controlled trial involved 312 women with breast cancer. Participants were randomly assigned to control, education, peer discussion, or education plus peer discussion groups. The groups met weekly, 1 to 2 hours per meeting, for 8 successive weeks. Helgeson et al. (1999) concluded the following: "Education-based group interventions facilitated the initial adjustment of women diagnosed with early stage breast cancer. There was no evidence of benefits from peer discussion group interventions" (p. 340). This study makes a strong argument for including a thorough educational component in cancer support groups. We should caution readers, however, that the negative results for peer discussion groups in the Helgeson et al. (1999) study may not generalize to all cancer patients and psychotherapists. For example, the group facilitators in the Helgeson study were experienced oncology nurses and social workers whose specific leadership styles may have particularly facilitated the educational intervention. Furthermore, a subsequent analysis suggests that patients with no social support system may indeed benefit from peer support (Helgeson, Cohen, Schulz, & Yasko, 2000; see also Compas et al., 1998; Davison et al., 2000; Helgeson & Cohen, 1996; Holland, 1998; Meyerowitz, Richardson, Hudson, & Leedham, 1998).

There are at least four possible reasons why these psychological interventions may be helpful for depressed cancer patients. First, psychological interventions help patients to adhere correctly to their medical regimens. These interventions also help patients to carry out sensible plans for their diet, exercise, substance use, and smoking reduction (Courneya & Friedenreich, 1999; Wing et al., 2000). In addition, psychological interventions help patients to cope effectively with their daily emotions and physical challenges (Antoni et al., 2001; Merluzzi & Sanchez, 1997). Second, psychological interventions help patients to improve their self-esteem, sense of control, optimism, under-standing, and emotional processing (Davison et al., 2000; Helgeson & Cohen, 1996). Third, psychological interventions help patients to improve specific areas of their lives, such as lessening their sleep disrup-tion (Morin et al., 1999; Roberts et al., 2000). Finally, psychological inter-ventions help patients to directly reduce their anxiety and depression, which then pays numerous dividends across most areas of their lives (Compas et al., 1998; Fawzy & Fawzy, 1998; Holland, 1998; Nezu et al., 1998; Richards & Perri, 1999, 2000).

There is little compelling evidence, however, that depression, person-ality, and stress can influence the *development* of cancer (e.g., McKenna et al., 1999) or that psychological interventions can strongly influence immune function (e.g., Miller & Cohen, 2001).

Clinical Guidelines

The following guidelines for cancer support groups and depressed cancer patients reflect reviews of the psychological-educational treat-ment literature in this area (e.g., Compas et al., 1998; Helgeson & Cohen, 1996; Holland, 1998; McKenna et al., 1999; Miller & Cohen, 2001; Nezu et al., 1998; Richards & Perri, 1999, 2000).

- Have a strong educational component in your cancer support groups, including presentations by an interdisciplinary team of experts.
- Consider the merits of brief skill-focused psychotherapies, such as cognitive behavior therapy and problem-solving therapy.
- Include an emphasis on adherence to medical and health promotion regimens, better self-esteem, concrete improvements in day-to-day experiences such as less sleep disruption, and reduced depression and anxiety.
- Consider the implications of research suggesting that peer support is primarily helpful for cancer support group members who do not have other support systems, rather than for all group members.
- Your cancer support groups should be carefully integrated with comprehensive and state-of-the-art medical care rather than set up as an independent treatment for cancer patients.

- Get some feedback from colleagues regarding your leadership style with cancer support groups.
- Be prepared to cope with extremely intense levels of anxiety, anger, and depression: Cancer support group participants are "looking death in the face" and they are often scared, angry, and depressed.
- When antidepressants are used, arrange for very careful physician supervision of the pharmacotherapy because of concerns regarding side effects and drug interactions. For example, the combinations of some chemotherapy and antidepressant-medication regimens are contraindicated because of serious drug interactions.
- Consider the advantages of adding booster sessions for your cancer support groups because depressive relapse is a common problem.
- Some of your cancer support group members will die: Be prepared to handle grieving among the group members.
- The research base for psychological interventions regarding depressed cancer patients is changing rapidly; keep up with your reading and continuing education in this area.
- Clinical work with depressed cancer patients can be hard on the practitioner—get help when you need it.

Dementia

Issues Regarding Depressed Patients

In this section of the chapter, we focus specifically on Alzheimer's disease, which is the most common type of dementia in older adults (Small et al., 1997). Alzheimer's disease affects at least 4 million Americans, evidences a gradual onset and progressive deterioration, is disabling and irreversible, and is frequently associated with depression (American Psychiatric Association, 2000b; American Psychological Association, 1998; National Institutes of Health [NIH], 1992; Small et al., 1997). The continuing expansion in the number of older adults in the United States will yield a continuing increase in Alzheimer's disease cases over the foreseeable future, and some experts are predicting a parallel increase in depression and other psychiatric disorders among older adults. For example, witness the following conclusion from a panel of experts: "It is anticipated that the number of people older than 65 years with psychiatric disorders in the United States will increase from about 4 million in 1970 to 15 million in 2030" (Jeste et al., 1999, p. 848). Thus, practitioners need to be very alert to the association of depression and dementia.

One of the controversial issues in this area is whether depression is an early manifestation or a predictor of dementia. Several large studies suggest the former rather than the latter, but this issue is not yet fully resolved, and investigations may produce different findings depending on the subgroup of dementia patients studied (e.g., Bassuk et al., 1998; Chen, Ganguli, Mulsant, & DeKosky, 1999; Heun, Papassotiropoulos, Jessen, Maier, & Breitner, 2001; Yaffe et al., 1999).

Individuals with depression and dementia often use inpatient services (Kales et al., 1999). They frequently evidence improvements in their depression following both psychological and pharmacological treatments (Dew et al., 1997; Niederehe & Schneider, 1998; Scogin & McElreath, 1994; Simon et al., 2001). Moreover, in recent years, depressed geriatric patients are increasingly likely to receive one of the selective serotonin reuptake inhibitors (SSRIs; e.g., fluoxetine or Prozac) as their pharmacological treatment for depressive symptomatology (Schatzberg, 2000).

Clinical Guidelines

The following guidelines for working with depressed patients who are experiencing dementia reflect several summaries developed by consensus panels of experts (e.g., American Psychiatric Association, 2000b; American Psychological Association, 1998; NIH, 1992; Small et al., 1997).

- Make your clinical work an interdisciplinary effort.
- Help your patients to receive thorough medical evaluations and treatments.
- Always conduct a thorough interview of your patient, with careful attention to the symptoms and signs of both depression and

dementia. Because some of the symptoms of depression and dementia overlap, a particularly cautious evaluation of your patient may be necessary here. For example, "feelings of worthlessness" are often intertwined with both depression and dementia in older adults.

- In virtually all work with depressed patients, things said simply are things said well. This guideline is particularly relevant here, where cognitive decline is an issue. Indeed, there is uncertainty whether Alzheimer's disease patients have sufficient capacity to competently give informed consent for their participation in treatment and research procedures (e.g., Kim, Caine, Currier, Leibovici, & Ryan, 2001).

- Attempt to get corroborative information about your patient from significant others and caregivers. This may be particularly helpful with dementia patients because they are often poor historians with inaccurate recall of recent symptoms and experiences.

- Use a battery of standard measures—including well-established measures for neuropsychological assessment—because severe depression can mimic symptoms of dementia in geriatric patients. This may not be possible with some dementia patients, and practitioners should adjust to each patient's level of toleration and capacity.

- Extensive neuropsychological assessment by an expert is warranted when your patient can tolerate it.

- Your minimum reassessment interval should be 3 to 6 months, and your minimum follow-up interval should be 1 year for depressed dementia patients.

- Consider the merits of empirically supported interventions for geriatric depression, including cognitive behavior therapy, interpersonal psychotherapy, problem-solving therapy, and pharmacotherapy. Patients with severe cognitive decline, however, may struggle with cognitive therapies.

- Consider the advantages of illness support groups for the *caregivers* and *family members* of depressed dementia patients. Taking care of a loved one who is experiencing depression and dementia can be very stressful for the caregiver.

- Provide constructive feedback, extensive support, thorough education, and an effective therapeutic alliance for your patient and his or her significant others.
- Help your patient to overcome the biases in our society against older adults.
- Extensive clinical work with depressed dementia patients can be difficult; you may occasionally need extra professional support for yourself.

Chapter Summary

Chronic health problems are frequently associated with depression. We discussed three examples: the association of cardiovascular disease, cancer, and dementia with depression. We discussed issues regarding depressed patients who have one of these chronic health problems, and we provided clinical guidelines in the context of each health problem.

If chronic depression follows a myocardial infarction, then the risk of exacerbated cardiovascular problems increases considerably. Chronic hopelessness also increases the risk for additional cardiovascular problems. Psychological treatments for reducing stress and depressive symptoms in cardiovascular disease patients have achieved some promising results. Better coping styles may also help the caregivers of patients with coronary heart disease. Pharmacotherapy for depression in patients with cardiovascular disease is effective in many cases, but very careful physician monitoring is necessary to make sure that the medication does not generate dangerous side effects or problematic interactions with other medications.

In addition, the coping and health behaviors of cardiovascular disease patients with depressive symptoms almost always need to change. Enhanced social support is helpful, whether it is through the natural support system of the patient or through organized social support groups. The social support groups also frequently include an educational component, with some attention given to promoting healthier behaviors.

Cancer patients are often confronted with extreme levels of stress. Many of these patients will experience depressive symptomatology, and if they stay depressed they are likely to function less effectively. How well they cope has implications for their emotional health and day-to-day adjustment, and perhaps also for their cancer. Negative emotions like depression can be successfully treated in cancer patients through empirically supported psychological procedures. These psychological treatments not only help the cancer patients to be happier and to cope more effectively with their day-to-day challenges but may also increase survival rates. More research, however, is needed to clarify the issue of survival rates. Nevertheless, it is clear that psychological interventions can help cancer patients and their caregivers to improve the quality of their lives. Pharmacotherapy for depression in cancer patients also has merit, but it requires very thorough supervision by physicians because of concerns with side effects and medication interactions.

Alzheimer's disease is the most common type of dementia in older adults. Dementia, including Alzheimer's disease, is frequently associated with depression. Most studies suggest that depression is an early manifestation, rather than a predictor, of dementia. Individuals with depression and dementia often use inpatient services. Depressed dementia patients typically show improvements in their mood and functioning following treatment with empirically supported interventions for depression. These interventions include empirically validated forms of psychotherapy and pharmacotherapy for depression.

Suggested Readings

Discussions

Assessment of Dementia

- A panel of experts representing the American Psychological Association (1998) developed a consensus statement that presents 10 guidelines for the evaluation of dementia. These guidelines are helpful.

Psychological Interventions for Patients With Cardiovascular Disease

- Dusseldorp et al. (1999) reviewed the literature and concluded that psychological programs for health education and stress management in cardiovascular disease patients resulted in considerable benefits, with 34% fewer cardiac-related deaths during the follow-up periods. This review offered a clear summary of promising psychological interventions for patients with cardiovascular disease (see also Rozanski et al., 1999).

Problem-Solving Therapy for Patients With Cancer

- Nezu et al. (1998) presented a treatment manual for teaching cancer patients effective problem-solving skills. This treatment approach is time limited (10 sessions), and it enjoys some empirical support (D'Zurilla & Nezu, 1999). Practitioners who work with depressed cancer patients will find this book helpful.

Coping With Health Problems

- Rosen (2000) discussed the varying "sequences of change" when coping with different health problems. This review is a sophisticated and insightful analysis of behavior change sequences for patients with chronic health problems.

Maintenance of Healthy Changes

- Wing et al. (2000) edited a series of reviews regarding research on maintaining healthy behavior changes. These interesting reviews cover the literature regarding smoking cessation, weight loss, exercise, and diet.

Studies

- Chen, Ganguli, et al. (1999) conducted a study with 1,366 older adults. Their findings suggested that Alzheimer's disease patients were 6.5 times more likely to evidence depression than participants without dementia. Preexisting depression, however, did not confer a significant increase in risk for the later development of Alzheimer's disease or other dementia.

- Druss et al. (2001) studied a national sample of 88,241 Medicare patients who were at least 65 years old and were hospitalized for myocardial infarction. The investigators' results at a 1-year follow-up suggested that depression was no longer a significant predictor of mortality once five quality-of-care variables (including counseling for smoking cessation) were adjusted for in the statistical prediction model. The researchers concluded that their investigation "suggests the potential importance of improving these patients' medical care as a step toward reducing their excess mortality" (p. 565).

- Ferketich et al. (2000) conducted a 10-year longitudinal investigation with 7,893 male and female participants. The results suggested that depression was associated with almost twice the risk for developing coronary heart disease in both men and women (see also Penninx et al., 2001).

- Ford et al. (1998) conducted a 40-year longitudinal study of 1,190 men. The findings indicated that, even in healthy men, depression was associated with double the risk for myocardial infarctions 10 years later.

- Helgeson et al. (1999) conducted a randomized controlled trial involving 312 women with breast cancer. The results suggested that education groups were more efficacious than peer discussion groups for enhancing day-to-day adjustment. Additional research, however, suggested that peer discussion groups were efficacious for participants who did not have social support from their partners and physicians (Helgeson et al., 2000).

- Simon et al. (2001) conducted a randomized controlled trial with 407 depressed patients participating in several HMOs. The findings suggested that patients who frequently use medical care systems, such as patients with chronic health problems, could be screened and treated efficiently for depression (primarily via patient education and pharmacotherapy). The clinical improvements were significant, and the cost increases for health services averaged between $1,008 and $2,475 per year.

9 Suicide and Depression

Overview

We begin this chapter with a case study involving a depressed adult who is contemplating suicide. We then discuss the prevalence of suicide in adults, and we review the empirically established risk factors, while using our case example to illustrate key elements. Next we provide a brief overview of the literature on assessment and treatment, and we highlight certain ethical and practical issues for crisis management. We also consider some future directions for theory and practice. Finally, we provide clinical guidelines, a chapter summary, and suggested readings.

Case Study

This is a case of a crisis phone call regarding suicide. It is 2:00 a.m. at a crisis hotline center in a large city.

Counselor: This is Contact Dallas, how may I help you?

Caller: I'm pretty upset. Things are a big mess. I don't know . . . maybe this is a bad idea? I should probably just go away.

Counselor: Please talk with me.

Caller: Well . . . let's see. I'm really upset about my kids. My ex-wife got this legal thing, I don't know, some kind of "Court Order," and I don't get to see my kids much. And this social worker has to be around. Damn! Anyway, my ex-wife moved our kids back to San Antonio, so I can't see them much. And I feel confused and depressed about this.

I don't see much hope. What can I do? . . . If I can't see my kids, then . . . well, there just seems to be no hope . . . just pain and guilt and sleepless nights and endless days.

Counselor: I think that we can help you with some of these things. Which issue would you like to talk about first?

Caller: I want to see my kids! This "Court Order" is bad. I'm living alone. I'm all alone. I'm so lonely . . . I can't deal with this . . . it seems hopeless.

Counselor: If you like, we can set up a meeting for tomorrow with a Legal Aid attorney.

Caller: Well, I don't know. I didn't like my last attorney. The Public Defender guy seemed . . . well, he didn't get what I wanted. I didn't mean to hit Billy. I just lost it . . . you know? I was drunk . . . you know? And then my ex-wife makes a big legal issue out of it. We had four kids in 8 years—it was pretty damn stressful, you know? And I really am a good father . . . most of the time. I'm not the scumbag that my ex-wife says I am. I'm broke—my plant has been closed for 3 months. It's just hopeless.

Counselor: Let's get you some legal advice tomorrow. And let's not drink any more tonight, okay?

Caller: Okay. But sometimes I just want to get drunk and then maybe put a bullet in my head.

Counselor: Do you have a gun?

Caller: Yes, I've been staring at my loaded pistol for hours, but I haven't had the courage to put it to my head.

Counselor: We need to unload your gun and then store it in a safe place. Okay?

Caller: I don't know. Anyway, I probably don't have the guts to shoot myself. Getting really drunk might give me more courage.

Counselor: We can help with your depression and drinking. We need to stop drinking tonight and to unload your gun and put it in a safe place. Okay?

Caller: Okay. But it just seems hopeless. You do seem nice though. . . . I really miss my kids!

Counselor: I understand! Would you like to start meeting in person with a counselor tonight? You should not drive now, after you've been drinking heavily, but if you want, we can arrange to have someone pick you up and give you a ride to our clinic in St. Francis Hospital. We can help!

Caller: I don't know—maybe. I could use some help.

Counselor: Let's get you some help tonight, but first we'll unload the gun. Okay?

Caller: Okay.

Discussion of the Case Study

The person in this case, who is calling the crisis hotline center, appears to be at a *very high* risk for suicide. He evidences 11 of the empirically established risk factors for suicide. We will discuss these risk factors later in the chapter.

Prevalence

At least 31,000 Americans commit suicide each year (Hirschfeld & Russell, 1997; Jacobs, 1999; Jamison, 1999; Maris et al., 2000; Westefeld et al., 2000). This estimate is probably much lower than the true number because many suicides go unreported and undetected (Bongar, 1991; Jacobs, 1999; Jobes et al., 2000). There are about 18 suicide attempts for every completed suicide. Women are more likely to attempt suicide, but men are more likely to complete suicide. About four times as many men as women kill themselves (Hirschfeld & Russell, 1997). One of the possible reasons for this gender difference is that men are more likely to use guns, whereas women are more likely to use poisons (or to overdose on medication). On average, guns are more lethal than poisons (or overdoses of medication). Indeed, guns account for 60% of the deaths by suicide in the United States (Hirschfeld & Russell, 1997), and easy access to lethal methods of injury, such as loaded guns, may explain some of the differences in suicide rates from one location to the next (Jamison, 1999; Sommers-Flanagan & Sommers-Flanagan, 1995).

Whites and Native Americans currently have higher suicide rates than other racial and ethnic groups in the United States (Hirschfeld & Russell, 1997). However, like many of the statistics on suicide, this one may be rapidly changing. For instance, there has recently been a dramatic increase in suicide rates among African American adolescents, with the suicide rate more than doubling for this group between 1980 and 1995 (Jamison, 1999). Suicide rates clearly go up for men who are over the age of 69, but not for women (Hirschfeld & Russell, 1997). For both genders during the last 40 years, suicide rates have increased at least 300% among adolescents and young adults (Brener et al., 1999; Jamison, 1999). Suicide is now the third leading cause of death among individuals between the ages of 15 and 24, and it is the fifth leading cause of death among people under the age of 45 (Hirschfeld & Russell, 1997). A review by Inskip et al. (1998) concluded that the lifetime risk of suicide for depressed individuals is 6%, which is more than 100 times the suicide rate for the population at large (Hirschfeld & Russell, 1997).

Risk Factors

Hirschfeld and Russell (1997) provided a summary of the empirically established risk factors for suicide in adults. We will briefly discuss each of these risk factors. We will also relate these risk factors to our case study.

Clinical Risk Factors

- *Depression.* "Over 90 percent of persons who commit suicide have diagnosable psychiatric illnesses at the time of death, usually depression, alcohol abuse, or both" (Hirschfeld & Russell, 1997, p. 911). For example, one large study found that 93% of the suicide victims had symptoms justifying a psychiatric diagnosis, including 59% with serious depression (Henriksson et al., 1993; see also American Psychiatric Association, 2000a; Conwell et al., 1996). In our case study, the caller is obviously depressed.

- *Substance abuse.* This is an important risk factor (Brener et al., 1999). The caller in our case study is abusing alcohol. Notice that the counselor quickly spotted the depression and the alcohol abuse and then tried to deal with these concerns in a clear, positive, and direct manner. Henriksson et al. (1993) also found a high rate of alcohol abuse (and dependence) among suicide victims—43% were abusing alcohol. Several other studies have found similar results (e.g., Statham et al., 1998).
- *Schizophrenia.* The distressed caller in our case study does not evidence psychotic thinking—that is, disordered and bizarre perception, thinking, and emotion—which is a hallmark of schizophrenia. Schizophrenia is a major risk factor, with about 4% of schizophrenic patients committing suicide (Inskip, Harris, & Barraclough, 1998).
- *Panic Disorder.* This is one of the more debilitating anxiety disorders (American Psychiatric Association, 2000a). The symptoms include sudden, unpredictable attacks of anxiety, intrusive thoughts about terror, and frightening physical sensations (difficult breathing, chest pain, dizziness, etc.). Our case study does not evidence this risk factor. Panic Disorder is an important risk factor for suicide, as demonstrated in several large investigations (e.g., Pilowsky, Wu, & Anthony, 1999). Furthermore, any severe anxiety disorder increases the risk for suicide, particularly when it is combined with depression, which it often is (Hirschfeld & Russell, 1997; Mineka et al., 1998). Finally, the combination of Panic Disorder and a chronic style of unstable relationships, self-image, and emotion (e.g., Borderline Personality Disorder) is a strong risk factor for suicide (American Psychiatric Association, 2000a; Linehan, Heard, & Armstrong, 1993).
- *Hopelessness.* Our distressed caller definitely has this risk factor. Numerous studies have illustrated that hopelessness is an important risk factor for suicide and a frequent component of suicidal thinking (e.g., Brown et al., 2000; Cooper-Patrick et al., 1994; Jamison, 1999; Maris et al., 2000; Young et al., 1996). Hopelessness is also one of the risk factors that can often be assessed accurately. Notice that the counselor in our case study was empathic but that she also

avoided getting mired in the caller's sense of doom and that she moved on to constructive thinking and action.

- *Severe inability to experience pleasure (anhedonia).* The caller in our case study has this risk factor—he is miserable, never has fun, is very lonely, hates being broke, and misses his children terribly. He has lost interest and pleasure in almost all of his activities, which, of course, is also one of the symptoms of Major Depressive Disorder (American Psychiatric Association, 2000a). It is important to carefully assess patients for this risk factor (Baumeister, 1990; Jacobs, 1999; Rudd & Joiner, 1998; Westefeld et al., 2000).

- *Previous suicidal attempts or a history of suicidal ideation.* In our case study, it is clear that the caller has been obsessed with suicidal ideation for a while (see Brown et al., 2000), but it is not clear if he has a history of suicidal attempts. Aborted suicidal attempts, however, are evident in this case. Aborted attempts are strongly associated with completed attempts (Jamison, 1999). We should caution that, even in the absence of recent suicidal attempts, suicide attempts that were made several years earlier are also a risk factor (Clark, Gibbons, Fawcett, & Scheftner, 1989). Of course, the absence of previous suicide attempts does not eliminate suicidal risk: For instance, a large study in Finland indicated that 56% of suicide victims died with their first suicide attempt (Isometsa & Lonnqvist, 1998).

- *Chronic sleep disruption.* We will mention one further clinical risk factor, which has received support in several recent studies: chronic sleep disruption. This symptom, of course, is one of the nine symptoms used to diagnose Major Depressive Disorder (American Psychiatric Association, 2000a). Sleep disturbance is among the most frequent symptoms in extremely depressed individuals. Several investigations indicate that if depressed patients have chronic and severe sleep disruption, then this makes treatment more challenging (American Psychiatric Association, 2000b; Cooper-Patrick et al., 1994; Giles et al., 1998; see also Jacobs, 1999; Maris et al., 2000). In our case study, the caller mentions "sleepless nights," so he has this risk factor.

Sociological and Demographic Risk Factors

- *Male gender.* "Men are more than four times as likely to commit suicide as are women" (Hirschfeld & Russell, 1997, p. 911; see also Isometsa & Lonnqvist, 1998; Statham et al., 1998). The caller in our case study is male.
- *White or Native American race/ethnicity.* Adults in these racial and ethnic groups currently evidence the highest suicide rates in the United States, although the suicide rate among African American young adults is increasing (Hirschfeld & Russell, 1997; Jamison, 1999; Maris et al., 2000). Our caller does not have this risk factor because he is Hispanic.
- *Being widowed or divorced.* The caller in our case study is divorced. Moreover, he is extremely upset about not being able to see much of his children (Beach, 2001; Statham et al., 1998).
- *Living alone.* Our caller is living alone. Plus, he feels very isolated and lonely (see Appleby, Cooper, Amos, & Faragher, 1999; Bongar, 1991).
- *Unemployment or serious financial problems.* The caller in our case study is currently unemployed because of strike layoffs, and he also has serious money problems (see Brown et al., 2000; Hawton, Houston, & Shepperd, 1999; Joiner & Rudd, 2000; Krug et al., 1998; Statham et al., 1998).
- *Recent negative event, such as the loss of a close relationship or a job.* Our caller has these risks. There is a large research literature on the association of depression and distressed close relationships (Appleby et al., 1999; Beach, 2001). For example, Moos et al. (1998) found that support, stability, and effectiveness in close relationships is a strong predictor of avoiding further depressions—even 10 years later.
- *Being over 69 years of age and male.* Our case study does not have this risk factor: The distressed male caller is about 35 years old. Reports by the U.S. National Center for Health Statistics (Hirschfeld & Russell, 1997), however, illustrate that suicide rates climb dramatically for males who are over the age of 69. In addition, chronic health problems, which are most common among older adults,

increase the risk for both depression and suicidal symptoms (Chen, Bierhals, et al., 1999; Jeste et al., 1999; Niederehe & Schneider, 1998; National Institutes of Health [NIH], 1992; Richards & Perri, 1999, 2000, 2001; Westefeld et al., 2000).

Overall, the distressed caller in our case study evidenced 11 of the empirically supported risk factors for suicide. This total implies *extremely* high risk.

Assessment

The valid assessment of suicidal risk is difficult to do (American Psychiatric Association, 2000b; Bongar et al., 1998; Bostwick & Pankratz, 2000; Jacobs, 1999; Maris et al., 2000; Sommers-Flanagan & Sommers-Flanagan, 1995). Practitioners are faced with the task of predicting a low-frequency event: suicide. For practical and statistical reasons, it is difficult to be accurate with this prediction. The practitioner must think through a complicated "mental calculus" of the known risk factors and then reach a decision on the overall risk. The practitioner may have to make decisions based on modest amounts of information. Sometimes decisions must be made quickly, particularly in crisis intervention cases. Furthermore, even among patients with a high overall risk, only a small fraction will commit suicide, so the practitioner is trying to predict a very infrequent—but extremely important—event, the kind of event that statisticians have concluded is a difficult prediction to make accurately. Thus, this is a challenging assessment situation.

Moreover, it is easy to make mistakes:

After a junior at Harvard University stabbed her roommate to death and then hanged herself last month, attention quickly turned to this question: Had [the student] shown signs of what was coming? . . . Health officials at many colleges say, however, that even when they get a tip about behavior much more overt than that—a tip, for instance, that a student has a plan to kill himself—the challenges are only beginning. (Shea, 1995, p. 35A)

Hence, many experts advise practitioners to do the following: Try to get your patient with several suicidal risk factors *extensive* and *immediate* treatment. Ideally, this entails an interdisciplinary effort. We acknowledge, however, that there are practical and resource limitations to this strategy (Jacobs, 1999; Jobes et al., 2000; Task Force on Education, 2000). Furthermore, some suicidal individuals will refuse treatment, no matter what. Nevertheless, we should always try to get our suicidal patients some treatment!

There is a sizable literature on assessment devices—questionnaires, interview schedules, and so on—that may be used to evaluate suicidal risk. As with the evaluation of depression in its own right, an interview should always be part of the assessment effort.

We recommend using a simple "mental calculus" during the first interview with a suicidal patient, such as the following example, which is in alignment (except for simplifications and minor revisions) with the clinical guidelines suggested by Hirschfeld and Russell (1997, p. 913):

1. Assess sociological and demographic risk factors.
2. Ask about stress.
3. Evaluate depression and anxiety.
4. Screen for alcohol and drug abuse.
5. Assess suicidal ideation and plans, along with previous suicidal attempts and family history of suicide.
6. Evaluate the overall suicidal risk, in part by summing the number of risk factors. Arrange for immediate and intensive care if the risk appears high due to the presence of several risk factors or an extremely strong risk factor (e.g., severe and relentless "hopelessness").

After this initial assessment, if patients appear to evidence imminent risk of suicide, then experts typically recommend the following procedures. The practitioner should not leave the patient alone. Ambulance personnel or the police should supervise transfer of the patient to a psychiatric facility. Hospitalization (day and night) should be sought immediately for the patient (Hirschfeld & Russell, 1997; Jacobs, 1999; Maris et al., 2000; Westefeld et al., 2000).

For lower-risk suicidal patients, the practitioner may sidestep the previous crisis intervention procedures and pursue less dramatic interventions (American Psychiatric Association, 2000b; Clark, 1995; Rudd & Joiner, 1998; Westefeld et al., 2000). The following treatments are typically recommended for lower-risk suicidal patients:

- Intervening with both psychotherapy and pharmacotherapy (preferably with limited prescriptions of the low-overdose-risk medications, such as the SSRIs; see Halbreich & Montgomery, 2000; Nemeroff & Schatzberg, 1998; Rankin, 2000; Thase & Kupfer, 1996)
- Enlisting the help of the patient's significant others
- Reducing the availability of suicidal methods (guns, poisons, etc.)
- Maintaining very frequent counseling contact
- Aggressively treating the patient's depression and, when relevant, the patient's substance abuse

The merits of a No-Suicide Contract should also be considered. For example, a simpler and partially revised version of the "Anti-Suicide Contract" illustrated by Bongar (1991, p. 291) is shown in Table 9.1.

We recommend that the advantages of a No-Suicide Contract be discussed with all of your suicidal patients. The patient and the clinic should keep signed copies.

Treatment

Pharmacotherapy is frequently part of the treatment package for suicidal patients (American Psychiatric Association, 2000b). Antidepressants are relatively inexpensive (Olfson, Marcus, et al., 1998). Furthermore, antidepressant medications are covered by most health insurance policies. In addition, there is a large research literature supporting the efficacy of pharmacotherapy for severe depression (Halbreich & Montgomery, 2000; Khan, Warner, & Brown, 2000; Leon et al., 1999; Nemeroff & Schatzberg, 1998; Rankin, 2000; Thase & Kupfer, 1996). The practitioner should keep in mind, however, that antidepressants take 4 to 6 weeks to realize a maximum therapeutic effect (American Psychiatric Association, 2000b).

As with severe depression in general, however, many experts maintain that a combined treatment approach—including both pharmacotherapy

TABLE 9.1 No-Suicide Contract

I, _____ , will try to live a better life, and I will persistently seek help during a crisis. In addition, I will not attempt suicide. I will seek further help if I am contemplating a suicide attempt.

I can be contacted at the following phone numbers: _____ .

My psychotherapist and health care providers can be contacted at the following phone numbers: _____ .

My spouse or closest family member is _____ , and his/her phone numbers are _____ .

My best friend is _____ , and his/her phone numbers are _____ .

The phone number and address of my hospital emergency room is _____ .

Police and crisis-hotline services are available if I need immediate help. I can call 911 or the crisis hotline at _____ .

I agree to sincerely work with my psychotherapist and other health care providers and to give effective coping strategies my best effort.

Patient's printed or typed name _____ .

Patient's signature _____ Date _____ .

Psychotherapist's signature _____ Date _____ .

Clinic supervisor's and/or attending physician's signatures _____ Date _____ .

SOURCE: Adapted from Bongar (1991, p. 291).

and psychotherapy—is the best intervention for suicidal patients. Moreover, there is evidence that this may be the most effective approach for severe depression in general (e.g., Keller et al., 2000; Thase et al., 1997). Of course, brief hospitalization (day and night) with physician supervision is also typically considered in the treatment options for suicidal patients.

In addition to pharmacotherapy, another biological treatment possibility is electro-convulsive therapy (ECT; Fava & Rosenbaum, 1995). ECT is sometimes effective for depressed and suicidal patients where none of the frontline interventions have worked (Hammen, 1997). Many patients are frightened by the prospect of ECT, however, and most medical experts consider ECT to be a backup treatment possibility for extremely severe depression rather than a first treatment option

(American Psychiatric Association, 2000b). There are concerns about serious memory loss in a small percentage of the patients treated with ECT. Furthermore, there is a potential for harmful interactions between ECT and some health problems and medications. Finally, patients treated with ECT evidence a very high relapse rate. For instance, a recent randomized controlled trial indicated that most of the patients (84%) treated with ECT and a placebo medication experienced a relapse within 6 months of completing ECT (Sackeim et al., 2001). Even with various long-term pharmacotherapy options as part of a combined-treatment program, approximately 50% of the treated ECT patients evidenced a relapse within 6 months of completing ECT (Sackeim et al., 2001).

Regardless of what else is in the treatment package for suicidal patients, we would argue that some form of psychotherapy should always be included. Furthermore, we would not get counterarguments from most experts–they agree that suicidal patients of all ages need to learn more adaptive ways of thinking, feeling, and behaving (American Psychiatric Association, 2000b; Byford et al., 1999; Evans, Tyrer, et al., 1999; Harrington, Whittaker, & Shoebridge, 1998; Lewinsohn et al., 1996; Westefeld et al., 2000). For suicidal patients, these improved styles of adaptation and coping are what psychotherapy often focuses on. Moreover, even if depressed patients are receiving pharmacotherapy, they are likely to benefit from psychotherapy too (DeRubeis et al., 1999; Keller et al., 2000; Rotheram-Borus et al., 2000; Thase et al., 1997).

Rudd et al. (1996) provided an example of a psychotherapy intervention, including 2 weeks of day hospitalizations, for suicidal patients. They compared an outpatient psychotherapeutic intervention with the "standard treatment" for suicidal adults (i.e., pharmacotherapy, general counseling, and day-and-night hospitalization in some cases). Their outpatient treatment emphasized improving problem-solving skills and interpersonal competence (see also D'Zurilla & Nezu, 1999; Gilbert, 2000; Leahy & Holland, 2000; Nezu et al., 1989). It should be noted that a few of the patients in this outpatient psychotherapy program were also given pharmacotherapy and brief overnight hospitalizations if their individual circumstances appeared to recommend these additional interventions. With their sample of 264 suicidal young adults, the problem-solving therapy and social skills intervention worked better than the standard treatment. We should caution, however, that this group of young adult participants might be particularly well suited to an intervention focusing on problem-solving therapy and interpersonal skills (D'Zurilla & Nezu, 1999; Gilbert, 2000). Therefore, replication and extension to other suicidal populations are needed to see if this outpatient psychotherapy intervention will successfully generalize across different samples.

Of course, many—and perhaps most—suicidal patients need pharmacotherapy, brief hospitalizations (day and night), and long-term monitoring. The Rudd et al. (1996) study, however, reminds us that not all of them do: For a majority of the suicidal patients in this study, an intensive and structured psychotherapy was quite efficacious. Furthermore, this group intervention was also practical: The treatment protocol was 9 hours each weekday, for 2 weeks, in a day hospital set-ting (Rudd et al., 1996, p. 182). The professional consensus, however, is that both pharmacotherapy and brief hospitalization (day and night) should always be considered for a suicidal patient as possible treatment additions to intensive psychotherapy (American Psychiatric Association, 2000b; Bongar et al., 1998; Jacobs, 1999; Jamison, 1999; Maris et al., 2000; Thase et al., 1997; Richards & Perri, 2001). The professional con-sensus also recommends considering pharmacotherapy, along with intensive psychotherapy and brief hospitalization (day and night), for all severely suicidal patients (American Psychiatric Association, 2000b; Jamison, 1999; Keller et al., 2000).

Ethical and Practical Issues

Some experts have argued that seriously depressed individuals are too risky and confused to give truly "informed consent" for their safe and ethical participation in research (e.g., Elliott, 1997). Empirical research does not support this argument (Appelbaum et al., 1999; Khan et al., 2000). Moreover, several experts have given passionate defenses for more research on depression and suicide (e.g., Jamison, 1999; Kupfer, 1999; Salzman, 1999a). In addition, U.S. investigators have excellent track records for protecting depressed participants and for providing them with effective care in approved studies (Beckham & Leber, 1995; Hammen, 1997; for ethical discussions, see Bersoff, 1999; Heyd & Bloch, 1999; Koocher & Keith-Spiegel, 1998; Pope & Vasquez, 1998).

There are numerous practical challenges to treating suicidal patients. For example, the crisis hotline counselor in our case study needed to stay calm, think fast, show empathy, problem-solve effectively, and be helpful—and she had to accomplish all of this counseling during a phone call that only lasted a few minutes. Also witness the following comment by a seasoned veteran of crisis intervention with suicidal college students: "How to intervene when students may be suicidally depressed is one of the toughest decisions that campus psychologists face. 'Frankly, a situation like that comes up in my counseling center once a month,' says Peter Cimbolic, director of the center at Catholic University of America. 'They are nail-biters'" (Shea, 1995, p. 35A; see also Drumm, 2000; Gose, 2000a).

Limitations on resources, finances, and treatment options may pose practical problems. The increases in "managed care" health insurance plans have further restricted treatment options. Indeed, suicidal patients must sometimes be treated without financial compensation for the treatment provider because the patient's health insurance is either inadequate or nonexistent. Patients who are suicidal present difficult clinical challenges for the practitioner. There are many "what-to-do" lists on this issue (Jacobs, 1999; Maris et al., 2000; Richards & Perri, 2001), and five frequently mentioned guidelines follow:

1. Stay calm, be helpful, and protect yourself.
2. Communicate that you care!
3. Get expert advice.
4. Remember that the "legal standard of care" is care that is "average, reasonable, and prudent."
5. Keep in mind that one of the limits to confidentiality is a case in which the patient presents a clear and immediate danger to him- or herself.

The crisis counselor in our case study was trying to follow these clinical guidelines. We think that she was effective with the "stay calm and be helpful" guideline. The counselor communicated that "she cared." We cannot tell if she sought "expert advice," but most crisis clinics have this professional consultation available. Her counseling effort appears to have been within the legal standard of care. Finally, although Caller ID may present confidentiality concerns, the counselor in our case study sought voluntary consent for help.

Future Directions

"Grand theories" are unlikely to work here. Suicide is too complex, multifaceted, and dependent on the unique features of individuals' circumstances for us to expect any one theory to explain all cases. A more realistic approach is developing a theory that may explain some cases–specifically, some cases that have many features in common. Thus, for example, Baumeister (1990) has developed a theory that a subgroup of suicides might be understood as follows: "Suicide is analyzed in terms of motivations to escape from aversive self-awareness. . . . Suicide can be seen as an ultimate step in the effort to escape from self and world" (p. 90).

A challenge for clinical practice is better education: We need to improve the education of practitioners—and the lay public—so that they cope more effectively with suicidal crises (Bongar, 1992; Garland & Zigler, 1993; Jamison, 1999; Task Force on Education, 2000; U.S. Public Health Service, 1999; Westefeld et al., 2000). In this context, we recommend a book by Jamison (1999). This book is clear, thorough, and appropriate for both practitioners and laypersons.

Severe depression is a horrible experience (Jamison, 1995). Depressed and suicidal patients need empathy from their treatment providers. Even a commentary arguing that depression may "possibly" have an adaptive function in some cases still acknowledges that "depression is one of humanity's most serious medical problems" (Nesse, 2000, p. 18). Practitioners should be very empathic with their depressed and suicidal patients.

Clinical Guidelines

- Stay calm, be helpful, and protect yourself.
- Repeatedly communicate that you care!

- Attempt to develop an effective therapeutic alliance, even in brief crisis interventions.
- Know the established risk factors for suicide.
- Remember that the "legal standard of care" is care that is "average, reasonable, and prudent."
- Get expert advice.
- Keep in mind that one of the limits to confidentiality is a case in which your patient presents a clear and immediate danger to him- or herself.
- Educate yourself about the complex ethical issues regarding suicide.
- Keep good records.
- Be thorough, but quick, in providing care.
- Consider the merits of the major interventions for severe depression, including empirically supported psychotherapies, pharmacotherapy, and brief hospitalization (day and night). In extreme cases where frontline treatments have failed, ECT deserves consideration as a backup treatment option.
- Consider the advantages of building a skill enhancement component into your psychotherapy efforts with suicidal patients.
- Enlist the help of the suicidal patient's significant others if this appears beneficial.
- When your suicidal patient clearly needs brief hospitalization (day and night), make decisions about the pros and cons of voluntary versus involuntary hospitalization (i.e., "commitment"). Police officers are typically involved with involuntary hospitalizations.
- Appropriate physician supervision should be consistently provided for all hospitalizations.
- Outpatient counseling of a suicidal case requires frequent patient contact, along with frequent consultation.
- For suicidal patients, it is often helpful to provide treatment in the context of an interdisciplinary effort.
- Be flexible.
- Consider the merits of your patient discussing and signing a No-Suicide Contract.
- Include booster sessions in your treatment program to enhance the maintenance of therapeutic gains.

- If your patient's attorney contacts you, then redirect that attorney correspondence through your clinic attorney (whenever feasible).
- Suicidal crises and deaths may traumatize the counselor, so seek expert consultation, support from colleagues, and other types of professional assistance as you need it.
- This area is changing rapidly; thus, pursue continuing education.
- The issue is not if, but how, you will deal with suicidal crises in some of your patients.

Chapter Summary

At least 31,000 Americans commit suicide each year. There are about 18 attempts for every completed suicide. During the last 40 years, suicide rates have increased approximately 300% among adolescents and young adults. The lifetime risk of suicide among depressed individuals is 6%, which is more than 100 times the suicide rate for the population at large.

Based on empirical research, the major risk factors for suicide in adults are the following: depression, substance abuse, schizophrenia, panic disorder, hopelessness, severe inability to experience pleasure, previous suicidal attempts or a history of suicidal thinking, chronic sleep disruption, male gender, white or Native American race/ethnicity, being widowed or divorced, living alone, being unemployed or experiencing serious financial problems, a recent negative event such as the loss of a close relationship or a job, and being over 69 years of age and male.

Even when you are in doubt about the overall suicidal risk, the standard approach is to encourage anyone with several risk factors to get professional help. Interacting with the person through an interview can facilitate this process, along with improving the accuracy of the assessment.

Antidepressants are well supported in general, and they show promise for treating depressed people who are suicidal. Many experts favor a *combined* approach to treatment, however, in which both pharmacotherapy and intensive psychotherapy are provided. Brief hospitalization (day and night) is also used in many of the more serious cases.

Electro-convulsive therapy (ECT) is sometimes an effective backup treatment option when standard frontline treatments have failed. Suicidal patients need to learn more adaptive ways of thinking, feeling, and behaving. Thus, in our opinion, psychotherapy should always be part of the treatment package.

Clinical guidelines for handling suicidal crises in your patients include the following. Stay calm, be helpful, and protect yourself. Communicate that you care! Get expert advice. Provide care that is "average, reasonable, and prudent." Keep in mind that there are limits to confidentiality for your suicidal patients.

Suggested Readings

Discussions

Risk Factors

- Hirschfeld and Russell (1997) discussed the empirically established risk factors for adult suicide. This review is clear, thorough, and insightful.

Practice Guidelines

- The practice guidelines for treating Major Depressive Disorder developed by the American Psychiatric Association (2000b) and a thoughtful commentary on these guidelines by Hollon and Shelton (2001) are helpful resources in this area.

Reviews of the Literature

- Jacobs (1999) edited a series of reviews on assessment and treatment issues regarding suicide. This book includes numerous how-to suggestions that are helpful (see also Bongar et al., 1998; Maris et al., 2000; Richards & Perri, 2001).
- Westefeld et al. (2000) presented an overview of risk factors, assessment methods, and interventions for suicidal patients. This is an excellent review.

Overview for Practitioners and Laypersons

- Jamison (1999) presented an overview of research on suicide. This book is beautifully written, thorough, and appropriate for both practitioners and laypersons.

Education for Crisis Intervention

- The Task Force on Education and Training of the Section on Clinical Emergencies and Crises, Division of Clinical Psychology, American Psychological Association (2000), developed a "consensus statement" that offers helpful recommendations regarding education for crisis intervention (see also Roberts, 2000).

Studies

- Brener et al. (1999) conducted an epidemiological survey with a nationally representative sample of 4,609 college students. The findings indicated that 10% of the undergraduate students had seriously contemplated suicide.
- Brown et al. (2000) conducted a 20-year longitudinal investigation with 6,891 psychiatric outpatients. The results provided further support regarding several of the established risk factors for suicide, including depression, suicidal ideation, hopelessness, and unemployment (see also Koivumaa-Honkanen et al., 2001).
- Evans, Morgan, et al. (1999) conducted a randomized controlled trial with 827 deliberate self-harm patients. All patients received treatment as usual, and some patients were randomly assigned to a telephone-support intervention for further crises. The findings indicated that crisis telephone consultations were most likely to benefit first-time patients.
- Kessler, Borges, and Walters (1999) conducted an epidemiological survey with 5,877 participants. The results suggested that concrete suicidal plans yielded about three times more risk than abstract suicidal thinking.

PART IV

Treatment of Depression

10 Psychotherapy

Overview

We begin this chapter with a case study. We focus the remainder of the chapter primarily on the two psychotherapies for adult depression that have enjoyed the most empirical support: cognitive behavior therapy and interpersonal psychotherapy. We briefly discuss several additional psychotherapy interventions for depression, however, that have evidenced promising but less extensive empirical support: problem-solving therapy, behavior therapy (without a cognitive emphasis), behavioral marital therapy, systems and family therapy, coping-skills training, and brief psychodynamic therapy. We then present clinical guidelines, and we conclude with a chapter summary and suggested readings.

Case Study

This depressed patient is participating in psychotherapy at her university's counseling center. She is in her fourth session of treatment, which includes some cognitive behavior therapy. The patient is a graduate student, and she is discussing an incident that occurred recently in one of her classes.

Patient: I was humiliated! Sheila is so smart that she makes me look retarded. And she has this genius for diplomatically putting her classmates down. It didn't help, of course, that some of the other students snickered and made knowing

> looks at each other. I'm upset! This kind of humiliation makes my depression worse!

Therapist: What did Sheila say?

Patient: Well, I'd just made some comments regarding one of the theories of criminology that we were discussing, and I noted a few relevant studies, when Sheila jumped in and said that she agreed with me but that she particularly liked another study.

Therapist: And you interpreted this as a putdown?

Patient: Yes. Sheila couldn't leave what I'd said alone. She had to add to it. She complimented my contributions to the discussion, but then she had to add that one study that I'd forgotten to mention.

Therapist: Did you see Sheila's comment about an additional study as hostile toward you personally?

Patient: Of course! Okay, okay, she didn't attack me personally, but she did add to what I'd already said. Well, okay, it was not a personal attack. But somehow I would have felt better if she had just let my comments stand by themselves. Well, okay, I suppose that we are all supposed to comment and contribute to the general discussion—Dr. Jones is basing half of our course grade on class participation. Maybe I overreacted. But I feel so vulnerable in this class that I interpret almost any comment by a classmate as potentially hostile.

Therapist: What happens then?

Patient: I get depressed, of course. I know. I know. This stuff relates to that homework that you asked me to do about incorrect attributions and dysfunctional thinking. And it also relates to the self-monitoring records that you asked me to keep—where I matched the "situation" to my "thinking" and "mood," and where I planned "fun activities." That homework was easy. Even the role-plays that we've practiced here are easy. But using this stuff in real life is hard! I just wish that I wasn't so scared of the class. Sheila is brilliant—I bet that she isn't scared of the class.

Therapist: Do you think that Sheila is purposely trying to be mean to you?

Patient: No, of course not. She is an okay person. She has never said anything obviously hostile to me. But she is so smart that I feel that anything she says is potentially hostile. I know. That doesn't make sense. But when you are there, and scared and trying so hard, it just seems like any comment by a classmate is a potential putdown. I know that I need to stop thinking like this—it's making me depressed!

Therapist: I understand that changing some of your thinking styles and interpretations is a difficult challenge for you. And you seem to understand that what you say to yourself in these situations has a major impact on your feelings.

Discussion of the Case Study

The first thing to emphasize is that cognitive behavior therapy, like any psychotherapy, requires effective clinical skill if it is going to work. Notice that the therapist is empathic, gentle, structured, and insightful. Moreover, the therapist does not overwhelm the patient but rather allows her to do most of the talking. The therapist primarily structures the counseling through gentle questions. Cognitive behavior therapy is a directive therapy, but it does not entail relentlessly telling the patient what to do, arguing with the patient, or "preaching" at the patient. Rather, the patient and the therapist should work effectively together, as professional and trusting collaborators who are pursuing enhanced problem-solving styles. The patient has to work hard and collaboratively or this intervention will not be effective. Moreover, the therapist has to work in a structured and empathic manner or this intervention will not be effective. The previous case example appears to reflect the therapeutic process that is effective in cognitive behavior therapy. This case also illustrates the substance and style of a depressed patient who is wrestling with her dysfunctional thinking.

Cognitive Behavior Therapy

Cognitive behavior therapy focuses on changing the depressed patient's dysfunctional thinking about his or her personal self, environment, and future. As it is usually practiced, there is also some attention to enhancing coping and interpersonal skills (Goldfried & Davison, 1994; Hammen, 1997; Leahy & Holland, 2000; Persons, 1989; Sacco & Beck, 1995; Young et al., 1993). Of the psychotherapies used for treating depression, cognitive behavior therapy is—by far—one of the best-supported psychotherapies. Systematic empirical investigations, including numerous randomized controlled trials, have yielded extensive empirical support for cognitive behavior therapy (American Psychiatric Association, 2000b; Clark & Beck, 1999; Craighead et al., 1998; DeRubeis & Crits-Christoph, 1998; DeRubeis et al., 1999; Hollon & Shelton, 2001; Keller et al., 2000). Nevertheless, experts acknowledge that we still do not have a complete understanding of why this psychotherapeutic approach works or when it will work best (Kazdin, 2000). But cognitive behavior therapy often does work. Therefore, it is important for practitioners to be familiar and comfortable with this psychological approach to treating depression. At the same time, it would be difficult for us to exaggerate the complexity of these therapeutic techniques; practitioners need thorough training and supervision in these techniques to use them effectively. This caution holds for all of the psychotherapies discussed in this chapter.

Several treatment manuals are available for cognitive behavior therapy of depression. The classic work of Beck and his colleagues is helpful, including discussions of the theoretical model (Clark & Beck, 1999) and how-to recommendations for psychotherapists (Beck et al., 1979; Young et al., 1993). Persons and her colleagues have developed how-to manuals and clinical guidelines for cognitive behavior therapy of depression (Persons, 1989; Persons et al., 2001). In addition, Goldfried and Davison (1994) have presented numerous practical suggestions regarding the use of cognitive behavior therapy for a broad array of psychological disorders, as have Leahy and Holland (2000).

Most of the same principles that apply to making any psychotherapy efficacious are also crucial here. For instance, an effective therapeutic alliance with the patient is necessary (American Psychiatric Association, 2000b; Martin, Garske, & Davis, 2000; Meier & Davis, 1997; Persons, 1989; Sacco & Beck, 1995; Tang & DeRubeis, 1999). Helping the patient to work hard, in therapy and outside of it (e.g., homework), is important (Burns & Spangler, 2000; Meier & Davis, 1997). This therapeutic approach lends itself to a structured and directive style, and the practitioner's ability to structure treatment effectively is an influential component of success (Goldfried & Davison, 1994; Meier & Davis, 1997; Persons, 1989; Shaw et al., 1999). At the same time, however, the practitioner must be careful to avoid the following kind of simple advice giving, "preaching," and berating of the patient.

Patient: Oh, I felt so depressed after Sheila made me look stupid in class! Why can't I be a genius like Sheila? I'm just a retarded bystander in the class. It doesn't help, of course, that they give us too much work to do—even if I never slept I couldn't keep up with these classes. The PhD program that I'm in is impossible. I'll flunk out—or drop out—sooner or later. It's hopeless. Maybe they'll just kick me out. Whatever . . . it just seems hopeless.

Therapist: I disagree! You primarily earned grades of A last year, and nothing below a B. Sheila just made a constructive comment in class. You're supposed to do that in the course. She didn't attack you. You need to immediately disengage from these dysfunctional thoughts when you start having them. You are not a bad person. Your future is not ruined. The concrete evidence suggests that you are one of the most effective students in your PhD program. But you need to learn to nip your depressive thinking in the bud, every time something makes you think that you're a bad person, or your world is bad, or your future is bad. That kind of thinking isn't accurate—and it just makes you depressed. You must learn to think differently about this.

In our assessment, the previous example is *not* an effective therapeutic technique. If depression could be simply whisked away by telling the patient to stop thinking in a depressive manner, then we would have a lot less depression in the world. Furthermore, the lack of empathy, graciousness, and sensitivity illustrated in the previous example will not be effective in any therapeutic approach. Rather, cognitive behavior therapy with depressed patients requires a warm and gentle inter personal style, an empathic sensitivity and insight, and a collaborative and respectful therapeutic relationship (Beck et al., 1979; Burns & Nolen-Hoeksema, 1992; Meier & Davis, 1997; Persons, 1989; Safran, 1998; Safran & Segal, 1990; Young et al., 1993).

Much of the structuring in cognitive behavior therapy is accomplished through brief and carefully thought out *questions*. This process is illustrated in the case example at the beginning of the chapter. Yet, here again, the interpersonal process should be gentle, empathic, and collaborative—and the questions should be limited and brief. Depressed patients do not want to be bombarded with a seemingly endless list of questions. Rather, they want an opportunity to talk comfortably, and the therapist needs a chance to listen carefully (American Psychiatric Association, 2000b; Beck et al., 1979; Goldfried & Davison, 1994; Haley, 1996; Othmer & Othmer, 1994; Persons, 1989; Young et al., 1993).

One of the more challenging aspects of cognitive behavior therapy is working collaboratively with depressed patients to help them *change dysfunctional thinking*. It is, of course, difficult for depressed patients to do this—particularly early in the therapeutic process (see Kuyken, Kurzer, DeRubeis, Beck, & Brown, 2001). The following therapy interaction is an example.

Patient: I totally botched the first take-home exam in my criminology course. I worked terribly hard on the exam. But, despite the determined effort, I didn't do well. I'm hopeless.

Therapist: What was your grade?

Patient: I got a grade of B+. I know. I know. That doesn't sound so bad. But I really did work hard on this. If B+ is the best I can ever do, even after a Herculean effort, then that is pretty pathetic.

Therapist: Why?

Patient: Well, because I should do better!

Therapist: I'm sorry, but maybe I'm missing some of your rationale here. Please explain the reasoning behind your "I should do better" conclusion.

Patient: Well, um, I don't always think through all of the reasons. They sort of pop up automatically. Let's see. I guess the reason is I think that if I work very hard then I should get a grade of A. Anything less is a putdown.

Therapist: So getting a B+ triggers the thought that anything less than an A is a putdown?

Patient: When you ask me to think this stuff through carefully, then I'll admit it sounds foolish. It's like I'm saying that if I'm not perfect then I'm a failure.

Therapist: And if you believe that getting a B+ means that you're a failure, what kind of feeling do you experience when you get a B+?

Patient: To be honest, I feel pretty miserable. Yeah, I feel depressed.

Therapist: So expecting yourself to be perfect has some negative emotional consequences?

Patient: It sure does!

Therapist: And when you're feeling depressed, how does that affect you?

Patient: I'm not sure I know what you mean.

Therapist: In what ways do you act differently when you are feeling depressed?

Patient: I don't want to be around people. I just want to be alone, and being alone only leads to my getting into a deeper depression.

Therapist: Okay, let's see if we can put these different pieces together to see how your beliefs influence your mood and behavior.

Patient: Well, looking back, it seems to fit together pretty well. My belief that I always need to be perfect is the setup for my depression.

Therapist: How so?

Patient: If I get a B+ I tell myself I'm a failure and that leads to my feeling miserable and depressed. When I feel that way I

> keep to myself, but that only ends up with my feeling even worse.
>
> *Therapist:* That's excellent! I really think that you have a good grasp of how your thoughts and beliefs play a major role in the emotions that you experience.
>
> *Patient:* Yeah, but it's easier to look back and understand this than it is to change how I think and feel when the professor hands me a test with a B+ grade.
>
> *Therapist:* You're right. That's why it would be helpful for us to set up a real-world homework assignment to help you monitor your thoughts and feelings.

This can be slow, hard work for both the patient and the therapist. In addition, many experts on cognitive behavior therapy (e.g., Persons, 1989) will point out that assessing and discussing patients' depression-related beliefs, which seem to lie behind their dysfunctional thoughts, will enhance the effectiveness of the psychotherapy. For instance, perhaps the patient in the previous example has been taught that "academic perfection is good," that "her academic perfection means that she is good," and that "her environment will systematically reinforce this belief and punish alternatives." Furthermore, perhaps her self-perceptions, social world, and interpersonal relationships relentlessly push her toward this academic perfectionism while leaving her ill prepared to consider alternatives. If so, this would be a good topic for therapy.

We also want to emphasize that a trusting and collaborative *therapeutic relationship* is crucial here. Cognitive behavior therapy will not work without it. In the therapeutic relationship, a strong alliance, respectful collaboration, and sincere empathy are the "psychological glue" that holds the therapeutic process together. For thorough discussions of this matter, practitioners will find the books by Gilbert (2000), Safran (1998), and Safran and Segal (1990) helpful because these authors have written extensively about the therapeutic relationship during cognitive behavior therapy. Depressed patients often feel miserable, setbacks are common, and tension is high. Sound theory and empirically validated techniques are crucially important, but they are not enough in this context—sometimes the therapeutic relationship has to "save the day." Witness the following case.

Patient: I feel miserable today! I did everything wrong today. I'm depressed and angry with myself, and I've made no attempt to use the mood diary that we set up in our last session. I'm afraid that I'm not a good patient. I don't think that you can really help me. And I can't help myself. I'm sorry. I like and respect you, but I just don't think this will work. I want to give up on therapy. I'm sorry.

Therapist: I like and respect you too. I'm hoping, of course, that you will not give up on therapy. We've both seen some progress—along with some setbacks—and we do work well together. I'd like to try a few more sessions, and then evaluate where we stand. But it is your decision—what do you want to do?

Patient: I don't know. I'm upset and confused. Maybe a few more sessions, and then some evaluation when I'm not so upset, would be sensible. I'm just very upset right now.... Okay, let's do a few more sessions.

Without a strong and effective therapeutic relationship, no psychotherapy in the world would have worked in this case.

Interpersonal Psychotherapy

Interpersonal psychotherapy has three phases, which focus on the following issues: assessment and goal setting, interpersonal problems that are related to the patient's depression, and supporting and practicing the interpersonal skills that are developed in the previous phase while planning for the future. In discussions with the patient, the present is emphasized, rather than the past. Four types of interpersonal problems that are often associated with depression provide guides for assessment, discussion, insight, skill development, and practice: grief, role disputes, role transitions, and interpersonal deficits. A trusting collaboration between the therapist and patient, education, emotional expression and regulation, role playing, and practice in the real world are the engines of change in this therapeutic approach. When interpersonal problems are discussed, there is an emphasis on better understanding of the situation, improved communication, and positive attempts at negotiating the interpersonal disputes. Although there is some attention to insight and enhanced self-understanding, this issue does not receive the emphasis that it does in psychodynamic approaches.

Several treatment manuals exist for interpersonal psychotherapy, including a classic work, *Interpersonal Psychotherapy of Depression* by Klerman et al. (1984), and more recent guidebooks, such as a manual for treating Dysthymic Disorder by Markowitz (1998). The recent *DSM-IV-TR* (American Psychiatric Association, 2000a, p. 379) emphasizes how important an active treatment approach, such as interpersonal psychotherapy, can be for Dysthymic Disorder. We should note again, however, that *thorough* training and supervision are necessary to use this therapeutic approach effectively with depressed patients (see Gilbert, 2000).

Interpersonal psychotherapy enjoys considerable empirical support for the treatment of depression (American Psychiatric Association, 2000b; Craighead et al., 1998; DeRubeis & Crits-Christoph, 1998; Hollon & Shelton, 2001; Spanier & Frank, 1998; Weissman & Markowitz, 1998). Indeed, among the available psychotherapies, only cognitive behavior therapy can currently offer a comparable profile of empirical validation. Moreover, with some specific populations of depressed patients, interpersonal psychotherapy may provide a particularly auspicious treatment option. For example, interpersonal psychotherapy has evidenced promising results for treating depression in Latino and Puerto Rican adolescents, postpartum patients, AIDS patients, and relapse-prone patients (Frank et al., 1990; Markowitz et al., 1998; Mufson et al., 1999; O'Hara et al., 2000; Reynolds et al., 1999; Rossello & Bernal, 1999). Therefore, it is important for practitioners to be familiar and comfortable with this psychotherapy for depression.

Psychotherapy transcripts of sessions during the last two phases of interpersonal psychotherapy also reveal a problem-solving focus that shares some emphases with problem-solving therapy for depression (D'Zurilla & Nezu, 1999; Nezu et al., 1989). The interpersonal psychotherapy approach to treating depression, however, stays focused on *one* type of problem—interpersonal difficulties—rather than the many types of problems that may be addressed with problem-solving therapy.

In addition, interpersonal psychotherapy tends to reflect a more non-directive approach than does cognitive behavior therapy or problem-solving therapy for depression.

The areas of role disputes and role transitions sometimes overlap when interpersonal psychotherapy is pursued with depressed patients. In the following case example, a depressed 41-year-old man who has recently been laid off from his job is struggling with the role issues of disputes and transitions. The disputes center on arguments with his wife about who does what at home and also about what his job loss means in terms of self-worth and humiliation. The transitions center on being suddenly unemployed and on the frustrations of looking for a new job.

Patient: My wife and I argue a lot! Helen says that I "need to get over my depression and start doing more around the house." Well, I suppose she is right, but I can't just eliminate my depression, and I hate housework and running the kids around to a million places. Before I lost my job, we could afford to hire people to help with some of this stuff, but now I'm supposed to do most of it. I hate it! Do you understand how humiliating it is to go from a good job to being suddenly unemployed and having to tell a million teachers, coaches, and other parents that "I'll be picking up the kids now because I lost my job"?

Therapist: I understand. The arguing with your wife, the job loss, and the humiliation are very difficult issues for you. Is the humiliation that you feel something we should talk about?

Patient: Probably. Looking for jobs, however, is also one of my problems. I hate job hunting . . . but I have to do it. I haven't had to apply for jobs for 17 years. I'm not good at it. My self-confidence and poise are in the toilet. Helen is trying to be supportive, but our financial situation forces her to work two jobs, and she's constantly worrying about money. Our relationship is pretty tense and cold right now. I'll have to take a low-level job and I hate this inevitable failure on my part. I've worked hard for

17 years, and now I'm kicked out on the street. I don't think that Helen understands my problems and my shame. It is very humiliating!

Therapist: Yes, I appreciate how difficult this is for you. Have you discussed this humiliation with Helen?

Patient: No.

Therapist: Would it be helpful to role-play some of this discussion with Helen?

Patient: Maybe. I'm not good at telling her what's going on with me. We have talked about this before. It is hard for me to talk about this stuff with my wife! And I hate having to do so much housework and errands with the kids—but I have to—we're broke. I feel like a jerk because I lost my job. And I'm angry! This is hard.

Therapist: Okay, let's role-play how you will discuss this with Helen. Then we can talk about our role-play. We can discuss your feelings and different ways of talking with Helen. I know that you find our role playing a bit awkward, but if you cannot discuss this with me, then you will probably not discuss it with Helen. I think that it would be very helpful for you to talk with Helen about this, and I think the role playing will help.

Patient: Okay. I don't particularly like it, but maybe it will help. Let's try it.

The previous case example illustrates several common themes in interpersonal psychotherapy for depression. The focus is on interpersonal problems, which are often complex. The patient and the therapist work collaboratively. The therapist helps the patient to cope more effectively with depressive emotions, cognitions, and behaviors. There is some attention to the patient's beliefs and insights about his or her self-worth. Moreover, there is specific processing about the patient's feelings of humiliation and loss. There is also some attention to problem-solving skills. The therapist's style is moderately directive but also gentle and empathic. Finally, the patient and the therapist work together on communication skills and problem-solving strategies that can be used in the patient's real world—with the people that are most important to this patient.

Additional Psychotherapy Interventions

Problem-solving therapy helps depressed patients to cope more effectively with their life by teaching them five problem-solving steps: (a) problem orientation, (b) problem definition, (c) generation of alternative solutions, (d) decision making, and (e) solution implementation and verification (D'Zurilla & Nezu, 1999; Nezu et al., 1989, 1998). This therapeutic approach overlaps with coping-skills training, but it is more specific and focused. Problem-solving therapy currently enjoys substantial empirical validation for treating depression, although not as much as cognitive behavior therapy or interpersonal psychotherapy (American Psychiatric Association, 2000b; DeRubeis & Crits-Christoph, 1998; D'Zurilla & Nezu, 1999; Hollon & Shelton, 2001).

Problem-solving therapy is easily and comfortably adapted to interventions with depressed patients. For instance, Nezu et al. (1989) have developed a detailed treatment manual and corresponding clinical guidelines for this therapeutic approach to treating depression. Furthermore, this approach may dovetail nicely with the challenges faced by depressed patients who are coping with a chronic physical illness such as cancer (e.g., Nezu et al., 1998) or with the more diverse array of chronic health problems that are common in the elderly (e.g., Arean et al., 1993). Finally, the treatment outcome research on problem-solving therapy for depressed patients is quite promising, if not conclusive (American Psychiatric Association, 2000b; DeRubeis & Crits Christoph, 1998; D'Zurilla & Nezu, 1999).

Behavior therapy for treating depression—with an emphasis on positive reinforcement, shaping, role playing of enhanced social and communication skills, and environmental improvement—has evidenced positive results, particularly with depressed children and adolescents (Clarke et al., 1992; Craighead et al., 1998; DeRubeis & Crits-Christoph, 1998; Lewinsohn et al., 1996, 1998). This treatment approach has a strong empirical underpinning and numerous supportive studies.

Thus, practitioners should consider the merits of building some of these behavior therapy components into their treatment programs, regardless of the theoretical approach they are focusing on. This behavior therapy approach, with its emphasis on skill enhancement, has some overlap with other skill development approaches such as problem-solving therapy and coping-skills training. With adult patients, however, there is more empirical support for a *cognitive* behavioral approach to treating depression, which *includes* an emphasis on dysfunctional cognitive styles, than there is for this more limited behavioral-only approach (Clark & Beck, 1999; Gortner et al., 1998; Jacobson et al., 1996). The broader cognitive behavioral approach may be particularly advantageous in terms of better maintenance of treatment effects (Hollon & Shelton, 2001; Jarrett et al., 2001; Sanders & McFarland, 2000; Teasdale et al., 2000, 2001).

Behavioral marital therapies for depressed spouses have evidenced some promising results. Chronic depression disrupts marriages. Furthermore, chronically distressed marriages tend to elicit depression (Beach, 2001; Joiner & Coyne, 1999; Prince & Jacobson, 1995; Whisman & Bruce, 1999). Therefore, a marital therapy approach deserves consideration when one or both members of a couple are seriously depressed (Baucom et al., 1998). We also discuss depression and close relationships in Chapter 7. Of the possible approaches to marital therapy with depressed patients, the behavioral approach has received some of the most elegant research evaluations (Baucom et al., 1998). This approach blends the components of cognitive behavior therapy, problem-solving therapy, and extensive training with communication skills into the format of marital therapy. For a distressed couple where one or both members are depressed, the merits of this approach deserve consideration; the research outcome literature is promising, though not conclusive (Baucom et al., 1998).

A *systems and family therapy* approach often makes sense for the same reasons that a marital therapy approach does: Depression is hard on families, and chronically distressed family members are hard on depression (e.g., Holahan et al., 2000). Within this framework, a behavioral version of systems and family therapy for depressed patients has received the most extensive research evaluation (Alexander,

Holtzworth-Munroe, & Jameson, 1994; Baucom et al., 1998; Prince and Jacobson, 1995). Moreover, recent outcome studies have yielded promising results (e.g., Birmaher et al., 2000; Kolko et al., 2000), although the specific therapeutic components responsible for success remain unclear (Kolko et al., 2000). Nevertheless, practitioners may find it beneficial to blend behavior therapy into their systems and family therapy when working with families that include depressed family members.

Coping-skills training, conducted in a group format, has been investigated with child and adolescent participants, and the results are promising but not conclusive (Kazdin & Weisz, 1998). Furthermore, the exact mechanisms of change for this promising therapeutic approach have not yet been established (Kazdin, 1999, 2000). Presumably, the depressed participants learn how to cope with stress more effectively, how to resolve problems and increase reinforcement in their environments, and how to enhance their interpersonal relationships. This reasonable hypothesis, however, is easier to state than it is to prove. Nevertheless, controlled outcome studies suggest that this group intervention does reliably reduce depressive symptomatology in children and adolescents (e.g., Gillham et al., 1995; Weisz et al., 1997).

Coping-skills interventions share some of the philosophy, strategies, and goals of problem-solving therapy, but the specific process and emphases are not the same. Problem-solving therapy sticks closely to the five-step model of problem resolution (described previously in this chapter), whereas coping-skills training relies on a broader array of models and techniques to teach enhanced coping skills. The coping-skills approach, of course, may also be extended to therapy with depressed adults, and again there are some promising results but not the extensive empirical validation that is available for cognitive behavior therapy and interpersonal psychotherapy (Craighead et al., 1998; Cronkite & Moos, 1995; DeRubeis & Crits-Christoph, 1998; Snyder, 1999).

Brief psychodynamic therapy has evidenced some promise with depression. For example, Barkham, Shapiro, Hardy, and Rees (1999) found promising results after only three sessions of psychodynamic-interpersonal psychotherapy with a group of mildly depressed participants. They found a similar outcome for a three-session version of cognitive behavior therapy, although the cognitive behavior therapy condition showed better results at a 1-year follow-up. Whether such extremely brief interventions will have merit for more seriously depressed participants is a question that awaits further investigation. Several other research teams have also found some positive outcomes with brief versions of psychodynamic therapy, which typically run from 20 to 30 sessions (Crits-Christoph, 1992; Henry, Strupp, Schacht, & Gaston, 1994). Although more time limited than classical psychodynamic approaches, these brief versions of psychodynamic therapy continue to emphasize the therapeutic alliance, transference within the therapeutic relationship, insight about interpersonal experiences, and—in some versions (e.g., Barkham et al., 1999)—attention to the skills for resolving interpersonal difficulties. The recent work with very brief versions of psychodynamic therapy is a reminder that in a "managed care world" most care is brief.

Clinical Guidelines

- *Get thorough* training and supervision in the psychotherapy techniques that you use. For example, cognitive behavior therapy and interpersonal psychotherapy are complex and challenging treatment interventions. Extensive training is necessary to use these therapeutic techniques effectively with depressed patients.
- Focus on the therapeutic alliance. Any effective psychotherapy for severely depressed patients requires a strong therapeutic alliance.
- Be empathic, gentle, structured, and insightful; never forget that your patient is depressed.
- You and your patient should work together as professional and trusting collaborators who are pursuing enhanced problem-solving styles and improved coping skills.
- If you find it difficult to interact with a particular patient in an empathic and structured manner, then you should discuss this with your patient.
- If your patient is not willing to work hard and collaboratively, then therapy will be difficult, and you should discuss this with your patient.
- Consider the merits of using cognitive behavior therapy. It is one of the two *most* empirically supported psychotherapies for severe depression in adults.

- During cognitive behavior therapy, expect your depressed patients to struggle with their dysfunctional thinking and to encounter roadblocks and setbacks in their quest for more adaptive styles of thinking.
- During cognitive behavior therapy, give attention to improved coping and interpersonal skills for your depressed patients. Changing dysfunctional thinking is not enough, your patients need to change their behavior too.
- When using cognitive behavior therapy in a *group* treatment format (e.g., several depressed patients or a family), take a very planned, careful, and structured approach. Talking about dysfunctional thinking in a group of depressed patients is complicated.
- Consider the merits of using interpersonal psychotherapy. It is one of the two *most* empirically supported psychotherapies for severe depression in adults.
- When using interpersonal psychotherapy, include some attention to skills: interpersonal skills for troubled relationships, along with coping and problem-solving skills for day-to-day adjustment.
- Use role playing as a component of interpersonal psychotherapy. If your depressed patients will not role-play discussions about their interpersonal problems with you, then they will probably not have these discussions with their significant others.
- We recommend *against* trying to combine all features of interpersonal psychotherapy and cognitive behavior therapy in a brief-therapy format. Trying to do everything from both approaches may be too ambitious in a time-limited format.
- Your adult patients should usually evidence a favorable response to cognitive behavior therapy or interpersonal psychotherapy within about 20 sessions. The dose-response literature on cognitive behavior therapy and interpersonal psychotherapy is fairly clear on this matter.
- Thus, if your patient has not evidenced *clinically* significant improvement (e.g., substantial improvement in depressive symptoms or movement out of the *DSM-IV-TR* [American Psychiatric Association, 2000a] diagnostic range) by approximately 20 sessions of these psychotherapies, then you and the patient should

discuss alternative treatment interventions. One alternative is pharmacotherapy. Another alternative is a combination of pharmacotherapy and continued psychotherapy. We discuss these treatment options in Chapter 11.

- If your patient is not progressing well, consult with colleagues and consider alternative, empirically supported interventions.

- Consider the advantages of adding a few booster sessions to your treatment protocol for relapse prevention. Even "very effective people" can relapse, and this is not a sign of weakness or failure. Tell your patients that it is perfectly acceptable for them to contact you if they do relapse. We discuss relapse prevention in Chapter 12.

- Keep up with the psychotherapy outcome literature on depression. This literature is changing rapidly, and it is the empirical backbone of our psychotherapeutic efforts.

Chapter Summary

In this chapter, we discussed psychotherapy for depression. We emphasized the two psychotherapies with the strongest empirical support for treating adult depression, which are cognitive behavior therapy and interpersonal psychotherapy. Cognitive behavior therapy focuses on helping depressed patients to change their dysfunctional thinking about their personal self, their environment, and their future. Cognitive behavior therapy also emphasizes positive behavior change and enhanced coping skill.

Interpersonal psychotherapy focuses on interpersonal problems and skills, with an emphasis on four types of interpersonal difficulties that are common in depression: grief, role disputes, role transitions, and interpersonal deficits. Interpersonal psychotherapy also emphasizes self-understanding and improved problem solving. We discussed several case examples involving these therapeutic approaches with depressed patients.

Several other psychotherapies that enjoy some empirical support for treating depression were briefly covered. We also presented a number of clinical guidelines for practitioners who are using cognitive behavior therapy or interpersonal psychotherapy with their depressed patients.

Suggested Readings

Discussions

Practice Guidelines

- Panels of experts representing the American Psychiatric Association (2000b) have presented practice guidelines regarding the treatment of numerous psychiatric disorders, including Major Depressive Disorder. These practice guidelines are very influential. Moreover, these guidelines are empirically based, thorough, and helpful.
- Hollon and Shelton (2001) offered a thoughtful commentary on the American Psychiatric Association's (2000b) practice guidelines for treating Major Depressive Disorder. The authors discussed numerous relevant issues, including the extensive empirical support for cognitive behavior therapy and interpersonal psychotherapy.

Cognitive Behavior Therapy

- Goldfried and Davison (1994) offered "how-to" discussions on cognitive behavior therapy, including several examples regarding depression. This book is interesting and useful (see also Leahy & Holland, 2000).
- Persons (1989) offered advice on cognitive behavior therapy, including discussions of case formulation, cognitive behavioral intervention, and the therapeutic relationship. This book is full of helpful clinical guidelines (see also Persons et al., 2001).
- Safran (1998) and Safran and Segal (1990) presented thorough discussions of the therapeutic relationship in cognitive behavior therapy (see also Gilbert, 2000).
- Young et al. (1993) presented clinical recommendations on cognitive behavior therapy for depression, and the chapter stays in close

alignment with Aaron Beck's influential theoretical model (Beck et al., 1979; Clark, 2001; Clark & Beck, 1999).

Interpersonal Psychotherapy

- Klerman et al. (1984) gave clinical guidelines for interpersonal psychotherapy of depression, along with a discussion of the theoretical rationale. The authors are credited with developing the theoretical foundation for interpersonal psychotherapy, and this book includes helpful clinical suggestions.
- Markowitz (1998) provided a "how-to" discussion of interpersonal psychotherapy for Dysthymic Disorder. This book has clinical guidelines and helpful treatment suggestions for using interpersonal psychotherapy (see also Gilbert, 2000).

Supervision of Psychotherapy

- Bernard and Goodyear (1998) provided a literature review and a thorough array of clinical guidelines for supervising psychotherapy. This book will help clinical supervisors who use any of the psychotherapy approaches discussed in this chapter.

Psychotherapy "Efficacy" Versus "Effectiveness"

- Nathan et al. (2000) discussed the distinctions between "efficacy" and "effectiveness" in psychotherapy studies, including the need to incorporate more effectiveness issues into research so that it is easier to generalize the results to the practical world of clinicians. If investigators follow the authors' recommendations, then the resulting studies may be more helpful to practitioners (see also Heppner, Kivlighan, & Wampold, 1999; Kazdin, 1998).

Studies

- Lewinsohn et al. (2000) conducted an interview study of 3,003 community participants, with samples spanning the age range of adolescents to older adults. The investigators' findings suggested that depressive symptoms not meeting diagnostic criteria were still associated with significant psychosocial dysfunction, so that these symptoms justified treatment (see also Flett et al., 1997; Santor & Coyne, 2001).

- Rossello and Bernal (1999) conducted a randomized controlled trial with 71 depressed adolescents who were living in Puerto Rico. This study evaluated cognitive behavior therapy and interpersonal psychotherapy. Results indicated that both treatments were efficacious with depressed adolescents, compared with a wait-list control group (see also DeRubeis et al., 1999; Keller et al., 2000; Mufson et al., 1999; O'Hara et al., 2000; Shea et al., 1992).
- Shaw et al. (1999) analyzed data from a large randomized controlled trial with depressed adults. The investigators' findings indicated that "the therapist's ability to structure the treatment" (Shaw et al., 1999, p. 837) was the feature of competence most strongly related to outcome when using cognitive behavior therapy to treat depression.
- Teasdale et al. (2000) conducted a randomized controlled trial to evaluate a relapse prevention strategy. Participants were 145 recurrently depressed patients. Results suggested that training patients to quickly recognize and then disengage from depressive thinking was a cognitive behavioral intervention that improved treatment maintenance (see also Teasdale et al., 2001).
- Young, Klap, Sherbourne, and Wells (2001) conducted a cross-sectional telephone survey with 1,636 adult participants who evidenced depressive or anxiety disorders. The researchers' results indicated that only 30% of the participants received "appropriate treatment" (i.e., medication or counseling that was in alignment with practice guidelines).

11 Pharmacotherapy

Overview

In this chapter, we *briefly* summarize pharmacotherapy for depression. We discuss reviews of the treatment outcome literature and randomized controlled trials. Then the major types of antidepressant medication are covered. We use a blend of classification schemes for antidepressant medications, taken from several reviews by experts (e.g., American Psychiatric Association, 2000b; Nemeroff & Schatzberg, 1998; Thase & Kupfer, 1996). The major types of Food and Drug Administration (FDA)-approved antidepressant medications are the following: (a) tricyclics, (b) selective serotonin reuptake inhibitors (SSRIs), (c) monoamine oxidase inhibitors (MAOIs), and (d) second-generation and other agents: tetracyclics, dopamine-norepinephrine reuptake inhibitors, serotonin-norepinephrine reuptake inhibitors, serotonin modulators, and norepinephrine-serotonin modulators. We summarize research on combined approaches to treatment where pharmacotherapy and psychotherapy are used together. Then we provide clinical guidelines for psychotherapists and other relevant nonphysician practitioners. We conclude with a chapter summary and suggested readings.

We wish to note at the outset that we are *not* physicians and that pharmacotherapy for depression should always be prescribed and closely supervised by a qualified physician. A diverse and complex array of potential contraindications, negative drug-drug interactions, comorbid medical conditions, and chronic disease issues need to be considered by a qualified physician in the context of providing pharmacotherapy for depression. (We realize, of course, that some nonphysician health care providers have special training and licensing to prescribe a limited range of medications in their area of expertise. For example, certified nurse practitioners with special training in obstetrics, gynecology, and associated medication regimens may be licensed—in some U.S. jurisdictions—to prescribe a limited range of FDA-approved medications that are frequently used regarding women's reproductive health care.)

In this brief chapter, we attempt to stay in very close alignment with several well-regarded reviews and practice guidelines on the topic of pharmacotherapy for depression. Some of these practice guidelines have been prepared by panels of experts that were appointed by appropriate national organizations (e.g., Agency for Health Care Policy Research, 1999; American Psychiatric Association, 2000b; *Physicians' Desk Reference*, 2000). Additional reviews and practice guidelines have been prepared by numerous well-regarded experts who were writing collaboratively (e.g., Halbreich & Montgomery, 2000; Nemeroff & Schatzberg, 1998; Rankin, 2000; Schatzberg & Nemeroff, 1998; Thase & Kupfer, 1996). We relied on all of these reviews.

Literature Reviews

Pharmacotherapy is an efficacious intervention for depression in adults. This is the conclusion of numerous reviews, which in turn have evaluated the results of hundreds of randomized, placebo-controlled trials (American Psychiatric Association, 2000b; Halbreich & Montgomery, 2000). Indeed, no other psychiatric disorder has received as much treatment evaluation regarding pharmacotherapy as has depression, and the success rates for pharmacotherapy of depression are comparable to medication treatment of several important medical disorders such as diabetes and hypertension (Nemeroff & Schatzberg, 1998). Moreover, these studies on the pharmacotherapy of depression often demonstrate methodological and statistical elegance (Thase & Kupfer, 1996).

Furthermore, there are several practice guidelines regarding pharmacotherapy and numerous drug handbooks—for example, *Practice Guidelines for the Treatment of Psychiatric Disorders* (American Psychiatric Association, 2000b); the *Merck Manual of Medical Information*

(Berkow et al., 1997); the *Consumer Reports Complete Drug Reference* (Consumer Reports, 2000); and the *Physicians' Desk Reference* (2000). These informational resources are available to practitioners, of course, and also to patients via many libraries and bookstores.

In addition to the conclusion that pharmacotherapy of depression is efficacious for adults, several other conclusions can be drawn from the treatment outcome literature. For example, no particular FDA-approved antidepressant has been demonstrated to be consistently and significantly more efficacious than another (Nemeroff & Schatzberg, 1998). Hence, considerations beyond differential efficacy play a role in physicians' decisions about which of the available antidepressant medications to prescribe. These considerations include concerns regarding side effects, toxicity, overdose, contraindications, drug interactions, dose-effect relationships, dosing convenience, cost, and patient preferences (American Psychiatric Association, 2000b; Bollini, Pampallona, Tibaldi, Kupelnick, & Munizza, 1999; Halbreich & Montgomery, 2000; Olfson, Marcus, et al., 1998; *Physicians' Desk Reference*, 2000; Schatzberg, 2000).

Although the evidence for pharmacotherapy efficacy with adult patients is quite compelling, this is not the case for children and younger adolescents. There is very little controlled research, using randomized controlled trials, with these younger populations (Nemeroff & Schatzberg, 1998). The few controlled trials that have been reported tend to find some positive but very modest treatment responses, particularly in terms of complete symptom remission (e.g., Emslie et al., 1997). Curiously, pharmacotherapy for depressed children, including preschool age children, has recently increased despite the lack of empirical evidence for treatment efficacy (see Zito et al., 2000).

In randomized controlled trials with placebo groups, the participants in the placebo group receive considerable attention from the investigators. This extensive contact—which may exceed the amount of practitioner contact in some fee-for-service settings—appears to yield some therapeutic benefit (Khan et al., 2000; Nemeroff & Schatzberg, 1998; Thase & Kupfer, 1996). Thus, the methodology of a randomized placebo-controlled trial seems to be a viable approach for evaluating antidepressants, although this topic is not without some controversial features and ethical issues (e.g., Bloch, Chodoff, & Green, 1999; Khan et al., 2000; Koocher & Keith-Spiegel, 1998; Moncrieff, Wessely, & Hardy, 1998; Quitkin, Rabkin, Gerald, Davis, & Klein, 2000). For example, some researchers and certain practitioners are uncomfortable withholding state-of-the-art treatments from research participants for any length of time. Nevertheless, many experts believe that placebo-controlled trials are the only possible method for validly assessing the physical impact and physiological mechanisms of an antidepressant medication (see panel discussion of experts reported in "Health Workers," 2000; also Heppner et al., 1999; Kazdin, 1998).

Reviews and treatment guidelines suggest that practitioners should expect antidepressants to take from 3 to 8 weeks to begin showing a therapeutic response (American Psychiatric Association, 2000b, p. 427; Halbreich & Montgomery, 2000; Nemeroff & Schatzberg, 1998; *Physicians' Desk Reference,* 2000; Rankin, 2000). If there is no therapeutic response after 8 weeks, then the treatment options are numerous and complex. These options include, of course, continued maintenance and evaluation of the current pharmacotherapy regimen for a few more weeks before deciding on alternative treatments, modified dosages, new medications, alternative interventions such as psychotherapy, and complementary approaches such as exercise and herbal remedies. The options for the physician practitioner, involving pharmacotherapy, are complicated and far beyond the scope of this book. For the psychotherapist practitioner whose patient is receiving combined treatment involving pharmacotherapy plus psychotherapy, perhaps a useful guideline is to talk with their patient about the merits of further assessment by the patient's physician if the pharmacotherapy appears to be yielding no benefit after 8 weeks. This is also a good place to remind psychotherapy practitioners that pharmacotherapy should entail regular and careful evaluation by the prescribing physician.

Many experts recommend maintaining a successful pharmacotherapy regimen for at least 6 months. Longer maintenance may be indicated for depressed patients who exhibit any of the following conditions: extremely severe depression, chronic depression or dysthymia, recurrent depression, high risk of relapse, slow response to treatment or great difficulty in treating, strong family history of depression, and comorbid medical or psychiatric conditions (American Psychiatric Association, 2000b; De Lima et al., 1999; Halbreich & Montgomery, 2000; Nemeroff & Schatzberg, 1998; *Physicians' Desk Reference*, 2000; Thase & Kupfer, 1996).

Comorbid conditions pose difficult challenges for practitioners and patients. Obviously, the prescribing physicians should be thorough in their assessments of possible drug interactions, toxicity, contraindications, side effects, and so forth (Nemeroff & Schatzberg, 1998). Furthermore, there is evidence that some groups of antidepressants have more favorable side-effect profiles with certain comorbid conditions. For instance, some SSRIs are better tolerated by depressed patients with cardiovascular disease than are some tricyclics (American Psychiatric Association, 2000b, p. 447; Glassman & Shapiro, 1998; Musselman et al., 1998; Roose et al., 1998; Schatzberg, 2000). As another example, some SSRIs have demonstrated an attractive combination of efficacy, along with favorable toxicity and side-effect profiles, for the treatment of Bulimia Nervosa (Ferguson & Pigott, 2000). Across the range of chronic health problems, however, there is considerable evidence that pharmacotherapy is an efficacious treatment option for depressed adults with comorbid medical disorders (American Psychiatric Association, 2000b; Halbreich & Montgomery, 2000; Nemeroff & Schatzberg, 1998; Rankin, 2000; Reynolds et al., 2000; Schatzberg, 2000).

Because comorbid medical disorders are most likely to be present in older adults (Niederehe & Schneider, 1998; Reynolds et al., 2000), we should note that potentially *in*appropriate psychotropic medications are prescribed at a distressingly common rate for this age group. For example, Mort and Aparasu (2000) reported that, for a large sample of geriatric patients, 27% of the psychotropic prescriptions were potentially inappropriate. Therefore, this is a good place to remind practitioners that if their depressed patients evidence comorbid conditions, these patients should be evaluated very carefully while the practitioners are planning and implementing a treatment regimen. This evaluation should typically include a thorough medical evaluation along with a complete psychological assessment. In addition, efforts to improve patient education may improve medication compliance and adherence (Katon et al., 1999; Lin et al., 1999).

Pharmacotherapy has a very important place among the treatment options for suicidal patients (Salzman, 1999b). The 3- to 8-week window for the appearance of a clear treatment response, however, argues for using a *combined* approach of pharmacotherapy and psychotherapy with suicidal patients. In addition to pharmacotherapy, this combined approach might include crisis counseling, risk reduction strategies, longer-term psychotherapy, and immediate hospitalization (day and night) in the more severe cases (Boes & McDermott, 2000; Maris et al., 2000; Westefeld et al., 2000). In addition, clinicians should be alert for the initial period of energy improvement that follows a treatment response, as this may actually increase patients' tendency to act on their suicidal ideation (Salzman, 1999b).

Several of the most important risk factors for suicide are modifiable variables regarding depression. These modifiable variables include the somatic symptoms of Major Depressive Disorder, suicidal thinking, hopelessness, and unemployment status (Brown et al., 2000; Jacobs, 1999). We should be treating these symptoms of suicidal risk (Jamison, 1999; Simon et al., 2001). Nevertheless, there is clear evidence that medications and psychological treatments are underused with suicidal and severely depressed patients (Isacsson, Holmgren, Druid, & Bergman, 1999; Steffens et al., 2000; Young et al., 2001). In Chapter 9, we discussed the topic of suicide and depression in much greater detail.

Tricyclic Antidepressants

The commonly used, FDA-approved tricyclic antidepressants are amitriptyline (Elavil), clomipramine (Anafranil), doxepin (Sinequan), imipramine (Tofranil), and trimipramine (Surmontil) [tertiary amine tricyclics], plus desipramine (Norpramin), nortriptyline (Aventyl), and protriptyline (Vivactil) [secondary amine tricyclics]. Desipramine and nortriptyline may be particularly attractive medications in the tricyclic category because patients typically experience fewer side effects with these medications (American Psychiatric Association, 2000b, p. 424). In terms of efficacy across numerous patient groups, the tricyclics appear to be comparable to the SSRIs (Nemeroff & Schatzberg, 1998).

The tricyclics inhibit the reuptake of norepinephrine into presynaptic neurons. The tricyclic antidepressants are potentially toxic for cardiovascular functioning if taken in overdose (American Psychiatric Association, 2000b, p. 447; Glassman & Shapiro, 1998; Musselman et al., 1998), and they are the most common cause of death from overdose regarding U.S. prescription drugs (Nemeroff & Schatzberg, 1998). Furthermore, tricyclics may be contraindicated for depressed patients who have comorbid conditions entailing cardiovascular disease or hypertension (American Psychiatric Association, 2000b, pp. 450–451). Common side effects of the tricyclics include tachycardia, sedation, weight gain, dry mouth, constipation, urinary hesitancy, blurred vision, and memory disturbance (American Psychiatric Association, 2000b, p. 447; Nemeroff & Schatzberg, 1998; *Physicians' Desk Reference*, 2000).

Compared with the tricyclics, the SSRIs appear to offer many patients a more favorable side-effect profile and a wider safety margin, but not more efficacy (Ferguson & Pigott, 2000; Halbreich & Montgomery, 2000; *Physicians' Desk Reference*, 2000; Rankin, 2000; Schatzberg, 2000). These advantages in the SSRI side-effect profile presumably account for the rapid increase in SSRI prescriptions over the last decade (Schatzberg, 2000). (We discuss SSRIs in the next section of the chapter.) Nevertheless, tricyclics remain an important pharmacotherapy option for specific patients (Nemeroff & Schatzberg, 1998).

Maintenance pharmacotherapy with tricyclics has been investigated with some encouraging results (e.g., Frank et al., 1990), and the most promising dose-effect relationships for preventing relapse appear to be maintenance at the same dosage levels that were found effective during acute treatment (Nemeroff & Schatzberg, 1998).

Selective Serotonin Reuptake Inhibitors

There has been an explosion in the use of SSRIs to treat depression. Many experts now consider SSRIs to be the frontline pharmacotherapy for depression, as evidenced in part by annual U.S. sales exceeding $6 billion (Schatzberg, 2000). As noted previously, the relatively favorable side-effect profiles and wider safety margins of SSRIs explain much of the popularity for this group of antidepressant medications. SSRIs block the reuptake of serotonin into presynaptic neurons.

The commonly used, FDA-approved SSRIs are citalopram (Celexa), fluoxetine (Prozac), paroxetine (Paxil), and sertraline (Zoloft) (American Psychiatric Association, 2000b, p. 424). (Fluvoxamine [Luvox] is an SSRI that is FDA approved in the United States for the treatment of Obsessive-Compulsive Disorder but not for Major Depressive Disorder, although it is used for treating depression in many other countries; Nemeroff & Schatzberg, 1998; Thase & Kupfer, 1996.) As noted previously, the SSRIs have equivalent efficacy to the tricyclics across a broad array of patient groups (Halbreich & Montgomery, 2000).

The side-effect profiles, however, tend to favor SSRIs over tricyclics. The SSRIs produce few—if any—side effects of dry mouth, constipation, urinary hesitance, sedation, weight gain, and overdose toxicity for cardio-vascular functioning (American Psychiatric Association, 2000b, p. 447; Nemeroff & Schatzberg, 1998; *Physicians' Desk Reference*, 2000; Rankin, 2000). The SSRIs are well tolerated and enjoy wide safety margins. There are some side effects from SSRI pharmacotherapy, of course, including insomnia, nervousness, sexual dysfunction (e.g., arousal and perfor-mance problems for males and females), headaches, nausea, and diarrhea (American Psychiatric Association, 2000b, p. 447; Nemeroff & Schatzberg, 1998; *Physicians' Desk Reference*, 2000; Thase & Kupfer, 1996).

Although the side-effect profiles of the SSRI medications are rela-tively favorable compared with those of tricyclic antidepressants, the side effects of SSRIs may still be quite medically serious and psycho-logically unpleasant in some cases, including considerable disruption of sexual functioning (Meston & Frohlich, 2000).

Low dosing will reduce or eliminate many of these side effects, with the exception of sexual dysfunction, which may remain as a side effect for approximately 30% of the patients (Nemeroff & Schatzberg, 1998). Moreover, recent studies have continued to indicate that SSRIs have a wide array of negative side effects regarding sexual function (Meston & Frohlich, 2000, p. 1023). SSRIs should not be administered with MAOIs, but SSRIs may be coadministered with tricyclics following a very cautious and careful pharmacotherapy evaluation (Nemeroff & Schatzberg, 1998; *Physicians' Desk Reference*, 2000).

Another positive feature of SSRIs is that there is already a large research base on these medications, and it is expanding rapidly (e.g., see Halbreich & Montgomery, 2000, for reviews, and Meyer et al., 2001, for a sample study). There have been comparisons of SSRIs and tricyclics with depressed patients who have comorbid conditions (e.g., Hoehn-Saric et al., 2000), comparisons of SSRIs and tricyclics regarding compliance (e.g., Thompson, Peveler, Stephenson, & McKendrick, 2000), and comparisons of SSRIs and tricyclics for treating patients with Atypical Depression (e.g., McGrath et al., 2000). In alignment with earlier research, recent studies usually find a more favorable side-effect profile for SSRIs than for tricyclics, but they do not consistently find that SSRIs are significantly more efficacious than tricyclics.

The high tolerability and wide safety margin of SSRIs suggest that SSRIs may offer a favorable pharmacotherapy option for *long-term* maintenance treatment. Moreover, long-term maintenance treatment with SSRIs does not appear to produce new side effects or renew old ones (Nemeroff & Schatzberg, 1998). Given this favorable side-effect profile, it is hardly surprising that "selective serotonin reuptake inhibitors (SSRIs) have become first-line agents for patients with major depression" (Schatzberg, 2000, p. 323).

Monoamine Oxidase Inhibitors

The commonly used, FDA-approved MAOIs for treating depression are phenelzine (Nardil) and tranylcypromine (Parnate) (American Psychiatric Association, 2000b, p. 424). Moclobemide (Manerex) is currently available in Canada and many other countries but not in the United States (Consumer Reports, 2000; Halbreich & Montgomery, 2000; *Physicians' Desk Reference*, 2000). The MAOIs prevent the degradation of monoamines such as serotonin and norepinephrine (Nemeroff & Schatzberg, 1998).

MAOIs have the least favorable side-effect profile of any group of antidepressants that are approved by the FDA. Their side effects can include tachycardia, cardiovascular orthostatic hypotension, hypertensive crises (see contraindications below), palpitations, dizziness, edema, weight gain, insomnia, and sexual dysfunction (American Psychiatric Association, 2000b, p. 447; Nemeroff & Schatzberg, 1998; *Physicians' Desk Reference*, 2000; Rankin, 2000; Thase & Kupfer, 1996). In addition, there are a number of drug-drug combinations (e.g., MAOIs and SSRIs or cold medications) and drug-food combinations (e.g., MAOIs and aged meat, cheese, chocolate, or Chianti wine) that are absolutely contraindicated. These combinations may cause severe hypertension and cerebrovascular reactions such as stroke (Nemeroff & Schatzberg, 1998). Symptoms of this hypertensive reaction include extreme headache, palpitations, flushing, and strong nausea. Therefore, dietary restrictions and avoidance of some drug-drug combinations are very important when a patient is receiving pharmacotherapy via the MAOIs.

Moreover, there are several other disadvantages to the MAOIs, such as the need for dosing several times per day (*Physicians' Desk Reference*, 2000). In summary, there are rather extreme side effects from MAOIs, along with a low safety margin, numerous dietary restrictions, and a requirement of multiple doses each day. Therefore, it is understandable that most experts consider the MAOIs to be a backup pharmacotherapy option, which is considered only when several other first-line agents and psychotherapy have failed (American Psychiatric Association, 2000b, p. 434; Halbreich & Montgomery, 2000; Nemeroff & Schatzberg, 1998; Rankin, 2000; Schatzberg & Nemeroff, 1998). Indeed, some experts have concluded that "MAOIs may become 'orphan' drugs in the United States" (Thase & Kupfer, 1996, p. 649).

Despite these disadvantages and gloomy predictions, however, MAOIs continue to be used and investigated with certain subgroups of depression, such as Atypical Depression (e.g., Jarrett et al., 1999). Extensive patient education, along with thorough and ongoing physician supervision, is obviously called for when the pharmacotherapy approach is MAOIs. Furthermore, there is some evidence that cognitive behavior therapy may offer comparable efficacy to an MAOI (phenelzine) for treating patients with Atypical Depression (Jarrett et al., 1999). This psychotherapy approach, of course, also has the advantage of avoiding the adverse side effects of MAOIs. Although MAOIs may be one of the more effective pharmacotherapy approaches for treating Atypical Depression, many experts recommend starting with the SSRIs and psychotherapy because of the more favorable side-effect profiles with these latter approaches (American Psychiatric Association, 2000b, p. 434).

Second-Generation and Other Agents

Tetracyclics share many of the pros and cons of tricyclics, including comparable efficacy (American Psychiatric Association, 2000b; Halbreich & Montgomery, 2000; Nemeroff & Schatzberg, 1998). The commonly used, FDA-approved tetracyclics are amoxapine (Ascendin) and maprotiline (Ludiomil) (American Psychiatric Association, 2000b, p. 424). Like the tricyclic medications that we have already discussed, the tetracyclics have a less favorable side-effect profile than the SSRIs (Nemeroff & Schatzberg, 1998; *Physicians' Desk Reference*, 2000; Thase & Kupfer, 1996).

Bupropion (Wellbutrin) is a commonly used, FDA-approved dopamine-norepinephrine reuptake inhibitor (American Psychiatric Association, 2000b, p. 424). This medication primarily blocks dopamine reuptake. Outcome research indicates that bupropion is effective for treating depression, with similar efficacy to tricyclics and SSRIs (Nemeroff & Schatzberg, 1998). A slow-release version of this medication has been developed to avoid multiple dosing per day and to reduce the risk of seizures under high doses. Bupropion does not have the cardiovascular side effects of tricyclics and the sexual dysfunction side effects of SSRIs (Nemeroff & Schatzberg, 1998). Thus, bupropion has a favorable side-effect profile, although approximately 28% of the patients treated with this medication exhibit a significant weight loss (*Physicians' Desk Reference*, 2000).

Venlafaxine (Effexor) is a commonly used, FDA-approved serotonin-norepinephrine reuptake inhibitor (American Psychiatric Association, 2000b, p. 424). This medication provides considerable blockage of both serotonin and norepinephrine reuptake. Although venlafaxine has a more favorable side-effect profile than the tricyclics, it still entails many of the side effects common to SSRIs and includes the side effects of hypertension, tachycardia, and perspiration (Nemeroff & Schatzberg, 1998). Unlike the tricyclics, venlafaxine is unlikely to be lethal in overdose. An extended-release version of this medication has been developed to avoid the need for multiple dosing per day (American Psychiatric Association, 2000b). One of the attractive features of venlafaxine is that it may be more efficacious than the SSRIs for very severe depression. Furthermore, patients who have failed to respond to other antidepressants, including the SSRIs, may respond to venlafaxine (Halbreich & Montgomery, 2000; Nemeroff & Schatzberg, 1998). The efficacy of venlafaxine for treatment-refractory patients is important, and this efficacy may counterbalance some concerns about venlafaxine's less favorable side-effect profile when compared with that of the SSRIs (American Psychiatric Association, 2000b).

The commonly used, FDA-approved serotonin modulators are nefazodone (Serzone) and trazodone (Desyrel) (American Psychiatric Association, 2000b, p. 424). Nefazodone inhibits serotonin and norepinephrine reuptake while also serving as a receptor antagonist for Serotonin Type 2. Trazodone primarily serves as a receptor antagonist for Serotonin Type 2, although it is also a weak serotonin reuptake inhibitor (Nemeroff & Schatzberg, 1998). Nefazodone has some favorable side-effect features, including no disruption of sexual functioning and sleep (American Psychiatric Association, 2000b, p. 447; Consumer Reports, 2000; Halbreich & Montgomery, 2000; *Physicians' Desk Reference*, 2000). Efficacy results are comparable to those for SSRIs. Disadvantages include the need for titration of the doses and multiple doses per day. Moreover, combinations with some antihistamines or benzodiazepines are contraindicated, with toxic cardiovascular effects possible following such combinations. Sedation is one of the more important side effects.

Trazodone has the advantages of once-per-day dosing (although twice-per-day dosing is common) and comparable efficacy to the tricyclics and SSRIs (Nemeroff & Schatzberg, 1998). Trazodone is not lethal if taken in overdose. Important side effects include sedation and orthostatic hypotension, particularly in geriatric patients (American Psychiatric Association, 2000b, p. 447; Consumer Reports, 2000; Halbreich & Montgomery, 2000). Furthermore, for patients with cardiovascular disease, trazodone is sometimes associated with arrhythmias. Because trazodone has sedative side effects, it is often combined with an SSRI to reduce the common insomnia side effects of SSRIs (Nemeroff & Schatzberg, 1998).

The commonly used, FDA-approved norepinephrine-serotonin modulators include mirtazapine (Remeron) (American Psychiatric Association, 2000b, p. 424). One of the newer antidepressants on the U.S. market, mirtazapine is believed to increase neurotransmission for both norepinephrine and serotonin (Nemeroff & Schatzberg, 1998). Because this medication is relatively recent, there is less efficacy data than for many of the other FDA-approved antidepressants, but the available data indicate significant efficacy (Halbreich & Montgomery, 2000). Advantages of mirtazapine include no side effects regarding sexual function, single dosing per day, and nonlethality in overdose (American Psychiatric Association, 2000b, p. 447; Consumer Reports, 2000; Halbreich & Montgomery, 2000; *Physicians' Desk Reference*, 2000). Disadvantages include the side effects of drowsiness, dizziness, weight gain, increased cholesterol, and—in a very small percentage (less than 0.1%) of cases—agranulocytosis (a blood disorder that generates disruption of the white blood cells, along with fever, ulcers, and weakness) (American Psychiatric Association, 2000b, p. 447; Nemeroff & Schatzberg, 1998; *Physicians' Desk Reference*, 2000). Mirtazapine should not be combined with MAOIs, as the adverse reactions are extensive and potentially fatal (*Physicians' Desk Reference*, 2000).

Combinations of Pharmacotherapy and Psychotherapy

The possibility that combinations of pharmacotherapy and psychotherapy will be the treatment of choice—particularly for severe or recurrent cases of depression—has received considerable discussion and some research attention (American Psychiatric Association, 2000b, pp. 437–438, 475; Hollon & Shelton, 2001; Jarrett, 1995; Klerman et al., 1994; Niederehe & Schneider, 1998; Sherbourne et al., 2001; Thase et al., 1997). We will summarize a few of the more recent studies on this matter, and then we will offer a speculative conclusion regarding the merits of combined therapy regimens.

An intervention study by Keller et al. (2000) indicated that combined pharmacotherapy and cognitive behavior therapy is more efficacious than either of these treatments is by itself. This randomized controlled trial involved 681 adult participants with chronic Major Depressive Disorder. Approximately 85% of the patients in the combined-treatment group evidenced significant improvement, versus about half of those in the individual-treatment groups. The pharmacotherapy was a serotonin modulator (nefazodone).

A randomized controlled trial by Reynolds et al. (1999) investigated the benefits of combined pharmacotherapy and interpersonal psycho-therapy with a sample of 187 geriatric participants. The pharmaco-therapy was a tricyclic (nortriptyline). Participants were at high risk for relapse because of chronic histories of recurrent Major Depressive Disorder. Following a combined-treatment regimen for all patients during acute treatment, various maintenance strategies were evaluated. Booster sessions with the combined approach were efficacious for reducing relapse. The combined-treatment booster group experienced only 20% relapse during the 3-year follow-up period, whereas the placebo-control group experienced 90% relapse. Separating the two booster interven-tions was less effective, yielding a relapse rate of 43% for maintenance pharmacotherapy and 64% for interpersonal psychotherapy booster ses-sions. A maintenance condition of medication clinic visits plus placebo, however, yielded 90% relapse. The authors concluded that "combined treatment using both appears to be the optimal clinical strategy in pre-serving recovery" (Reynolds et al., 1999, p. 39).

Several other randomized controlled trials have suggested that adding various forms of cognitive behavior therapy, as booster sessions, to an acute intervention with pharmacotherapy will enhance the dura-bility of the initial treatment effects (e.g., Fava et al., 1998; Paykel et al., 1999; Teasdale et al., 2000). We present a detailed discussion of relapse prevention strategies in Chapter 12. There is also evidence that cogni-tive behavior therapy may augment the effects of pharmacotherapy for patients with dysthymia (e.g., Ravindran et al., 1999).

Our major purpose in this section of the chapter is to discuss *com-bined* pharmacotherapy and psychotherapy (particularly cognitive behavior therapy and interpersonal psychotherapy) rather than to dis-cuss a potential "competition" between the two. Both approaches have evidenced a large amount of efficacy when used singly (e.g., American

Psychiatric Association, 2000b; Bovasso, Eaton, & Armenian, 1999; Craighead et al., 1998; DeRubeis et al., 1999; Halbreich & Montgomery, 2000; Hollon & Shelton, 2001). For especially severe or *recurrent* cases of depression, however, the combined approach may be more efficacious. We tentatively conclude that it is. Hence, we recommend a combined-intervention approach, using both pharmacotherapy and one of the empirically supported psychotherapies, when treating patients with particularly severe or recurrent depression (see Sherbourne et al., 2001).

Furthermore, this combined-treatment approach seems to be common. For instance, approximately 50% of the treatment regimens, used for participants who evidenced depression in the 1996 National Depression Screening Day, entailed a combined-treatment approach (Greenfield et al., 2000).

Clinical Guidelines

Keep in mind that pharmacotherapy for depression, using FDA-approved medications, should always be prescribed and closely supervised by a qualified physician.

- Become familiar with the major types of pharmacotherapy for depression. Many depressed patients receive pharmacotherapy. It is often efficacious. Therefore, psychotherapists and other relevant nonphysician practitioners should be familiar with this important treatment option.
- Become familiar with the common side effects of pharmacotherapy. Your patients may want to discuss some of these side effects in their psychotherapy sessions.
- Be extremely thorough in your assessment, consultation, and referral efforts when your depressed patients evidence *comorbid medical conditions.* Pharmacotherapy options for these patients may be more limited and hazardous than for physically healthy adults. A wide array of additional side effect, toxicity, and drug-drug concerns can be important for these patients. Depressed patients with comorbid medical conditions will typically need a thorough and ongoing medical evaluation, along with a complete psychological assessment.

- Take your patient's preferences, treatment history, and symptom severity into account when considering the pros and cons of mono-therapy versus combined-therapy approaches.
- Consider the merits of a *combined*-treatment approach, using both pharmacotherapy and psychotherapy, when your patient is experiencing severe or recurrent depression.
- Talk with your patients about the advantages of further assessment by their physician if the pharmacotherapy that they are receiving appears to be yielding no benefit after 8 weeks.
- Be collaborative, cautious, and vigilant when your patient is receiving a combined-treatment approach. Combined approaches are more complicated than mono-therapy approaches; for example, a cooperative and professional collaboration with the prescribing physician is necessary when your patient is receiving both psychotherapy and pharmacotherapy. Severely depressed patients, who often receive a combined-treatment regimen, warrant more therapeutic caution and vigilance than mildly depressed patients do.

Chapter Summary

We summarized the literature on pharmacotherapy for depression and discussed the major types of antidepressant medication: tricyclics, SSRIs, MAOIs, and second-generation or other agents. Our discussion included information on efficacy and side effects. Pharmacotherapy for depression has been extensively researched, and the evidence for efficacy is impressive. All pharmacotherapy options for treating depression have side effects, with the side-effect profiles ranging from mild to severe depending on the medication and the patient.

SSRIs are currently the frontline antidepressants in the United States and Canada. Tricyclics are potentially problematic for cardiovascular disease patients, and MAOIs have numerous contraindications. Some second-generation and other antidepressants offer promising efficacy and side-effect profiles regarding carefully evaluated subgroups of depressed patients.

We provided clinical guidelines for psychotherapists and other relevant nonphysician practitioners. Pharmacotherapy of depression with FDA-approved medications requires prescription and careful supervision by a qualified physician. However, psychotherapists should become familiar with the typical side-effect profiles for commonly used antidepressants. Combined treatment, using both pharmacotherapy and psychotherapy, may be the treatment of choice for patients with severe or recurrent depression. A combined-treatment approach should include a cooperative and professional collaboration between the psychotherapist and the prescribing physician.

Suggested Readings

Discussions

Practice Guidelines

- Panels of experts representing the American Psychiatric Association (2000b) have presented practice guidelines regarding pharmacotherapy (and psychotherapy). The psychiatric disorders covered include Major Depressive Disorder, along with several other disorders that are relevant because of the comorbid conditions that are often associated with depression (e.g., Dementia, Substance Use, Bipolar Disorder, Panic Disorder, and Eating Disorders). Practitioners will find this book to be a very helpful addition to their professional library (also see Hollon & Shelton, 2001).
- The *Physicians' Desk Reference* (2000) has offered guidelines and recommendations for FDA-approved medications. Extensive information is given on dosage and administration, contraindications, drug interactions, side effects, and overdose. This informational resource is updated yearly. This book is very useful.

Literature Reviews

- Halbreich and Montgomery (2000) edited a series of reviews on pharmacotherapy for several disorders, including Major Depressive Disorder, Bipolar Disorder, Anxiety Disorders, and Dementia. This book may be challenging reading for the nonphysician, but it is very scholarly, thorough, and helpful.

- Nemeroff and Schatzberg (1998) presented a summary of the major antidepressants. This review is readable and thorough.
- Rankin (2000) edited a series of reviews on psychopharmacology for numerous psychiatric disorders, and these summaries are readable for nonphysician practitioners. This book is very helpful.
- Thase and Kupfer (1996) discussed pharmacotherapy for Major Depressive Disorder and Bipolar Disorder. This review was written primarily for nonphysician practitioners and researchers.

Dose-Effect Relationships

- Bollini et al. (1999) presented a meta-analysis of dose-effect relationships. Their review concluded that low doses of antidepressants somewhat reduce the odds of improvement but also somewhat reduce the odds of adverse reactions.

Pharmacotherapy Versus Cognitive Behavior Therapy

- DeRubeis et al. (1999) reviewed four randomized controlled trials that compared pharmacotherapy and cognitive behavior therapy. The authors' analysis suggests that either intervention (medication or cognitive behavior therapy) is equivalently efficacious for the treatment of severely depressed outpatients.

Pharmacotherapy and Psychotherapy Combinations

- Thase et al. (1997) reviewed six randomized controlled trials on the treatment of depression. The authors concluded that combined interventions may be the most efficacious for treating severe and recurrent depressions.

Dysthymic Disorder

- De Lima et al. (1999) reviewed the relevant literature and concluded that pharmacotherapy is efficacious for treating dysthymia.

Older Adults

- Reynolds et al. (2000) summarized the clinical recommendations for pharmacotherapy with depressed geriatric patients. This is a helpful review for practitioners.

Suicidal Patients

- Salzman (1999b) discussed treatment strategies when using pharmacotherapy for suicidal patients. This review includes how-to advice and clinical guidelines.

Studies

- Jarrett et al. (1999) conducted a randomized controlled trial. The participants were 108 patients with Atypical Depression, and the pharmacotherapy was an MAOI (phenelzine). The investigators' findings suggested that there were equivalently positive results (58% response rates) for pharmacotherapy and cognitive behavior therapy interventions.
- Keller et al. (2000) conducted a randomized controlled trial for 681 adult participants with chronic Major Depressive Disorder. The researchers' findings indicated that combined pharmacotherapy and cognitive behavior therapy was more efficacious than either of these treatments was by itself. Approximately 85% of the patients in the combined-treatment group evidenced significant improvement, versus about 50% of those in the individual-treatment groups. The pharmacotherapy was a serotonin modulator (nefazodone).
- Mort and Aparasu (2000) analyzed data from several large surveys. The findings suggested that potentially inappropriate psychotropic medications are commonly (27%) prescribed for geriatric patients.
- Sherbourne et al. (2001) evaluated a short-term quality improvement intervention for treating 1,299 depressed patients in 46 primary care practices. This intervention, which focused on combined treatment via pharmacotherapy and psychotherapy, did yield

improved patient outcomes over a 2-year follow-up interval. The authors concluded that "integrated psychotherapy and medication-based treatment strategies in primary care have the potential for relatively long-term patient benefits" (p. 696).

• Steffens et al. (2000) conducted an epidemiological survey in Utah with 4,559 older adults. The investigators' results indicated that 48% of the participants with lifetime Major Depressive Disorder had received pharmacotherapy for their depression at some point in their lives (see also Young et al., 2001).

12 Relapse Prevention

Overview

We begin this chapter with a case study. Relapse is a major problem for depressed individuals, so we discuss the risk factors for relapse. We then review the literature regarding people who cope with depression on their own, without professional help; this literature may enhance our knowledge of relapse prevention. We discuss practical issues for relapse prevention. Then we review maintenance strategies, including the use of booster sessions—this strategy has yielded some very promising findings. Finally, we present clinical guidelines, a chapter summary, and suggested readings.

As we noted in Chapter 1, we use the term relapse to cover both a worsening of depressive symptoms after the symptoms have partially improved and a new episode of depression after full recovery from a previous episode. Some experts prefer to call the new episode a recurrence rather than a relapse (American Psychiatric Association, 2000a, 2000b; Beckham & Leber, 1995; Clark & Beck, 1999; Gilbert, 2000; Hammen, 1997; Hollon & Shelton, 2001; Markowitz, 1998). The literature on depression, however, does *not* offer compelling evidence that effective relapse prevention strategies significantly vary depending on whether the symptoms fit the term *relapse* or *recurrence*. Hence, for the sake of simplicity, we will call *all* depressive deterioration that follows substantial improvement a "relapse."

Case Study

This student is 17 years old, a junior in high school, and physically healthy. She has relapsed back into depression. In addition, she has been depressed three other times in the last 2 years. In this session with her high school counselor, the student describes her feelings.

Student: I don't understand. I seem to do okay for a while, even when things get bad at home, you know? I thought that I'd learned how to cope when Mom is depressed. But then it seems that something new happens, I make mistakes, I get down, and things just get worse and worse. I hate this!

Counselor: Have you thought about why things get worse for you?

Student: Well, I've got lots of problems. I wish I looked better. Before my friend Heather and I had that big fight, we used to tease each other about being "fat." I look like a mess! I'm very unhappy.

Counselor: I hear how upset you are. How depressed are you?

Student: I have most of those symptoms of depression that we discussed last week . . . or was it 2 weeks ago? I don't remember. I can't think straight now. I can barely put one foot in front of the other, you know? I'm just falling apart. I worry about everything. I fight with everybody . . . even my sister, Ann. Why do I do this? This is awful.

Counselor: Are there some small steps we can work on for gradually making things better?

Student: Maybe. Changing almost anything would probably help me. I wish I could sleep better. Nothing is fun. I'm just sad all of the time. I cry a lot. I don't seem to do anything—I don't get much done. And I don't understand it! I've broken up with guys before. Plus, Dave is a jerk anyway—he is so uncool. And I've coped with Mom's depression for years. No problem. Well, Dad's drinking is worse . . . but he's feeling bummed out about work problems. I'm always worrying about stuff.

Counselor: You are covering a lot of issues. We need to focus on one or two. What can we deal with today?

Student: This may sound strange, but I read about a high school student who was so depressed that he shot himself. I thought about how desperate he must have felt, and I began to get really sad. That poor guy!

Counselor: Have you had any thoughts about suicide or harming yourself?

Student: No. No. I'm not that depressed. Actually, right now I'm more upset about my parents hammering me because of my low grades. So what if I'm getting Cs instead of As? I can't think straight. I'm doing the best I can! Like, give me a break!

Counselor: It's okay to get angry in here. I know that you really do care about people, especially the people close to you. That's good! For right now, let's focus on ways to make things better for you. If you could get a little more fun into your daily life, might that help your moods and your grades?

Student: Probably. I never do anything fun now. I used to do stuff. Now I do very little. This is awful.

Counselor: Should we talk about doing something fun today?

Student: Okay. I'm feeling guilty about those awful things I said to Ann. I'm worried that she hates me now. I need to do better.

Counselor: Yes, and you will do better! Let's talk about something fun that you can do with Ann—today!

Discussion of the Case Study

Our case study reflects a typical case of relapse in adolescent depression. The counselor in our case study is seeing this student after school. They meet every week to talk. The counselor's style in our case study may seem a tad abrupt, but she is trying to help the student focus and not get further confused and exasperated. Moreover, this student does need to focus and problem-solve—she is sinking into another depressive episode, and she has done this several times before. The counselor wants to gently help the student to enhance her coping and problem solving.

Preventing relapse is a challenging treatment issue for depression. Approximately 80% of all depressed patients will relapse several times during the course of their lives (Judd et al., 2000; Kessing et al., 1998;

Mueller et al., 1999; Ormel, 2000; Solomon et al., 2000). Depression can usually be treated with success. Over 50% of the successfully treated patients, however, will relapse within 5 years (Blackburn & Moore, 1997; Evans et al., 1992; Frank et al., 1990; Gortner et al., 1998; Jarrett et al., 1998; Kupfer et al., 1992; Shea et al., 1992).

In addition, the relapse problem is not new or limited to depression. For example, about 25 years ago Richards and Perri (1978) wrote that "treatment effects often do not last. Counselors are frequently chagrined to find that their budding posttreatment successes soon wilt in the hot sun of time" (p. 376).

Risk Factors

The risk factors for relapse are typically evaluated during the interview of the depressed patient. Naturally, some relevant information may also be collected through questionnaires about depression and through a summary of demographic information (age, gender, living situation, education, and so on). In addition, information from significant others can be helpful because the quality of close relationships has a strong impact on the risk for relapse (Holahan et al., 2000; Whisman et al., 2000).

There are many risk factors for depressive relapse, but these factors may be clustered into a few categories. The symptoms of current or previous depression experienced by the patient typically affect relapse: More severe depressions or more previous depressions increase the risk of relapse (Kendler & Gardner, 1998; Mueller et al., 1999; Pine et al., 1999; Solomon et al., 2000). The presence of an additional psychiatric disorder increases the risk for relapse, particularly anxiety, eating, personality, and psychotic disorders (e.g., Flint & Rifat, 1998; Strakowski et al., 1998). Chronic health problems increase the risk (e.g., Judd et al., 2000; Musselman et al., 1998). Chronic substance abuse also increases the risk (e.g., Strakowski et al., 1998; Van Gorp, Altshuler, Theberge, Wilkins, & Dixon, 1998).

Furthermore, specific and focused symptoms may increase the risk for relapse. For example, the risk of relapsing back into depression is higher for patients with any of the following conditions: serious sleep problems (Thase, Fasiczka, Berman, Simons, & Reynolds, 1998), extreme hopelessness (Young et al., 1996), low self-esteem (Andrews & Brown, 1995), a tendency to worry even when under mild stress (Zonderman, Herbst, Schmidt, Costa, & McCrae, 1993), a chronic depression such as Dysthymic Disorder (Keller et al., 2000; Markowitz, 1998; McCullough, 2000; Mueller et al., 1999), and exposure to extreme stress (Davila et al., 1995).

The "scar hypothesis" suggests that the experience of depression often produces a cognitive diathesis or "scar" that puts the patient at increased risk for relapse. Thus, certain types of stress (that are relevant to the patient's depressive experiences) may be combined with the cognitive diathesis ("scar") of a tendency to cycle into dysfunctional thinking when under stress. If this diathesis-stress combination occurs, then the patient is more likely to relapse back into depression (e.g., Clark & Beck, 1999; Ingram et al., 1998).

Certain demographic factors increase the risk. Women may be at more risk for experiencing relapse than men are, although the findings on this issue are mixed (Hankin et al., 1998; Mueller et al., 1999; Wichstrom, 1999). Relapse is most common during the ages of 15 to 35. Economic adversity increases the risk: Depressed patients are more likely to experience relapse if they are poor or unemployed (e.g., Sherbourne, Hays, & Wells, 1995). Frequent social or academic problems in school are risk factors, especially among children and adolescents (e.g., Cole, Martin, Powers, & Truglio, 1996; Lewinsohn et al., 1998). Finally, living alone is a risk factor, especially in the context of suicidal risk (Bongar, 1991; Hirschfeld & Russell, 1997; Jacobs, 1999; Jamison, 1999; Maris et al., 2000).

Some of the risk factors involve close relationships. A chaotic or hostile family is a risk factor for all ages—children, adolescents, and adults (Butzlaff & Hooley, 1998). Moreover, having a chronically depressed parent is an important risk factor. A 10-year follow-up of the offspring of depressed parents (Weissman et al., 1997) provided an example of this risk: The study suggested that the children of depressed parents are at greatly increased risk for experiencing depression themselves. A dysfunctional relationship with a partner or spouse is also a risk factor (e.g., Andrews & Brown, 1995).

Drastic changes in the family situation, even if they are primarily positive changes, may increase the likelihood of relapse. For instance, the complex biological, psychological, and day-to-day changes that immediately follow the birth of a child put mothers at an increased risk for relapse (Frank, 2000; Gotlib, Whiffen, Wallace, & Mount, 1991; O'Hara et al., 2000; Quindlen, 2001; Shea, 1998).

Even a positive move across the country may put some individuals— especially adolescents—at increased risk for relapse. Indeed, any large increase in social stress or any large decrease in social support is a risk factor (e.g., Hammen, 1997; Lara, Leader, & Klein, 1997). An example would be divorce (e.g., Kessler & Magee, 1993). A less common, but horrible, example would be child abuse; this tragedy increases the risk in children and adolescents for numerous psychiatric disorders, including Major Depressive Disorder and Dysthymic Disorder (American Psychiatric Association, 2000a). For adolescents, the suicide of a peer or a close friend is a risk factor: These adolescents are more likely to experience depression, relapse back into depression, and attempt suicide (e.g., Lewinsohn, Rohde, & Seeley, 1994; Lewinsohn et al., 1996).

What the person *does* makes a difference: How the person copes with stress has a strong impact on relapse. In general, active coping strategies that emphasize problem solving, along with planned improvements in one's behavior and situation, are the most effective strategies for dealing with depression (Davila et al., 1995; D'Zurilla & Nezu, 1999; Hammen, 1997; Nezu et al., 1989; Shea, 1998). In contrast, passive coping strategies, which emphasize focusing on one's negative emotions and obsessing about one's problems, are typically less effective. Numerous studies have suggested that men are more likely to use an active coping style, whereas women are more likely to use a passive coping style (Cyranowski et al., 2000; Frank, 2000; Hammen, 1997; Nolen-Hoeksema & Girgus, 1994; Shea, 1998; Taylor, Klein, et al., 2000). These gender differences may partially account for the higher relapse rates among women.

Some broad theoretical models of relapse have been developed, particularly regarding issues such as alcohol abuse, cardiovascular health, drug addiction, exercise adherence, obesity, smoking reduction, and so forth (e.g., see American Psychiatric Association, 2000b;

McCrady & Ziedonis, 2001; Muehrer, 2000; Perri, 1998; Rosen, 2000; Wing et al., 2000). However, assessing and treating the specific risk factors for *depressive* relapse is probably more helpful for preventing relapse in depressed patients. The broad theoretical models developed for *other* disorders and health concerns are interesting and helpful within the areas in which they were developed. Nevertheless, the utility of these broad models for relapse prevention in depressed patients is unclear (Clark & Beck, 1999; Hammen, 1997; Hollon & Shelton, 2001; Lewinsohn et al., 1998; Markowitz, 1998; McCullough, 2000; Nezu et al., 1989).

If we compare this summary of risk factors with the situation facing the student in our case study, then it is not surprising that a relapse has occurred. This student has risk factors from most of the categories. Nevertheless, people with a history of repeated depressions and a situation that is very stressful can still be remarkably resilient. Indeed, the student in our case has apparently coped effectively for some time. Now, however, she needs some counseling.

People Coping on Their Own

We might get some ideas about how to prevent relapse from studying people who cope on their own regarding depression, without professional help. This is what most depressed people do: They cope on their own (Cicchetti & Toth, 1998; Hirschfeld et al., 1997; Steffens et al., 2000; Young et al., 2001). Differences between those who cope successfully and those who do not might have implications for treatment maintenance strategies. Of course, we have to be careful here. People who cope on their own may not be the same as people who seek out professional treatment, and the process of developing coping strategies on one's own may not be the same as developing these strategies with the help of a counselor.

When people cope effectively with depression on their own, they are active: They attempt to do things, to get involved in new activities, and to change their situations. They emphasize the positive: They focus on the belief that things get better with time, that there is something positive in every day, and that optimism is more helpful than pessimism. They avoid focusing on the negative: They stay away from thinking about the negative over and over again, and they do this through distraction, activity, and an appreciation that obsessing about bad things—especially bad thoughts or anger regarding oneself—is not helpful. They make positive changes in their social environment: They spend more time with best friends, more time in social situations that make them happy, some time with new friends, and less time with enemies and social situations that make them miserable. Finally, they are strategic: They plan and problem-solve. They try to solve their problems, reduce their stress, and increase their fun by carefully defining problems, outlining solutions, and trying the best solutions. Moreover, they *continue* to try solutions until they find a combination that works (e.g., Doerfler & Richards, 1981, 1983; D'Zurilla & Nezu, 1999; Faller, Bulzebruck, Drings, & Lang, 1999; McDaniel & Richards, 1990; Moeller, Richards, Hooker, & Ursino, 1992; Parker, Brown, & Blignault, 1986; Salovey, Bedell, Detweiler, & Mayer, 1999).

When people cope effectively with depression on their own, there are also some things that they do *not* do. They do not keep records of negative experiences and thoughts. They do not spend a lot of time being angry—especially being angry with themselves; rather, they limit and distract themselves from their anger. They do not ruminate—over and over again—about unfortunate experiences, lost chances, and missed opportunities; instead, they understand that regret is the "cancer of life," and they get on with their own life. Finally, they avoid substance abuse in general, and they avoid using alcohol and drugs as a stress reduction strategy in particular (e.g., Doerfler & Richards, 1981, 1983; D'Zurilla & Nezu, 1999; Faller et al., 1999; Fava, 1999; McDaniel & Richards, 1990; Moeller et al., 1992; Parker et al., 1986).

Practical Issues

For particularly severe cases of depression, many experts think that a *combination* of psychotherapy and pharmacotherapy is the best treatment option for preventing relapse (e.g., American Psychiatric Association, 2000b; Frank et al., 1990; Keller et al., 2000; Markowitz, 1998; McCullough, 2000; Reynolds et al., 1999; Spanier & Frank, 1998; Thase et al., 1997).

Continuing treatment for a long time appears to be a successful relapse prevention strategy, but this may not be practical. We cannot expect patients to pursue weekly psychotherapy for years, and at least some patients do not want to take antidepressant medications for years. Insurance policies do not pay for years of psychotherapy, and many patients do not want to deal with the side effects of long-term pharmacotherapy.

Nevertheless, if severely depressed patients do not continue with some treatment or coping effort, they will probably relapse. Perhaps we should think about relapse prevention for depression the way we think about this for chronic physical diseases (e.g., Kumanyika et al., 2000; Muehrer, 2000; Perri, 1998; Wing et al., 2000). Dealing effectively with depression requires a lifelong coping effort; it requires a new way of thinking and behaving that is maintained and adjusted over many years; and it requires a permanent change in some close relationships and interpersonal strategies.

Part of the solution to the relapse problem may be a change in focus. Practitioners should teach their depressed patients how to think like a therapist, how to cope on their own, and how to solve problems without professional help so that they can cope effectively when the therapy is over.

The empirically supported skill-oriented psychotherapies offer promise for relapse prevention. Cognitive behavior therapy is an attractive option because it focuses on teaching the patient to think and behave more adaptively (Clark & Beck, 1999; Craighead et al., 1998; DeRubeis et al., 1999; Persons et al., 2001). In addition, there is a rapidly expanding empirical literature suggesting that cognitive behavior therapy has a substantial relapse prevention effect (e.g., see Hollon & Shelton, 2001; Jarrett et al., 2001; Teasdale et al., 2001). Problem-solving therapy is relevant here because it focuses on teaching the patient to solve problems more effectively (D'Zurilla & Nezu, 1999; Nezu et al., 1989). Interpersonal psychotherapy is a positive option because depression is so interwoven into interpersonal problems (Gilbert, 2000). Moreover, there are some impressive randomized controlled trials suggesting that interpersonal psychotherapy has a considerable relapse prevention effect (see, e.g., Frank et al., 1990; Hollon & Shelton, 2001; Markowitz, 1998; Reynolds et al., 1999).

Finally, practitioners should consider the merits of maintenance pharmacotherapy. Long-term pharmacotherapy is a very promising relapse-prevention strategy, particularly for the most severe cases of depression (Agency for Health Care Policy Research, 1999; American Psychiatric Association, 2000b; Halbreich & Montgomery, 2000; Hollon & Shelton, 2001; Kocsis et al., 1996; Kupfer et al., 1992; Rankin, 2000; Schatzberg, 2000; Sherbourne et al., 2001). The side effects and cost of long-term pharmacotherapy may have to be tolerated by some severely depressed patients. The option is almost inevitable relapse, which is worse (Jamison, 1999; Judd et al., 2000; Ormel, 2000; Reynolds et al., 1999, 2000).

Booster Sessions

Based on several randomized controlled trials, an *especially promising* relapse prevention strategy is the use of booster sessions (Jarrett et al., 1998; Jarrett et al., 2001; Richards, 1999). For instance, Fava et al. (1998) reduced relapse rates from 80% to 25%, during the 2 years of follow-up, via booster sessions of cognitive behavior therapy. Paykel et al. (1999) reduced relapse rates from 47% to 29%, during the 16 months of follow-up, through offering booster sessions of cognitive therapy.

Booster sessions of *combined* psychotherapy and pharmacotherapy look even more promising. For example, Frank et al. (1990) reduced relapse rates from approximately 90% to 25%, during the 3-year follow-up period, by offering booster sessions of combined interpersonal psychotherapy and pharmacotherapy. Booster sessions of interpersonal psychotherapy without medication were less effective, reducing relapse to about 65%. Moreover, Reynolds et al. (1999) found parallel results with a sample of depressed geriatric patients: Booster sessions of combined interpersonal psychotherapy and pharmacotherapy reduced relapse from 90% (placebo control) to 20% (combined boosters) during the 3 years of follow-up (see also Katon et al., 2001). As was found in the Frank et al. (1990) study, Reynolds et al. (1999) showed that booster sessions of interpersonal psychotherapy without medication were less effective, reducing relapse to 64%.

In summary, booster sessions—particularly those with *combined* psychotherapy and maintenance pharmacotherapy—appear to significantly reduce relapse (American Psychiatric Association, 2000b). Practitioners should consider the merits of adding booster sessions to their treatment protocols for depressed patients.

Clinical Guidelines

- Consider clinical guidelines for relapse prevention to be tentative and incomplete; this problem has not been solved yet.
- Provide a thorough, comprehensive, and extensive treatment intervention for your high-risk patients.
- Help your depressed patients to learn more effective problem-solving skills.
- Consider the merits of the empirically supported skill-oriented psychotherapies for depression, such as cognitive behavior therapy, interpersonal psychotherapy, and problem-solving therapy.
- Consider the merits of maintenance or long-term pharmacotherapy, under close physician supervision, for your depressed patients who are at high risk for relapse.
- Prepare your depressed patients for the possibility of relapse, and discuss various coping and help-seeking strategies that they can pursue if they do relapse.
- Help your depressed patients to understand that relapse is common and that it does not mean they have failed or should feel guilty—it is okay to pursue treatment again!
- Include some *booster sessions* in your treatment protocols for depressed patients.
- Many of your severely depressed patients *will* relapse, despite their best efforts and your best treatments. Be prepared to help these patients with further treatment if they need it.

Chapter Summary

Over 50% of the patients who are successfully treated for depression will relapse within 5 years. Thus, relapse prevention is a major challenge in treating depression. The risk of relapse is greater if the depressive symptoms are severe, if relapse has occurred before, if stress is high, if social support is low, if close relationships are dysfunctional, or if coping styles are passive rather than active.

People who cope with depression on their own, without professional help, are more likely to be successful if the coping has certain qualities. They should be active, make positive changes in their social environment, emphasize the positive, problem-solve, and avoid alcohol abuse and ruminating about negative experiences.

Less than 50% of all seriously depressed individuals receive adequate treatment for their depression. There would be less depression, and fewer relapses back into depression, if more individuals received thorough treatment for their depressive episodes. To prevent relapse, it may be necessary to think of depression as an experience that includes a chronic vulnerability. Thus, a lifelong coping effort may be required to avoid further depressions. In addition, booster sessions of psychotherapy and/or maintenance pharmacotherapy appear to reduce relapse. Practitioners should consider the merits of adding *booster sessions* to their treatment protocols for depressed patients.

Psychotherapies that emphasize helping depressed patients to cope more effectively with their thinking and behaving (e.g., cognitive behavior therapy and problem-solving therapy), and to deal more effectively with their close relationships (e.g., interpersonal psychotherapy), hold promise for reducing relapse. The most effective relapse prevention strategy for particularly severe depressions, however, may be long-term pharmacotherapy *combined* with booster sessions of psychotherapy. This long-term treatment approach, of course, raises concerns about financial hardships and side effects. In summary, effective relapse prevention is a major challenge when treating depression.

Suggested Readings

Discussions

Cognitive Theories

- Clark and Beck (1999) included a discussion of the cognitive theories of relapse and why some depressed patients are at more risk for relapse (see also Ingram et al., 1998; Teasdale et al., 2000; Teasdale et al., 2001). Aaron Beck has developed the most influential cognitive theory of depression, and this review coauthored with David Clark is scholarly and thorough.

Inadequate Treatment

- Hirschfeld et al. (1997) developed a "consensus statement" regarding inadequate treatment and discussed findings that at least half of all seriously depressed individuals receive either no treatment or inadequate treatment for their depression (see also Steffens et al., 2000; Young et al., 2001). This discussion is a sobering reminder that many depressed people do not receive adequate treatment.

Problem Solving

- Nezu et al. (1989) provided an overview of research on problem-solving treatments for depression. This book includes numerous clinical guidelines, how-to recommendations, and case examples (see also D'Zurilla & Nezu, 1999; Nezu et al., 1998).

Self-Administered Treatments

- Scogin et al. (1996) concluded that self-administered treatments often yield positive outcomes if the depressed participants are adequately prepared for these self-control treatments. This review discussed the promising future for self-administered treatments, while warning that appropriate screening and preparation are necessary.

Studies

- Fava et al. (1998) conducted a randomized controlled trial, and the findings suggested that booster sessions of cognitive behavior therapy reduced relapse from 80% to 25% during the 2-year follow-up period.
- Frank et al. (1990) conducted a randomized controlled trial, and the results indicated that booster sessions of interpersonal

psychotherapy conducted on a monthly basis reduced relapse from 90% to 65% over a 3-year follow-up.

- Jarrett et al. (2001) conducted a randomized controlled trial, and the findings suggested that 8 months of booster sessions, entailing cognitive behavior therapy with a strong cognitive emphasis, "significantly reduces relapse and recurrence in the highest-risk patients with recurrent MDD [Major Depressive Disorder]" (p. 381). For patients with early-onset depression, booster sessions reduced relapse from 67% to 16% at the 2-year follow-up.

- Paykel et al. (1999) conducted a randomized controlled trial, and the findings indicated that booster sessions of cognitive psychotherapy reduced relapse from 47% to 29% during the 16 months of follow-up.

- Reynolds et al. (1999) conducted a randomized controlled trial, and the results suggested that booster sessions of *combined* interpersonal psychotherapy and pharmacotherapy reduced relapse from 90% (placebo-control group) to 20% (combined booster group) over a 3-year follow-up (see also Katon et al., 2001).

Epilogue

Overview

We begin this brief epilogue with a letter from one of our former patients. The letter describes what therapy was like for the patient and how he has coped since therapy ended. After discussing key facets of the letter, we highlight some of the difficult therapeutic challenges for practitioners who are working with depressed patients. Next, we provide an overview of some of the prominent clinical guidelines for practitioners. These clinical guidelines pervade many of the chapters in our primer. We also discuss certain therapeutic themes that arise from these clinical guidelines. Finally, we provide a short list of suggested readings on depression that should be helpful for practitioners. These readings are relatively broad in their coverage, in contrast to some of the more specific readings that are suggested at the end of each chapter.

Case Study

The following letter was written by one of our former patients some months after therapy had ended. A number of personal details and phrases in the letter have been changed to protect the identity of the patient.

Dear Doctor,
I'm writing to let you know how I'm doing and to say a special "thanks" for your help. It's been nearly 5 months since our last session, and I'm actually doing pretty well right now. When I look back

to where I was when I first saw you about a year ago, I realize that I've made a lot of progress since then. In fact, back then I wasn't sure that I was going to make it. I was so terribly depressed that life truly did not seem worth living. Looking back, it's hard to believe how dark and scary those days were and how close I was to "checking out."

You were a big part of my continuing the struggle and not giving up, even when I was facing my darkest hours. As you know, at times therapy itself was a struggle for me. One of the things that made a difference for me was knowing that you cared—that you really cared about me as a person. I think back to that night when I called and told you I was suicidal. I probably would not be here today if you had not been there for me. I know how resistant I was to the idea of going to the hospital, but your going with me to the emergency room that Saturday night made the difference. I would not have gone on my own, and God only knows what would have happened if I hadn't been able to reach you! It seems like such a long time ago, but it was less than a year.

Things are going better now. I'm not 100%, but I'm doing pretty well. I'm still on an antidepressant and that seems to help, but I do want to let you know that the work we did in therapy is something that helped back then and is still helping now. I've been through some stressful times in the past few months. I didn't get the promotion at work that you know I'd been hoping for. But I didn't get depressed.

You'll be proud to know that I've been real careful to examine my thinking for those "hot" thoughts—you know the ones that tend to trigger my feeling down and depressed. When I didn't get the promotion, I was disappointed and down for a while. But then I asked myself, "What's so terrible about not getting the promotion?" One of the important things I learned in therapy was not to judge my self-worth based on the need to have approval from my boss for everything I do. I also looked at the flip side of the situation and realized that there were some good things associated with not getting the promotion—like less stress on the job and more time for myself and for my family. The more I thought about it from that perspective the better I felt.

Anyway, I don't mean to ramble on, but I did want to let you know that I'm doing well. I also want to tell you that I really appreciate all that you have done to help me. Right now I seem to be doing pretty well. But I also realize that if I hit a bump in the road, then I know that I can count on you to help me get back on track. I want to say thank you for your concern and helpful therapy!

Sincerely,

George

Discussion of the Case

Working with depressed patients can be rewarding as well as challenging. It is particularly gratifying when patients respond to treatment and their lives are improved as a result of our interventions. George initially came into treatment at the urging of his wife, who saw him as getting "stressed out" from work-related problems. Our assessment indicated that George was experiencing a Major Depressive Episode, which was triggered in part by his perception that he was a "failure" in his professional life. Like many high-achieving individuals, George's standards for judging his performance at work were unrealistically high. In fact, by any objective indication, his work performance was fully satisfactory and he was in no danger of losing his job. Our evaluation and detailed history taking also indicated that although this was probably not the most severe episode of depression that George had experienced it was part of a pattern of recurrent depression. Yet he had never been treated previously by a mental health professional, in large part due to his fears about the stigma associated with having a psychiatric disorder.

One month into treatment, George's depression worsened and he became suicidal. Fortunately, he contacted his therapist. After some crisis counseling, he trusted his therapist enough to allow himself to be hospitalized. He was in the hospital less than 2 weeks and was started on an antidepressant medication. Following his discharge, he resumed outpatient treatment that focused heavily on cognitive behavior therapy.

George responded well to the combination of cognitive behavior therapy and pharmacotherapy (an SSRI antidepressant). His letter highlights several important aspects about the treatment of depression. First, the development of a close working relationship appears to have been instrumental to successful treatment. George trusted the therapist enough to contact him when he was suicidal and to allow himself to be hospitalized when the therapist indicated it was necessary. Second, George appears to recognize the value of both antidepressant medication and cognitive behavior therapy. Indeed, he appears to be effectively implementing some key strategies in cognitive behavior therapy, such as his coping strategies when he did not get the promotion he wanted at work. Finally, George also appears aware that at some point in the future he may again need the therapist's assistance, and he seems receptive to getting additional treatment if needed.

Difficult Therapeutic Challenges

Depression is a horrible experience for many patients. Therefore, it can be challenging for the sensitive and concerned practitioner to avoid distress. Cultivating a strong professional identity, a resilient perspective, and a good sense of humor are helpful. Consultation with trusted colleagues is also beneficial. In addition, substantial knowledge of the empirical literature on depression is very helpful.

Depressed patients are sometimes difficult to work with. Therefore, it can be challenging for the goal-oriented and ambitious practitioner to avoid disappointment. A structured and organized approach to psychotherapy is helpful. A calm and empathic therapeutic style makes a positive impact. Furthermore, some reality testing is helpful: Psychotherapy is hard work, and it is not always effective.

Awful traumas are sometimes part of the depressed patient's life. Therefore, the practitioner may get traumatized too. Patient suicide is an obvious example. Patients who have experienced child abuse or rape are additional examples (from a potentially long list). Practitioners should not hesitate to get help for themselves if their patients' traumas are intensely upsetting them. Moreover, this is an issue where consulting with experts, collaborating with trusted colleagues, and working with an interdisciplinary team can be very beneficial.

Some depressed patients do not get better, and many patients relapse after they do improve. Therefore, the practitioner may get discouraged. Psychotherapy can be tough, disappointing work. Most patients treated with empirically supported therapies do get better, however, and that helps a lot. Furthermore, we are making progress on developing efficacious relapse prevention strategies, which is also encouraging.

Even the strongest practitioners may occasionally make a therapeutic or professional mistake with their depressed patients. Therefore, the practitioner may feel vulnerable. A subtle mistake about "crossing the lines of competence" or "a lapse in confidentiality" is an obvious example of this concern. Following professional ethics codes and laws of the jurisdiction will be very helpful. Keeping careful records will be beneficial. Moreover, staying in alignment with a cautious and prudent treatment plan, using empirically supported treatments, and consulting frequently with experts are effective therapeutic strategies, as well as reliable ways to reduce vulnerability.

Prominent Clinical Guidelines

Conduct careful interviews. Among the prominent clinical guidelines that run through most of the chapters is the theme that practitioners should conduct careful interviews of their depressed patients. This will afford the practitioner an opportunity to observe signs, discuss symptoms, clarify issues, and corroborate information. These interviews, of course, also allow the practitioner and the patient to begin developing their therapeutic relationship and collaborative working style. Furthermore, these interviews provide the patient with a chance to self-disclose and express emotion, while providing the practitioner with a chance to be empathic and understanding. Finally, practitioners should routinely assess for suicidal risk factors during their first interview of the patient.

Be empathic. Practitioners should evidence empathy with their depressed patients. This clinical guideline is apparent in most of the chapters, and research supports the association of effective empathy and effective psychotherapy. Moreover, being empathic with all patients—including those who are suffering from the horrible effects of severe depression—seems to be the decent and gracious thing to do. In addition, the empirical literature indicates that effective therapeutic alliances and positive treatment outcomes are related to clear empathy from the practitioner.

Assess and treat the symptoms, signs, problems, and comorbid conditions that are frequently associated with depression. There are many symptoms, signs, and problems associated with depression. Examples include severely distressed close relationships, employment problems, economic difficulties, and recent personal traumas. Furthermore, additional psychiatric disorders, such as anxiety disorders and alcohol abuse, frequently occur as comorbid conditions with depression. Chronic health problems, such as cardiovascular disease, cancer, and dementia, are often associated with depression. Finally, increased suicidal risk is common in cases of severe and chronic depression. Our clinical guidelines have repeatedly suggested that practitioners look for these associated problems and comorbid conditions, and that they aggressively treat them within the context of cooperative, interdisciplinary interventions.

Use empirically supported treatments. Certainly a very prominent clinical guideline, mentioned repeatedly throughout this primer, is that practitioners should study and use empirically supported treatments for their depressed patients. We need treatments that work. Empirical studies, particularly the more systematic studies such as randomized controlled trials, tell us what will work. Cognitive behavior therapy, interpersonal psychotherapy, and pharmacotherapy enjoy considerable empirical support as treatments for depression. Practitioners should use these empirically supported treatments. Moreover, both practitioners and patients benefit from education about the current state of these treatment interventions.

Pursue cognitive change. Depressed patients need to change their dysfunctional thinking. This point is evident in much of the empirical literature, and it is reflected in many of our clinical guidelines.

Pursue behavior change. Depressed patients need to change their ineffective behaviors. These patients need behavior change and skill enhancement that will yield the following improvements: more efficacious communication styles, interpersonal skills, social support, problem-solving strategies, coping skills, emotional regulation, and reinforcing activities. This conclusion is prominent in much of the empirical literature and in many of our clinical guidelines.

Consider the ethical, legal, and professional issues. Depressed patients sometimes present the practitioner with a complex array of ethical, legal, and professional issues. For example, there may be limits to confidentiality when a suicidal patient presents a clear and immediate danger to him- or herself. The professional challenges for practitioners in these cases include staying calm, being prepared to take immediate action, and protecting themselves. Ethical and legal issues include the legal standard of care, which is typically defined as care that is "average, reasonable, and prudent." Our clinical guidelines have repeatedly argued for getting expert consultation and for working in a cooperative, interdisciplinary manner. A crisis intervention case, such as a severely depressed and suicidal patient, is a good context for reviewing these clinical guidelines. Finally, pharmacotherapy for depression should be prescribed and carefully supervised by a qualified physician.

Include relapse prevention strategies. Most depressed patients relapse, even following successful treatment. Thus, relapse prevention strategies should be incorporated into the treatment programs for depressed patients. Booster sessions of psychotherapy, following the completion of the initial treatment program, seem to be a particularly promising relapse prevention strategy. This has been demonstrated in several randomized controlled trials that included large samples of severely depressed patients. Booster sessions of cognitive behavior therapy or interpersonal psychotherapy enjoy the strongest empirical support as psychotherapeutic relapse prevention strategies. Long-term maintenance pharmacotherapy is another well-supported strategy for relapse prevention. Planning for relapse prevention is a theme that pervades many of our clinical guidelines. Practitioners should prepare their depressed patients for the possibility of relapse, they should discuss coping and help-seeking strategies that patients can pursue if they do relapse, and they should emphasize that it is okay to pursue treatment again. Solving the relapse problem is one of the remaining frontiers for depression treatment.

Suggested Readings

These suggested readings are expository and relatively broad in scope, as befits an Epilogue. In contrast, the suggested readings at the end of each chapter are typically more focused and include both expository and empirical publications. We kept this list of suggested readings short–10 of the most helpful references for practitioners.

- The *DSM-IV-TR* (American Psychiatric Association, 2000a) is an indispensable resource for empirically based information on the symptoms, signs, course, and diagnosis of depression (and other psychiatric disorders). Practitioners who work with seriously depressed patients will find it helpful to have this manual on their bookshelves and to consult it regularly.
- Panels of experts representing the American Psychiatric Association (2000b) have provided a compendium of practice guidelines for numerous psychiatric disorders, including Major Depressive Disorder. The practice guidelines regarding pharmacotherapy for depression are empirically based, thorough, and helpful. The practice guidelines regarding psychosocial interventions for depression are also helpful. Some experts argue, however, that cognitive behavior therapy and interpersonal psychotherapy do not receive the full credit that these psychotherapies have earned through many randomized controlled trials (see Hollon & Shelton, 2001).
- The cognitive behavior therapy of depression, developed by Beck, Rush, Shaw, and Emery, and their numerous colleagues, is clearly described in their classic treatment manual (Beck et al., 1979). This influential book includes case examples, discussion of practical issues, and clinical guidelines.
- Gilbert (2000) provided a clear overview of psychotherapy for depression. This book includes brief literature reviews, how-to examples, and clinical guidelines. The therapeutic emphasis is an eclectic blend of cognitive behavior therapy, interpersonal psychotherapy, and biological/evolutionary perspectives.

- Jacobs (1999) presented a series of reviews on evaluating and treating suicidal patients. This edited book includes helpful literature reviews, clinical examples, and how-to advice.
- Jamison (1999) provided a well-written overview of what is currently known about suicide. This book is appropriate for both practitioners and laypersons.
- The interpersonal psychotherapy of depression, developed by Klerman, Weissman, Rounsaville, and Chevron, and their numerous colleagues, is clearly described in their classic treatment manual (Klerman et al., 1984). This influential book includes case examples, how-to suggestions, and clinical guidelines.
- Koocher and Keith-Spiegel (1998) provided a well-written review of the ethical issues in psychotherapy (and related instructional and research settings). This book includes helpful case examples, literature reviews, and summary guidelines.
- Markowitz (1998) provided a contemporary treatment manual for interpersonal psychotherapy of chronic depression (Dysthymic Disorder; see also McCullough, 2000). The numerous how-to suggestions and clinical guidelines in this book may be generalized to other serious forms of depression, such as Major Depressive Disorder.
- Persons et al. (2001) provided a contemporary discussion of cognitive behavior therapy for depression, with many case examples, how-to suggestions, and clinical guidelines (see also Persons, 1989). In addition, this book includes a very detailed case study in Chapter 7 that illustrates an insightful perspective on the dysfunctional thoughts and ineffective behaviors that are evidenced by many depressed patients.

References

Achat, H., Kawachi, I., Spiro, A., DeMolles, D. A., & Sparrow, D. (2000). Optimism and depression as predictors of physical and mental health functioning: The normative aging study. *Annals of Behavioral Medicine, 22,* 127–130.

Ackerson, J., Scogin, F., McKendree-Smith, N., & Lyman, R. D. (1998). Cognitive bibliotherapy for mild and moderate adolescent depressive symptomatology. *Journal of Consulting and Clinical Psychology, 66,* 685–690.

Agency for Health Care Policy Research. (1999). *Evidence report on treatment of depression: Newer pharmacotherapies.* San Antonio Evidence-Based Practice Center. Washington, DC: Agency for Health Care Policy Research.

Alexander, J. F., Holtzworth-Munroe, A., & Jameson, P. B. (1994). The process and outcome of marital and family therapy: Research review and evaluation. In A. E. Bergin & S. L. Garfield (Eds.), *Handbook of psychotherapy and behavior change* (4th ed., pp. 595–630). New York: John Wiley.

Alexopoulos, G. S. (2001). New concepts for prevention and treatment of late-life depression. *American Journal of Psychiatry, 158,* 835–838.

Alexopoulos, G. S., Bruce, M. L., Hull, J., Sirey, J. A., & Kakuma, T. (1999). Clinical determinants of suicidal ideation and behavior in geriatric depression. *Archives of General Psychiatry, 56,* 1048–1053.

Alexopoulos, G. S., Meyers, B. S., Young, R. C., Kalayam, B., Kakuma, T., Gabrielle, M., Sirey, J. A., & Hull, J. (2000). Executive dysfunction and long-term outcomes of geriatric depression. *Archives of General Psychiatry, 57,* 285–290.

Allumbaugh, D. L., & Hoyt, W. T. (1999). Effectiveness of grief therapy: A meta-analysis. *Journal of Counseling Psychology, 46,* 370–380.

American Psychiatric Association (1994). *Diagnostic and statistical manual of mental disorders* (4th ed.). Washington, DC: American Psychiatric Association.

American Psychiatric Association (2000a). *Diagnostic and statistical manual of mental disorders* (4th ed., text revision). Washington, DC: American Psychiatric Association.

American Psychiatric Association. (2000b). *Practice guidelines for the treatment of psychiatric disorders: Compendium 2000.* Washington, DC: American Psychiatric Association.

223

American Psychological Association. (1992). Ethical principles of psychologists and code of conduct. *American Psychologist, 47,* 1597–1611.

American Psychological Association. (1998). Guidelines for the evaluation of dementia and age-related cognitive decline. *American Psychologist, 53,* 1298–1303.

Anderson, J. C., Williams, S., McGee, R., & Silva, P. A. (1987). *DSM-III* disorders in preadolescent children: Prevalence in a large sample from the general population. *Archives of General Psychiatry, 44,* 69–76.

Anderson, P., Beach, S. R. H., & Kaslow, N. J. (1999). Marital discord and depression: The potential of attachment theory to guide integrative clinical intervention. In T. Joiner & J. C. Coyne (Eds.), *The interactional nature of depression* (pp. 271–297). Washington, DC: American Psychological Association.

Andrews, B., & Brown, G. W. (1995). Stability and change in low self-esteem: The role of psychosocial factors. *Psychological Medicine, 25,* 23–31.

Angold, A., & Costello, E. J. (1993). Depressive comorbidity in children and adolescents: Empirical, theoretical, and methodological issues. *American Journal of Psychiatry, 150,* 1779–1791.

Antoni, M. H., Lehman, J. M., Kilbourn, K. M., Boyers, A. E., Culver, J. L., Alferi, S. M., Yount, S. E., McGregor, B. A., Arena, P. L., Harris, S. D., Price, A. A., & Carver, C. S. (2001). Cognitive-behavioral stress management intervention decreases the prevalence of depression and enhances benefit finding among women under treatment for early-stage breast cancer. *Health Psychology, 20,* 20–32.

Appelbaum, P. S., Grisso, T., Frank, E., O'Donnell, S., & Kupfer, D. J. (1999). Competence of depressed patients for consent to research. *American Journal of Psychiatry, 156,* 1380–1384.

Appleby, L., Cooper, J., Amos, T., & Faragher, B. (1999). Psychological autopsy study of suicides by people aged under 35. *British Journal of Psychiatry, 175,* 168–174.

Arean, P. A., Perri, M. G., Nezu, A. M., Schein, R. L., Joseph, T. X., & Christopher, F. (1993). Comparative effectiveness of social problem-solving and reminiscence therapy as treatments for depression in older adults. *Journal of Consulting and Clinical Psychology, 61,* 1003–1010.

Bach, P. B., Cramer, L. D., Warren, J. L., & Begg, C. B. (1999). Racial differences in the treatment of early-stage lung cancer. *New England Journal of Medicine, 341,* 1198–1205.

Baldessarini, R. J., & Tondo, L. (2000). Does lithium treatment still work? Evidence of stable responses over three decades. *Archives of General Psychiatry, 57,* 187–190.

Barkham, M., Shapiro, D. A., Hardy, G. E., & Rees, A. (1999). Psychotherapy in two-plus-one sessions: Outcomes of a randomized controlled trial of cognitive-behavioral and psychodynamic-interpersonal therapy for subsyndromal depression. *Journal of Consulting and Clinical Psychology, 67,* 201–211.

Barlow, D. H. (2000). Unraveling the mysteries of anxiety and its disorders from the perspective of emotion theory. *American Psychologist, 55,* 1247–1263.

Barlow, D. H., Esler, J. L., & Vitali, A. E. (1998). Psychosocial treatments for Panic Disorders, Phobias, and Generalized Anxiety Disorder. In P. E. Nathan & J. M. Gorman (Eds.), *A guide to treatments that work* (pp. 288–318). New York: Oxford University Press.

Barnett, P. A., & Gotlib, I. H. (1988). Psychosocial functioning and depression: Distinguishing among antecedents, concomitants, and consequences. *Psychological Bulletin, 104*, 97–126.

Bassuk, S. S., Berkman, L. F., & Wypij, D. (1998). Depressive symptomatology and incident cognitive decline in an elderly community sample. *Archives of General Psychiatry, 55*, 1073–1081.

Baucom, D. H., Shoham, V., Mueser, K. T., Daiuto, A. D., & Stickle, T. R. (1998). Empirically supported couple and family interventions for marital distress and adult mental health problems. *Journal of Consulting and Clinical Psychology, 66*, 53–88.

Baumeister, R. F. (1990). Suicide as escape from self. *Psychological Review, 97*, 90–113.

Beach, S. R. H. (Ed.). (2001). *Marital and family processes in depression: A scientific foundation for clinical practice.* Washington, DC: American Psychological Association.

Beardslee, W. R., Versage, E. M., Wright, E. J., Salt, P., Rothberg, P. C., Drezner, K., & Gladstone, T. R. G. (1997). Examination of preventive interventions for families with depression: Evidence of change. *Development and Psychopathology, 9*, 109–130.

Beardslee, W. R., Wright, E., Rothberg, P. C., Salt, P., & Versage, E. (1996). Response of families to two preventive intervention strategies: Long-term differences in behavior and attitude change. *Journal of the American Academy of Child and Adolescent Psychiatry, 35*, 774–782.

Beck, A. T., Rush, A. J., Shaw, B. F., & Emery, G. (1979). *Cognitive therapy of depression.* New York: Guilford.

Beck, A. T., Steer, R. A., & Brown, G. K. (1996). *Beck Depression Inventory–II.* San Antonio, TX: Psychological Corporation.

Beck, A. T., Steer, R. A., & Garbin, M. G. (1988). Psychometric properties of the Beck Depression Inventory: Twenty-five years of evaluation. *Clinical Psychology Review, 8*, 77–100.

Beckham, E. E., & Leber, W. R. (Eds.). (1995). *Handbook of depression* (2nd ed.). New York: Guilford.

Beekman, A. T. F., De Beurs, E., Van Balkom, A. J. L. M., Deeg, D. J. H., Van Dyck, R., & Van Tilburg, W. (2000). Anxiety and depression in later life: Co-occurrence and communality of risk factors. *American Journal of Psychiatry, 157*, 89–95.

Berger, A. K., Small, B. J., Forsell, Y., Winblad, B., & Backman, L. (1998). Preclinical symptoms of major depression in very old age: A prospective longitudinal study. *American Journal of Psychiatry, 155*, 1039–1043.

Berkow, R., Beers, M. H., & Fletcher, A. J. (Eds.). (1997). *Merck manual of medical information* (home ed.). West Point, PA: Merck, Simon & Schuster.

Bernard, J. M., & Goodyear, R. K. (1998). *Fundamentals of clinical supervision* (2nd ed.). Boston: Allyn & Bacon.

Bersoff, D. N. (Ed.). (1999). *Ethical conflicts in psychology* (2nd ed.). Washington, DC: American Psychological Association.

Bierut, L. J., Heath, A. C., Bucholz, K. K., Dinwiddie, S. H., Madden, P. A. F., Statham, D. J., Dunne, M. P., & Martin, N. G. (1999). Major Depressive Disorder in a community-based twin sample: Are there different genetic and environmental contributions for men and women? *Archives of General Psychiatry, 56,* 557–563.

Birmaher, B., Brent, D. A., Kolko, D., Baugher, M., Bridge, J., Holder, D., Iyengar, S., & Ulloa, R. E. (2000). Clinical outcome after short-term psychotherapy for adolescents with Major Depressive Disorder. *Archives of General Psychiatry, 57,* 29–36.

Birmaher, B., Ryan, N. D., Williamson, D. E., Brent, D. A., & Kaufman, J. (1996). Childhood and adolescent depression: A review of the past 10 years. Part II. *Journal of the American Academy of Child and Adolescent Psychiatry, 35,* 1575–1583.

Birmaher, B., Ryan, N. D., Williamson, D. E., Brent, D. A., Kaufman, J., Dahl, R. E., Perel, J., & Nelson, B. (1996). Childhood and adolescent depression: A review of the past 10 years. Part I. *Journal of the American Academy of Child and Adolescent Psychiatry, 35,* 1427–1439.

Blackburn, I. M., & Moore, R. G. (1997). Controlled acute and follow-up trial of cognitive therapy and pharmacotherapy in out-patients with recurrent depression. *British Journal of Psychiatry, 171,* 328–334.

Blazer, D. G., Kessler, R. C., McGonagle, K. A., & Swartz, M. S. (1994). The prevalence and distribution of major depression in a national community sample: The National Comorbidity Survey. *American Journal of Psychiatry, 151,* 979–986.

Bloch, S., Chodoff, P., & Green, S. A. (Eds.). (1999). *Psychiatric ethics* (3rd ed.). New York: Oxford University Press.

Block, J. H., Gjerde, P. F., & Block, J. H. (1991). Personality antecedents of depressive tendencies in 18–year-olds: A prospective study. *Journal of Personality and Social Psychology, 60,* 726–738.

Blumenthal, J. A., Jiang, W., Babyak, M. A., Krantz, D. S., Frid, D. J., Coleman, R. E., Waugh, R., Hanson, M., Appelbaum, M., O'Connor, C., & Morris, J. J. (1997). Stress management and exercise training in cardiac patients with myocardial ischemia: Effects on prognosis and evaluation of mechanisms. *Archives of Internal Medicine, 157,* 2213–2223.

Boes, M., & McDermott, V. (2000). Crisis intervention in the hospital emergency room. In A. R. Roberts (Ed.), *Crisis intervention handbook: Assessment, treatment, and research* (2nd ed., pp. 389–411). New York: Oxford University Press.

Bollini, P., Pampallona, S., Tibaldi, G., Kupelnick, B., & Munizza, C. (1999). Effectiveness of antidepressants: Meta-analysis of dose–effect relationships in randomised clinical trials. *British Journal of Psychiatry, 174,* 297–303.

Boney-McCoy, S., & Finkelhor, D. (1996). Is youth victimization related to trauma symptoms and depression after controlling for prior symptoms and family relationships? A longitudinal, prospective study. *Journal of Consulting and Clinical Psychology, 64,* 1406–1416.

Bongar, B. (1991). *The suicidal patient: Clinical and legal standards of care.* Washington, DC: American Psychological Association.

Bongar, B. (1992). The ethical issue of competence in working with the suicidal patient. *Ethics and Behavior, 2,* 75–89.

Bongar, B., Berman, A. L., Maris, R. W., Silverman, M. M., Harris, E. A., & Packman, W. L. (Eds.). (1998). *Risk management with suicidal patients.* New York: Guilford.

Bostwick, J. M., & Pankratz, V. S. (2000). Affective disorders and suicide risk: A reexamination. *American Journal of Psychiatry, 157,* 1925–1932.

Bovasso, G. B., Eaton, W. W., & Armenian, H. K. (1999). The long-term outcomes of mental health treatment in a population-based study. *Journal of Consulting and Clinical Psychology, 67,* 529–538.

Brener, N. D., Hassan, S. S., & Barrios, L. C. (1999). Suicidal ideation among college students in the United States. *Journal of Consulting and Clinical Psychology, 67,* 1004–1008.

Brown, G. K., Beck, A. T., Steer, R. A., & Grisham, J. R. (2000). Risk factors for suicide in psychiatric outpatients: A 20-year prospective study. *Journal of Consulting and Clinical Psychology, 68,* 371–377.

Brown, R. A., Evans, D. M., Miller, I. W., Burgess, E. S., & Mueller, T. I. (1997). Cognitive-behavioral treatment for depression in alcoholism. *Journal of Consulting and Clinical Psychology, 65,* 715–726.

Buchwald, A. M., & Rudick-Davis, D. (1993). The symptoms of major depression. *Journal of Abnormal Psychology, 102,* 197–205.

Burns, D. D., & Eidelson, R. J. (1998). Why are depression and anxiety correlated? A test of the tripartite model. *Journal of Consulting and Clinical Psychology, 66,* 461–473.

Burns, D. D., & Nolen-Hoeksema, S. (1992). Therapeutic empathy and recovery from depression in cognitive-behavioral therapy: A structural equation model. *Journal of Consulting and Clinical Psychology, 60,* 441–449.

Burns, D. D., Sayers, S. L., & Moras, K. (1994). Intimate relationships and depression: Is there a causal connection? *Journal of Consulting and Clinical Psychology, 62,* 1033–1043.

Burns, D. D., & Spangler, D. L. (2000). Does psychotherapy homework lead to improvements in depression in cognitive-behavioral therapy or does improvement lead to increased homework compliance? *Journal of Consulting and Clinical Psychology, 68,* 46–56.

Burns, D. D., & Spangler, D. L. (2001). Do changes in dysfunctional attitudes mediate changes in depression and anxiety in cognitive behavioral therapy? *Behavior Therapy, 32,* 337–369.

Butzlaff, R. L., & Hooley, J. M. (1998). Expressed emotion and psychiatric relapse: A meta-analysis. *Archives of General Psychiatry, 55,* 547–552.

Byford, S., Harrington, R., Torgerson, D., Kerfoot, M., Dyer, E., Harrington, V., Woodham, A., Gill, J., & McNiven, F. (1999). Cost-effectiveness analysis of a home-based social work intervention for children and adolescents who have deliberately poisoned themselves: Results of a randomised controlled trial. *British Journal of Psychiatry, 174*, 56–62.

Campbell, S. B., Cohn, J. F., & Meyers, T. (1995). Depression in first-time mothers: Mother-infant interaction and depression chronicity. *Developmental Psychology, 31*, 349–357.

Caspi, A., Moffitt, T. E., Newman, D. L., & Silva, P. A. (1996). Behavioral observations at age 3 years predict adult psychiatric disorders: Longitudinal evidence from a birth cohort. *Archives of General Psychiatry, 53*, 1033–1039.

Chassin, L., Pitts, S. C., DeLucia, C., & Todd, M. (1999). A longitudinal study of children of alcoholics: Predicting young adult substance use disorders, anxiety, and depression. *Journal of Abnormal Psychology, 108*, 106–119.

Chen, J. H., Bierhals, A. J., Prigerson, H. G., Kasl, S. V., Mazure, C. M., & Jacobs, S. (1999). Gender differences in the effects of bereavement-related psychological distress in health outcomes. *Psychological Medicine, 29*, 367–380.

Chen, P., Ganguli, M., Mulsant, B. H., & DeKosky, S. T. (1999). The temporal relationship between depressive symptoms and dementia: A community-based study. *Archives of General Psychiatry, 56*, 261–266.

Chorpita, B. F., Albano, A. M., & Barlow, D. H. (1998). The structure of negative emotions in a clinical sample of children and adolescents. *Journal of Abnormal Psychology, 107*, 74–85.

Christensen, H., Jorm, A. F., MacKinnon, A. J., Korten, A. E., Jacomb, P. A., Henderson, A. S., & Rodgers, B. (1999). Age differences in depression and anxiety symptoms: A structural equation modelling analysis of data from a general population sample. *Psychological Medicine, 29*, 325–339.

Cicchetti, D., & Toth, S. L. (1998). The development of depression in children and adolescents. *American Psychologist, 53*, 221–241.

Clark, D. A. (2001). The persistent problem of negative cognition in anxiety and depression: New perspectives and old controversies. *Behavior Therapy, 32*, 3–12.

Clark, D. A., & Beck, A. T. (1999). *Scientific foundations of cognitive theory and therapy of depression.* New York: John Wiley.

Clark, D. A., Cook, A., & Snow, D. (1998). Depressive symptom differences in hospitalized, medically ill, depressed psychiatric inpatients and nonmedical controls. *Journal of Abnormal Psychology, 107*, 38–48.

Clark, D. C. (1995). Epidemiology, assessment, and management of suicide in depressed patients. In E. E. Beckham & W. R. Leber (Eds.), *Handbook of depression* (2nd ed., pp. 526–538). New York: Guilford.

Clark, D. C., Gibbons, R. D., Fawcett, J., & Scheftner, W. A. (1989). What is the mechanism by which suicide attempts predispose to later suicide attempts? A mathematical model. *Journal of Abnormal Psychology, 98*, 42–49.

Clarke, G., Hops, H., Lewinsohn, P. M., Andrews, J., Seeley, J. R., & Williams, J. (1992). Cognitive-behavioral group treatment of adolescent depression: Prediction of outcome. *Behavior Therapy, 23,* 341–354.

Classen, C., Butler, L. D., Koopman, C., Miller, E., DiMiceli, S., Giese-Davis, J., Fobair, P., Carlson, R. W., Kraemer, H. C., & Spiegel, D. (2001). Supportive-expressive group therapy and distress in patients with metastatic breast cancer: A randomized clinical intervention trial. *Archives of General Psychiatry, 58,* 494–501.

Cole, D. A., Martin, J. M., Powers, B., & Truglio, R. (1996). Modeling causal relations between academic and social competence and depression: A multitrait-multimethod longitudinal study of children. *Journal of Abnormal Psychology, 105,* 258–270.

Cole, D. A., Peeke, L. G., Martin, J. M., Truglio, R., & Seroczynski, A. D. (1998). A longitudinal look at the relation between depression and anxiety in children and adolescents. *Journal of Consulting and Clinical Psychology, 66,* 451–460.

Cole, M. G., Bellavance, F., & Mansour, A. (1999). Prognosis of depression in elderly community and primary care populations: A systematic review and meta-analysis. *American Journal of Psychiatry, 156,* 1182–1189.

Compas, B. E., Ey, S., & Grant, K. E. (1993). Taxonomy, assessment, and diagnosis of depression during adolescence. *Psychological Bulletin, 114,* 323–344.

Compas, B. E., Haaga, D. A. F., Keefe, F. J., Leitenberg, H., & Williams, D. A. (1998). Sampling of empirically supported psychological treatments from health psychology: Smoking, chronic pain, cancer, and bulimia nervosa. *Journal of Consulting and Clinical Psychology, 66,* 89–112.

Compas, B. E., Oppedisano, G., Connor, J. K., Gerhardt, C. A., Hinden, B. R., Achenbach, T. M., & Hammen, C. (1997). Gender differences in depressive symptoms in adolescence: Comparison of national samples of clinically referred and nonreferred youths. *Journal of Consulting and Clinical Psychology, 65,* 617–626.

Consumer Reports. (2000). *Consumer Reports complete drug reference* (20th ed.). Yonkers, NY: Micromedex, Inc. & Consumer Reports, Division of Consumers Union.

Conwell, Y., Duberstein, P. R., Cox, C., Herrmann, J. H., Forbes, N. T., & Caine, E. D. (1996). Relationships of age and Axis I diagnoses in victims of completed suicide: A psychological autopsy study. *American Journal of Psychiatry, 153,* 1001–1008.

Cooper-Patrick, L., Crum, R. M., & Ford, D. E. (1994). Identifying suicidal ideation in general medical patients. *Journal of the American Medical Association, 272,* 1757–1762.

Copeland, J. R. M., Beekman, A. T. F., Dewey, M. E., Jordan, A., Lawlor, B. A., Linden, M., Lobo, A., Magnusson, H., Mann, A. H., Fichter, M., Prince, M. J., Saz, P., Turrina, C., & Wilson, K. C. M. (1999). Cross-cultural comparison of depressive symptoms in Europe does not support stereotypes of ageing. *British Journal of Psychiatry, 174,* 322–329.

Coryell, W., Akiskal, H. S., Leon, A. C., Winokur, G., Maser, J. D., Mueller, T. I., & Keller, M. B. (1994). The time course of nonchronic Major Depressive Disorder: Uniformity across episodes and samples. *Archives of General Psychiatry, 51,* 405–410.

Courneya, K. S., & Friedenreich, C. M. (1999). Physical exercise and quality of life following cancer diagnosis: A literature review. *Annals of Behavioral Medicine, 21*, 171–179.

Coyne, J. C. (1999). Thinking interactionally about depression: A radical restatement. In T. Joiner & J. C. Coyne (Eds.), *The interactional nature of depression* (pp. 365–392). Washington, DC: American Psychological Association.

Craighead, W. E., Craighead, L. W., & Ilardi, S. S. (1998). Psychosocial treatments for Major Depressive Disorder. In P. E. Nathan & J. M. Gorman (Eds.), *A guide to treatments that work* (pp. 226–239). New York: Oxford University Press.

Craske, M. G., & Zucker, B. G. (2001). Consideration of the APA Practice Guideline for the Treatment of Patients With Panic Disorder: Strengths and limitations for behavior therapy. *Behavior Therapy, 32*, 259–281.

Crits-Christoph, P. (1992). The efficacy of brief dynamic psychotherapy: A meta-analysis. *American Journal of Psychiatry, 149*, 151–158.

Cronkite, R. C., & Moos, R. H. (1995). Life context, coping processes, and depression. In E. E. Beckham & W. R. Leber (Eds.), *Handbook of depression* (2nd ed., pp. 569–587). New York: Guilford.

Cummings, E. M., & Davies, P. T. (1999). Depressed parents and family functioning: Interpersonal effects and children's functioning and development. In T. Joiner & J. C. Coyne (Eds.), *The interactional nature of depression* (pp. 299–327). Washington, DC: American Psychological Association.

Cyranowski, J. M., Frank, E., Young, E., & Shear, M. K. (2000). Adolescent onset of the gender difference in lifetime rates of major depression: A theoretical model. *Archives of General Psychiatry, 57*, 21–27.

Daley, S. E., Hammen, C., Burge, D., Davila, J., Paley, B., Lindberg, N., & Herzberg, D. S. (1997). Predictors of the generation of episodic stress: A longitudinal study of late adolescent women. *Journal of Abnormal Psychology, 106*, 251–259.

Daley, S. E., Hammen, C., Davila, J., & Burge, D. (1998). Axis II symptomatology, depression, and life stress during the transition from adolescence to adulthood. *Journal of Consulting and Clinical Psychology, 66*, 595–603.

Davila, J., Hammen, C., Burge, D., Paley, B., & Daley, S. E. (1995). Poor interpersonal problem solving as a mechanism of stress generation in depression among adolescent women. *Journal of Abnormal Psychology, 104*, 592–600.

Davis, M. C., Matthews, K. A., & Twamley, E. W. (1999). Is life more difficult on Mars or Venus? A meta-analytic review of sex differences in major and minor life events. *Annals of Behavioral Medicine, 21*, 83–97.

Davison, K. P., Pennebaker, J. W., & Dickerson, S. S. (2000). Who talks? The social psychology of illness support groups. *American Psychologist, 55*, 205–217.

De Lima, M. S., Hotoph, M., & Wessely, S. (1999). The efficacy of drug treatments for dysthymia: A systematic review and meta-analysis. *Psychological Medicine, 29*, 1273–1289.

DeRubeis, R. J., & Crits-Christoph, P. (1998). Empirically supported individual and group psychological treatments for adult mental disorders. *Journal of Consulting and Clinical Psychology, 66*, 37–52.

DeRubeis, R. J., Gelfand, L. A., Tang, T. Z., & Simons, A. D. (1999). Medications versus cognitive behavior therapy for severely depressed outpatients: Mega-analysis of four randomized comparisons. *American Journal of Psychiatry, 156*, 1007–1013.

Dew, M. A., Goycoolea, J. M., Stukas, A. A., Switzer, G. E., Simmons, R. G., Roth, L. H., & DiMartini, A. (1998). Temporal profiles of physical health in family members of heart transplant recipients: Predictors of health change during caregiving. *Health Psychology, 17*, 138–151.

Dew, M. A., Reynolds, C. F., Houck, P. R., Hall, M., Buysse, D. J., Frank, E., & Kupfer, D. J. (1997). Temporal profiles of the course of depression during treatment: Predictors of pathways toward recovery in the elderly. *Archives of General Psychiatry, 54*, 1016–1024.

Doerfler, L. A., & Richards, S. (1981). Self-initiated attempts to cope with depression. *Cognitive Therapy and Research, 5*, 367–371.

Doerfler, L. A., & Richards, S. (1983). College women coping with depression. *Behaviour Research and Therapy, 21*, 221–224.

Downey, G., & Coyne, J. C. (1990). Children of depressed parents: An integrative review. *Psychological Bulletin, 108*, 50–76.

Dozois, D. J. A., & Dobson, K. S. (2001). Information processing and cognitive organization in unipolar depression: Specificity and comorbidity issues. *Journal of Abnormal Psychology, 110*, 236–246.

Drumm, K. (2000, July 7). When open-access colleges enroll mentally ill students. *Chronicle of Higher Education*, p. B7.

Druss, B. G., Bradford, W. D., Rosenheck, R. A., Radford, M. J., & Krumholz, H. M. (2001). Quality of medical care and excess mortality in older patients with mental disorders. *Archives of General Psychiatry, 58*, 565–572.

Dusseldorp, E., Elderen, T. V., Maes, S., Meulman, J., & Kraaij, V. (1999). A meta-analysis of psychoeducational programs for coronary heart disease patients. *Health Psychology, 18*, 506–519.

D'Zurilla, T. J., & Nezu, A. M. (1999). *Problem-solving therapy* (2nd ed.). New York: Springer.

Eaton, W. W., Anthony, J. C., Gallo, J., Cai, G., Tien, A., Romanoski, A., Lyketsos, C., & Chen, L. (1997). Natural history of Diagnostic Interview Schedule/DSM-IV major depression: The Baltimore Epidemiologic Catchment Area follow-up. *Archives of General Psychiatry, 54*, 993–999.

Eaton, W. W., Neufeld, K., Chen, L. S., & Cai, G. (2000). A comparison of self-report and clinical diagnostic interviews for depression: Diagnostic Interview Schedule and Schedules for Clinical Assessment in Neuropsychiatry in the Baltimore Epidemiologic Catchment Area follow-up. *Archives of General Psychiatry, 57*, 217–222.

Eist, H. I. (1998). Treatment for major depression in managed care and fee-for-service systems. *American Journal of Psychiatry, 155,* 859–860.

Elliott, C. (1997). Caring about risks: Are severely depressed patients competent to consent to research? *Archives of General Psychiatry, 54,* 113–116.

Emmanuel, J., Simmonds, S., & Tyrer, P. (1998). Systematic review of the outcome of anxiety and depressive disorders. *British Journal of Psychiatry, 173,* 35–41.

Emslie, G. J., Rush, A. J., Weinberg, W. A., Kowatch, R. A., Hughes, C. W., Carmody, T., & Rintelmann, J. (1997). A double-blind, randomized, placebo-controlled trial of fluoxetine in children and adolescents with depression. *Archives of General Psychiatry, 54,* 1031–1037.

Ernst, E., Rand, J. I., & Stevinson, C. (1998). Complementary therapies for depression: An overview. *Archives of General Psychiatry, 55,* 1026–1032.

Estrada, R. (1998, June 1). Mental illness' conspiracy of silence. *Dallas Morning News,* p. A13.

Evans, K., Tyrer, P., Catalan, J., Schmidt, U., Davidson, K., Dent, J., Tata, P., Thornton, S., Barber, J., & Thompson, S. (1999). Manual-assisted cognitive-behaviour therapy (MACT): A randomized controlled trial of a brief intervention with bibliotherapy in the treatment of recurrent deliberate self-harm. *Psychological Medicine, 29,* 19–25.

Evans, M. D., Hollon, S. D., DeRubeis, R. J., Piasecki, J. M., Grove, W. M., Garvey, M. J., & Tuason, V. B. (1992). Differential relapse following cognitive therapy and pharmaco-therapy for depression. *Archives of General Psychiatry, 49,* 802–808.

Evans, M. O., Morgan, H. G., Hayward, A., & Gunnell, D. J. (1999). Crisis telephone consultation for deliberate self-harm patients: Effects on repetition. *British Journal of Psychiatry, 175,* 23–27.

Everson, S. A., Goldberg, D. E., Kaplan, G. A., Cohen, R. D., Pukkala, E., Tuomilehto, J., & Salonen, J. T. (1996). Hopelessness and risk of mortality and incidence of myocardial infarction and cancer. *Psychosomatic Medicine, 58,* 113–121.

Faller, H., Bulzebruck, H., Drings, P., & Lang, H. (1999). Coping, distress, and survival among patients with lung cancer. *Archives of General Psychiatry, 56,* 756–762.

Fava, G. A. (1999). Subclinical symptoms in mood disorders: Pathophysiological and therapeutic implications. *Psychological Medicine, 29,* 47–61.

Fava, G. A., Rafanelli, C., Grandi, S., Conti, S., & Belluardo, P. (1998). Prevention of recurrent depression with cognitive behavioral therapy: Preliminary findings. *Archives of General Psychiatry, 55,* 816–820.

Fava, M., & Rosenbaum, J. F. (1995). Pharmacotherapy and somatic therapies. In E. E. Beckham & W. R. Leber (Eds.), *Handbook of depression* (2nd ed., pp. 280–301). New York: Guilford.

Fawzy, F. I., & Fawzy, N. W. (1998). Psychoeducational interventions. In J. C. Holland (Ed.), *Psycho-Oncology* (pp. 676–693). New York: Oxford University Press.

Fawzy, F. I., Fawzy, N. W., Hyun, C. S., Elashoff, R., Guthrie, D., Fahey, J. L., & Morton, D. L. (1993). Malignant melanoma: Effects of an early structured psychiatric intervention, coping, and affective state on recurrence and survival 6 years later. *Archives of General Psychiatry, 50,* 681–689.

Ferguson, C. P., & Pigott, T. A. (2000). Anorexia and Bulimia Nervosa: Neurobiology and pharmacotherapy. *Behavior Therapy, 31,* 237–263.

Ferketich, A. K., Schwartzbaum, J. A., Frid, D. J., & Moeschberger, M. L. (2000). Depression as an antecedent to heart disease among women and men in the NHANES I Study. *Archives of Internal Medicine, 160,* 1261–1268.

Ferro, T., Verdeli, H., Pierre, F., & Weissman, M. M. (2000). Screening for depression in mothers bringing their offspring for evaluation or treatment of depression. *American Journal of Psychiatry, 157,* 375–379.

Field, T. M. (1998). Massage therapy effects. *American Psychologist, 53,* 1270–1281.

Finney, J. W., & Moos, R. H. (1998). Psychosocial treatments for alcohol use disorders. In P. E. Nathan & J. M. Gorman (Eds.), *A guide to treatments that work* (pp. 156–166). New York: Oxford University Press.

First, M. B., Gibbon, M., Spitzer, R. L., & Williams, J. B. W. (1997). *Structured clinical interview for DSM-IV Axis I disorders: Clinician version (SCID-I).* Washington, DC: American Psychiatric Press.

Flett, G. L., Vredenburg, K., & Krames, L. (1997). The continuity of depression in clinical and non-clinical samples. *Psychological Bulletin, 121,* 395–416.

Flint, A. J., & Rifat, S. L. (1998). Two-year outcome of psychotic depression in late life. *American Journal of Psychiatry, 155,* 178–183.

Foa, E. B., Dancu, C. V., Hembree, E. A., Jaycox, L. H., Meadows, E. A., & Street, G. P. (1999). A comparison of exposure therapy, stress inoculation training, and their combination for reducing posttraumatic stress disorder in female assault victims. *Journal of Consulting and Clinical Psychology, 67,* 194–200.

Fombonne, E. (1998). Suicidal behaviours in vulnerable adolescents: Time trends and their correlates. *British Journal of Psychiatry, 173,* 154–159.

Ford, D. E., Mead, L. A., Chang, P. P., Cooper-Patrick, L., Wang, N. Y., & Klag, M. J. (1998). Depression is a risk factor for coronary artery disease in men: The precursors study. *Archives of Internal Medicine, 158,* 1422–1426.

Foster, T., Gillespie, K., McClelland, R., & Patterson, C. (1999). Risk factors for suicide independent of DSM-III-R Axis I disorder: Case-control psychological autopsy study in Northern Ireland. *British Journal of Psychiatry, 175,* 175–179.

Fowler, R. C., Rich, C. L., & Young, D. (1986). San Diego Suicide Study: II. Substance abuse in young cases. *Archives of General Psychiatry, 43,* 962–965.

Frank, E. (Ed.). (2000). *Gender and its effects on psychopathology.* Washington, DC: American Psychiatric Press.

Frank, E., Kupfer, D. J., Perel, J. M., Cornes, C., Jarrett, D. B., Mallinger, A. G., Thase, M. E., McEachran, A. B., & Grochocinski, V. J. (1990). Three-year outcomes for maintenance therapies in recurrent depression. *Archives of General Psychiatry, 47,* 1093–1099.

Franklin, M. E., & Foa, E. B. (1998). Cognitive-behavioral treatments for Obsessive Compulsive Disorder. In P. E. Nathan & J. M. Gorman (Eds.), *A guide to treatments that work* (pp. 339–357). New York: Oxford University Press.

Frasure-Smith, N., Lesperance, F., Gravel, G., Masson, A., Juneau, M., Talajic, M., & Bourassa, M. G. (2000). Social support, depression, and mortality during the first year after myocardial infarction. *Circulation, 101,* 1919–1924.

Frasure-Smith, N., Lesperance, F., Prince, R. H., Verrier, P., Garber, R. A., Juneau, M., Wolfson, C., & Bourassa, M. G. (1997, August 16). Randomised trial of home-based psychosocial nursing intervention for patients recovering from myocardial infarction. *Lancet, 350,* 473–479.

Frasure-Smith, N., Lesperance, F., & Talajic, M. (1995). Depression and 18-month prognosis after myocardial infarction. *Circulation, 91,* 999–1005.

Fristad, M. A., Emery, B. L., & Beck, S. J. (1997). Use and abuse of the Children's Depression Inventory. *Journal of Consulting and Clinical Psychology, 65,* 699–702.

Funder, D. C. (2001). *The personality puzzle* (2nd ed.). New York: Norton.

Futterman, A., Thompson, L., Gallagher-Thompson, D., & Ferris, R. (1995). Depression in later life: Epidemiology, assessment, etiology, and treatment. In E. E. Beckham & W. R. Leber (Eds.), *Handbook of depression* (2nd ed., pp. 494–525). New York: Guilford.

Gallagher-Thompson, D., & Steffen, A. M. (1994). Comparative effects of cognitive-behavioral and brief psychodynamic psychotherapies for depressed family caregivers. *Journal of Consulting and Clinical Psychology, 62,* 543–549.

Garland, A. F., & Zigler, E. (1993). Adolescent suicide prevention: Current research and social policy implications. *American Psychologist, 48,* 169–182.

Gemar, M. C., Segal, Z. V., Sagrati, S., & Kennedy, S. J. (2001). Mood-induced changes on the Implicit Association Test in recovered depressed patients. *Journal of Abnormal Psychology, 110,* 282–289.

Gilbert, P. (2000). *Counselling for depression* (2nd ed.). Thousand Oaks, CA: Sage.

Giles, D. E., Kupfer, D. J., Rush, A. J., & Roffwarg, H. P. (1998). Controlled comparison of electrophysiological sleep in families of probands with unipolar depression. *American Journal of Psychiatry, 155,* 192–199.

Gillham, J. E., Reivich, K. J., Jaycox, L. H., & Seligman, M. E. P. (1995). Prevention of depressive symptoms in schoolchildren: Two-year follow-up. *Psychological Science, 6,* 343–351.

Glassman, A. H., & Shapiro, P. A. (1998). Depression and the course of coronary artery disease. *American Journal of Psychiatry, 155,* 4–11.

Goldfried, M. R., & Davison, G. C. (1994). *Clinical behavior therapy* (2nd ed.). New York: John Wiley.

Goodwin, F. K., & Ghaemi, S. N. (1998). Understanding manic-depressive illness. *Archives of General Psychiatry, 55,* 23–25.

Goodyer, I. M., Herbert, J., Tamplin, A., & Altham, P. M. E. (2000). First-episode major depression in adolescents: Affective, cognitive and endocrine characteristics of risk status and predictors of onset. *British Journal of Psychiatry, 176,* 142–149.

Gortner, E. T., Gollan, J. K., Dobson, K. S., & Jacobson, N. S. (1998). Cognitive-behavioral treatment for depression: Relapse prevention. *Journal of Consulting and Clinical Psychology, 66,* 377–384.

Gose, B. (2000a, February 25). Elite colleges struggle to prevent student suicides. *Chronicle of Higher Education,* pp. A54–A55.

Gose, B. (2000b, March 24). Harvard researchers note a rise in college students who drink heavily and often. *Chronicle of Higher Education,* p. A55.

Gotlib, I. H., Lewinsohn, P. M., & Seeley, J. R. (1998). Consequences of depression during adolescence: Marital status and marital functioning in early adulthood. *Journal of Abnormal Psychology, 107,* 686–690.

Gotlib, I. H., Whiffen, V. E., Wallace, P. M., & Mount, J. H. (1991). Prospective investigation of postpartum depression: Factors involved in onset and recovery. *Journal of Abnormal Psychology, 100,* 122–132.

Gottman, J. M., Coan, J., Carrere, S., & Swanson, C. (1998). Predicting marital happiness and stability from newlywed interactions. *Journal of Marriage and the Family, 60,* 5–22.

Graham, P. (1999). Ethics and child psychiatry. In S. Bloch, P. Chodoff, & S. A. Green (Eds.), *Psychiatric ethics* (3rd ed., pp. 301–315). New York: Oxford University Press.

Greenberger, E., Chen, C., Tally, S. R., & Dong, Q. (2000). Family, peer, and individual correlates of depressive symptomatology among U.S. and Chinese adolescents. *Journal of Consulting and Clinical Psychology, 68,* 209–219.

Greenfield, S. F., Reizes, J. M., Muenz, L. R., Kopans, B., Kozloff, R. C., & Jacobs, D. G. (2000). Treatment for depression following the 1996 National Depression Screening Day. *American Journal of Psychiatry, 157,* 1867–1869.

Greenfield, S. F., Weiss, R. D., Muenz, L. R., Vagge, L. M., Kelly, J. F., Bello, L. R., & Michael, J. (1998). The effect of depression on return to drinking: A prospective study. *Archives of General Psychiatry, 55,* 259–265.

Grundy, C. T., Lunnen, K. M., Lambert, M. J., Ashton, J. E., & Tovey, D. R. (1994). The Hamilton Rating Scale for Depression: One scale or many? *Clinical Psychology: Science and Practice, 1,* 197–205.

Halbreich, U. (2000). Gonadal hormones, reproductive age, and women with depression. *Archives of General Psychiatry, 57,* 1163–1164.

Halbreich, U., & Montgomery, S. A. (Eds.). (2000). *Pharmacotherapy for mood, anxiety, and cognitive disorders.* Washington, DC: American Psychiatric Press.

Haley, J. (1996). *Learning and teaching therapy.* New York: Guilford.

Hammen, C. (1997). *Depression.* Bristol, PA: Psychology Press/Taylor & Francis.

Hammen, C., & Brennan, P. A. (2001). Depressed adolescents of depressed and nondepressed mothers: Tests of an interpersonal impairment hypothesis. *Journal of Consulting and Clinical Psychology, 69,* 284–294.

Hammen, C., Henry, R., & Daley, S. E. (2000). Depression and sensitization to stressors among young women as a function of childhood adversity. *Journal of Consulting and Clinical Psychology, 68,* 782–787.

Hankin, B. L., Abramson, L. Y., Moffitt, T. E., Silva, P. A., McGee, R., & Angell, K. E. (1998). Development of depression from preadolescence to young adulthood: Emerging gender differences in a 10-year longitudinal study. *Journal of Abnormal Psychology, 107,* 128–140.

Harkness, K. L., Monroe, S. M., Simons, A. D., & Thase, M. (1999). The generation of life events in recurrent and non-recurrent depression. *Psychological Medicine, 29,* 135–144.

Harrington, R., Kerfoot, M., Dyer, E., McNiven, F., Gill, J., Harrington, V., Woodham, A., & Byford, S. (1998). Randomized trial of a home-based family intervention for children who have deliberately poisoned themselves. *Journal of the American Academy of Child and Adolescent Psychiatry, 37,* 512–518.

Harrington, R., Whittaker, J., & Shoebridge, P. (1998). Psychological treatment of depression in children and adolescents: A review of treatment research. *British Journal of Psychiatry, 173,* 291–298.

Harris, T., Brown, G. W., & Robinson, R. (1999). Befriending as an intervention for chronic depression among women in an inner city: I. Randomised controlled trial. *British Journal of Psychiatry, 174,* 219–224.

Hawton, K., Houston, K., & Shepperd, R. (1999). Suicide in young people: Study of 174 cases, aged under 25 years, based on coroners' and medical records. *British Journal of Psychiatry, 175,* 271–276.

Hayes, A. M., & Strauss, J. L. (1998). Dynamic systems theory as a paradigm for the study of change in psychotherapy: An application to cognitive therapy for depression. *Journal of Consulting and Clinical Psychology, 66,* 939–947.

Health workers defend placebo use against critical document: Many believe it is justified even with available treatments. (2000, November 25). *Dallas Morning News,* p. A11.

Helgeson, V. S., & Cohen, S. (1996). Social support and adjustment to cancer: Reconciling descriptive, correlational, and intervention research. *Health Psychology, 15,* 135–148.

Helgeson, V. S., Cohen, S., Schulz, R., & Yasko, J. (1999). Education and peer discussion group interventions and adjustment to breast cancer. *Archives of General Psychiatry, 56,* 340–347.

Helgeson, V. S., Cohen, S., Schulz, R., & Yasko, J. (2000). Group support interventions for women with breast cancer: Who benefits from what? *Health Psychology, 19,* 107–114.

Hendrick, C., & Hendrick, S. S. (Eds.). (2000). *Close relationships: A sourcebook.* Thousand Oaks, CA: Sage.

Hendrick, S. S. (1995). Close relationships research: Applications to counseling psychology. *Counseling Psychologist, 23,* 649–665.

Henriksson, M. M., Aro, H. M., Marttunen, M. J., Heikkinen, M. E., Isometsa, E. T., Kuoppasalmi, K. I., & Lonnqvist, J. K. (1993). Mental disorders and comorbidity in suicide. *American Journal of Psychiatry, 150,* 935–940.

Henry, W. P., Strupp, H. H., Schacht, T. E., & Gaston, L. (1994). Psychodynamic approaches. In A. E. Bergin & S. L. Garfield (Eds.), *Handbook of psychotherapy and behavior change* (4th ed., pp. 467–508). New York: John Wiley.

Heppner, P. P., Kivlighan, D. M., & Wampold, B. E. (1999). *Research design in counseling* (2nd ed.). Belmont, CA: Wadsworth.

Heun, R., Papassotiropoulos, A., Jessen, F., Maier, W., & Breitner, J. C. S. (2001). A family study of Alzheimer disease and early- and late-onset depression in elderly patients. *Archives of General Psychiatry, 58,* 190–196.

Heyd, D., & Bloch, S. (1999). The ethics of suicide. In S. Bloch, P. Chodoff, & S. A. Green (Eds.), *Psychiatric ethics* (3rd ed., pp. 441–460). New York: Oxford University Press.

Hinden, B. R., Compas, B. E., Howell, D. C., & Achenbach, T. M. (1997). Covariation of the anxious-depressed syndrome during adolescence: Separating fact from artifact. *Journal of Consulting and Clinical Psychology, 65,* 6–14.

Hirschfeld, R. M. A., Keller, M. B., Panico, S., Arons, B. S., Barlow, D., Davidoff, F., Endicott, J., Froom, J., Goldstein, M., Gorman, J. M., Guthrie, D., Marek, R. G., Maurer, T. A., Meyer, R., Phillips, K., Ross, J., Schwenk, T. L., Sharfstein, S. S., Thase, M. E., & Wyatt, R. J. (1997). The National Depressive and Manic-Depressive Association consensus statement on the undertreatment of depression. *Journal of the American Medical Association, 277,* 333–340.

Hirschfeld, R. M. A., & Russell, J. M. (1997). Assessment and treatment of suicidal patients. *New England Journal of Medicine, 337,* 910–915.

Hoehn-Saric, R., Ninan, P., Black, D. W., Stahl, S., Greist, J. H., Lydiard, B., McElroy, S., Zajecka, J., Chapman, D., Clary, C., & Harrison, W. (2000). Multicenter double-blind comparison of sertraline and desipramine for concurrent Obsessive-Compulsive and Major Depressive Disorders. *Archives of General Psychiatry, 57,* 76–82.

Holahan, C. J., Moos, R. H., Holahan, C. K., & Cronkite, R. C. (2000). Long-term post-treatment functioning among patients with unipolar depression: An integrative model. *Journal of Consulting and Clinical Psychology, 68,* 226–232.

Holland, J. C. (Ed.). (1998). *Psycho-Oncology.* New York: Oxford University Press.

Hollon, S. D., & Shelton, R. C. (2001). Treatment guidelines for Major Depressive Disorder. *Behavior Therapy, 32,* 235–258.

Hurry, J., & Storey, P. A. (2000). Assessing young people who deliberately harm themselves. *British Journal of Psychiatry, 176,* 126–131.

Ilardi, S. S., & Craighead, W. E. (1994). The role of nonspecific factors in cognitive-behavior therapy for depression. *Clinical Psychology: Science and Practice, 1,* 138–156.

Ingram, R. E., Miranda, J., & Segal, Z. V. (1998). *Cognitive vulnerability to depression.* New York: Guilford.

Inskip, H. M., Harris, E. C., & Barraclough, B. (1998). Lifetime risk of suicide for affective disorder, alcoholism and schizophrenia. *British Journal of Psychiatry, 172,* 35–37.

Irvin, J. E., Bowers, C. A., Dunn, M. E., & Wang, M. C. (1999). Efficacy of relapse prevention: A meta-analytic review. *Journal of Consulting and Clinical Psychology, 67,* 563–570.

Isacsson, G., Holmgren, P., Druid, H., & Bergman, U. (1999). Psychotropics and suicide prevention: Implications from toxicological screening of 5281 suicides in Sweden 1992–1994. *British Journal of Psychiatry, 174,* 259–265.

Isometsa, E. T., & Lonnqvist, J. K. (1998). Suicide attempts preceding completed suicide. *British Journal of Psychiatry, 173,* 531–535.

Jacobs, D. G. (Ed.). (1999). *The Harvard Medical School guide to suicide assessment and intervention.* San Francisco: Jossey-Bass.

Jacobson, N. S., Dobson, K. S., Truax, P. A., Addis, M. E., Koerner, K., Gollan, J. K., Gortner, E., & Prince, S. E. (1996). A component analysis of cognitive-behavior treatment for depression. *Journal of Consulting and Clinical Psychology, 64,* 295–304.

Jamison, K. R. (1995). *An unquiet mind.* New York: Vintage.

Jamison, K. R. (1999). *Night falls fast: Understanding suicide.* New York: Knopf.

Jarrett, R. B. (1995). Comparing and combining short-term psychotherapy and pharmacotherapy for depression. In E. E. Beckham & W. R. Leber (Eds.), *Handbook of depression* (2nd ed., pp. 435–464). New York: Guilford.

Jarrett, R. B., Basco, M. R., Risser, R., Ramanan, J., Marwill, M., Kraft, D., & Rush, A. J. (1998). Is there a role for continuation phase cognitive therapy for depressed outpatients? *Journal of Consulting and Clinical Psychology, 66,* 1036–1040.

Jarrett, R. B., Kraft, D., Doyle, J., Foster, B. M., Eaves, G. G., & Silver, P. C. (2001). Preventing recurrent depression using cognitive therapy with and without a continuation phase: A randomized clinical trial. *Archives of General Psychiatry, 58,* 381–388.

Jarrett, R. B., Schaffer, M., McIntire, D., Witt-Browder, A., Kraft, D., & Risser, R. C. (1999). Treatment of Atypical Depression with cognitive therapy or phenelzine: A double-blind, placebo-controlled trial. *Archives of General Psychiatry, 56,* 431–437.

Jeste, D. V., Alexopoulos, G. S., Bartels, S. J., Cummings, J. L., Gallo, J. J., Gottlieb, G. L., Halpain, M. C., Palmer, B. W., Patterson, T. L., Reynolds, C. F., & Lebowitz, B. D. (1999). Consensus statement on the upcoming crisis in geriatric mental health: Research agenda for the next 2 decades. *Archives of General Psychiatry, 56,* 848–853.

Jobes, D. A., Berman, A. L., & Martin, C. E. (2000). Adolescent suicidality and crisis intervention. In A. R. Roberts (Ed.), *Crisis intervention handbook: Assessment, treatment, and research* (2nd ed., pp. 131–151). New York: Oxford University Press.

Johnson, J. G., Cohen, P., Skodol, A. E., Oldham, J. M., Kasen, S., & Brook, J. S. (1999). Personality disorders in adolescence and risk of major mental disorders and suicidality during adulthood. *Archives of General Psychiatry, 56,* 805–811.

Johnson, S. L., & Jacob, T. (2000). Sequential interactions in the marital communication of depressed men and women. *Journal of Consulting and Clinical Psychology, 68,* 4–12.

Joiner, T., Catanzaro, S. J., & Laurent. J. (1996). Tripartite structure of positive and negative affect, depression, and anxiety in child and adolescent psychiatric inpatients. *Journal of Abnormal Psychology, 105,* 401–409.

Joiner, T., & Coyne, J. C. (Eds.). (1999). *The interactional nature of depression.* Washington, DC: American Psychological Association.

Joiner, T., Coyne, J. C., & Blalock, J. (1999). On the interpersonal nature of depression: Overview and synthesis. In T. Joiner & J. C. Coyne (Eds.), *The interactional nature of depression* (pp. 3–19). Washington, DC: American Psychological Association.

Joiner, T., & Rudd, M. D. (2000). Intensity and duration of suicidal crises vary as a function of previous suicide attempts and negative life events. *Journal of Consulting and Clinical Psychology, 68,* 909–916.

Jones, D. A., & West, R. R. (1996, December 14). Psychological rehabilitation after myocardial infarction: Multicentre randomised controlled trial. *British Medical Journal, 313,* 1517–1521.

Jones, D. J., Forehand, R., & Neary, E. M. (2001). Family transmission of depressive symptoms: Replication across Caucasian and African-American mother-child dyads. *Behavior Therapy, 32,* 123–138.

Jorm, A. F. (2000). Does old age reduce the risk of anxiety and depression? A review of epidemiological studies across the adult life span. *Psychological Medicine, 30,* 11–22.

Jorm, A. F., Christensen, H., Henderson, A. S., Jacomb, P. A., Korten, A., & Rodgers, B. (2000). Predicting anxiety and depression from personality: Is there a synergistic effect of neuroticism and extraversion? *Journal of Abnormal Psychology, 109,* 145–149.

Judd, L. L. (1997). The clinical course of unipolar Major Depressive Disorders. *Archives of General Psychiatry, 54,* 989–991.

Judd, L. L., Akiskal, H. S., Zeller, P. J., Paulus, M., Leon, A. C., Maser, J. D., Endicott, J., Coryell, W., Kunovac, J. L., Mueller, T. I., Rice, J. P., & Keller, M. B. (2000). Psychosocial disability during the long-term course of unipolar Major Depressive Disorder. *Archives of General Psychiatry, 57,* 375–380.

Kales, H. C., Blow, F. C., Copeland, L. A., Bingham, R. C., Kammerer, E. E., & Mellow, A. M. (1999). Health care utilization by older patients with coexisting dementia and depression. *American Journal of Psychiatry, 156,* 550–556.

Katon, W., Rutter, C., Ludman, E. J., Von Korff, M., Lin, E., Simon, G., Bush, T., Walker, E., & Unutzer, J. (2001). A randomized trial of relapse prevention of depression in primary care. *Archives of General Psychiatry, 58,* 241–247.

Katon, W., & Sullivan, M. D. (1990). Depression and chronic medical illness. *Journal of Clinical Psychiatry, 51,* 3–11.

Katon, W., Von Korff, M., Lin, E., Simon, G., Walker, E., Unutzer, J., Bush, T., Russo, J., & Ludman, E. (1999). Stepped collaborative care for primary care patients with persistent symptoms of depression: A randomized trial. *Archives of General Psychiatry, 56,* 1109–1115.

Katz, I. R., & Parmelee, P. A. (1997). Overview. In R. L. Rubinstein & M. P. Lawton (Eds.), *Depression in long term and residential care: Advances in research and treatment* (pp. 1–25). New York: Springer.

Katz, R., Shaw, B. F., Vallis, M., & Kaiser, A. S. (1995). The assessment of severity and symptom patterns in depression. In E. E. Beckham & W. R. Leber (Eds.), *Handbook of depression* (2nd ed., pp. 61–85). New York: Guilford.

Kazdin, A. E. (Ed.). (1998). *Methodological issues and strategies in clinical research* (2nd ed.). Washington, DC: American Psychological Association.

Kazdin, A. E. (1999, November 26). Child and adolescent psychotherapy: It works, but why? *Chronicle of Higher Education*, p. B9.

Kazdin, A. E. (2000). Developing a research agenda for child and adolescent psychotherapy. *Archives of General Psychiatry, 57*, 829–835.

Kazdin, A. E., & Weisz, J. R. (1998). Identifying and developing empirically supported child and adolescent treatments. *Journal of Consulting and Clinical Psychology, 66*, 19–36.

Keane, T. M. (1998). Psychological and behavioral treatments of Post-Traumatic Stress Disorder. In P. E. Nathan & J. M. Gorman (Eds.), *A guide to treatments that work* (pp. 398–407). New York: Oxford University Press.

Keitner, G. I., Ryan, C. E., Miller, I. W., Kohn, R., Bishop, D. S., & Epstein, N. B. (1995). Role of the family in recovery and major depression. *American Journal of Psychiatry, 152*, 1002–1008.

Keller, M. B., McCullough, J. P., Klein, D. N., Arnow, B., Dunner, D. L., Gelenberg, A. J., Markowitz, J. C., Nemeroff, C. B., Russell, J. M., Thase, M. E., Trivedi, M. H., & Zajecka, J. (2000). A comparison of nefazodone, the cognitive behavioral-analysis system of psychotherapy, and their combination for the treatment of chronic depression. *New England Journal of Medicine, 342*, 1462–1470.

Kendall, P. C., Cantwell, D. P., & Kazdin, A. E. (1989). Depression in children and adolescents: Assessment issues and recommendations. *Cognitive Therapy and Research, 13*, 109–146.

Kendall, P. C., Hollon, S. D., Beck, A. T., Hammen, C. L., & Ingram, R. E. (1987). Issues and recommendations regarding use of the Beck Depression Inventory. *Cognitive Therapy and Research, 11*, 289–299.

Kendler, K. S., & Gardner, C. O. (1998). Boundaries of major depression: An evaluation of DSM-IV criteria. *American Journal of Psychiatry, 155*, 172–177.

Kessing, L. V. (1998). Cognitive impairment in the euthymic phase of affective disorder. *Psychological Medicine, 28*, 1027–1038.

Kessing, L. V., Andersen, P. K., Mortensen, P. B., & Bolwig, T. G. (1998). Recurrence in affective disorder I: Case register study. *British Journal of Psychiatry, 172*, 23–28.

Kessler, R. C., Borges, G., & Walters, E. E. (1999). Prevalence of and risk factors for lifetime suicide attempts in the National Comorbidity Survey. *Archives of General Psychiatry, 56*, 617–626.

Kessler, R. C., & Magee, W. J. (1993). Childhood adversities and adult depression: Basic patterns of association in a U.S. national survey. *Psychological Medicine, 23*, 679–690.

Kessler, R. C., McGonagle, K. A., Zhao, S., Nelson, C. B., Hughes, M., Eshleman, S., Wittchen, H. U., & Kendler, K. S. (1994). Lifetime and 12-month prevalence of DSM-III-R psychiatric disorders in the United States: Results from the National Comorbidity Survey. *Archives of General Psychiatry, 51*, 8–19.

Kessler, R. C., Soukup, J., Davis, R. B., Foster, D. F., Wilkey, S. A., Van Rompay, M. I., & Eisenberg, D. M. (2001). The use of complementary and alternative therapies to treat anxiety and depression in the United States. *American Journal of Psychiatry, 158,* 289–294.

Kessler, R. C., Stang, P. E., Wittchen, H. U., Ustun, T. B., Roy-Burne, P. P., & Walters, E. E. (1998). Lifetime panic-depression comorbidity in the National Comorbidity Survey. *Archives of General Psychiatry, 55,* 801–808.

Khan, A., Warner, H. A., & Brown, W. A. (2000). Symptom reduction and suicide risk in patients treated with placebo in antidepressant clinical trials: An analysis of the Food and Drug Administration database. *Archives of General Psychiatry, 57,* 311–317.

Kim, S. Y. H., Caine, E. D., Currier, G. W., Leibovici, A., & Ryan, J. M. (2001). Assessing the competence of persons with Alzheimer's disease in providing informed consent for participation in research. *American Journal of Psychiatry, 158,* 712–717.

Klein, D. N., Lewinsohn, P. M., Seeley, J. R., & Rohde, P. (2001). A family study of Major Depressive Disorder in a community sample of adolescents. *Archives of General Psychiatry, 58,* 13–20.

Klein, D. N., Norden, K. A., Ferro, T., Leader, J. B., Kasch, K. L., Klein, L. M., Schwartz, J. E., & Aronson, T. A. (1998). Thirty-month naturalistic follow-up study of early onset Dysthymic Disorder: Course, diagnostic stability, and prediction of outcome. *Journal of Abnormal Psychology, 107,* 338–348.

Klerman, G. L., Weissman, M. M., Markowitz, J., Glick, I., Wilner, P. J., Mason, B., & Shear, M. K. (1994). Medication and psychotherapy. In A. E. Bergin & S. L. Garfield (Eds.), *Handbook of psychotherapy and behavior change* (4th ed., pp. 734–782). New York: John Wiley.

Klerman, G. L., Weissman, M. M., Rounsaville, B. J., & Chevron, E. S. (1984). *Interpersonal psychotherapy of depression.* New York: Basic Books.

Kocsis, J. H., Friedman, R. A., Markowitz, J. C., Leon, A. C., Miller, N. L., Gniwesch, L., & Parides, M. (1996). Maintenance therapy for chronic depression: A controlled clinical trial of desipramine. *Archives of General Psychiatry, 53,* 769–774.

Koenig, H. G., George, L. K., & Peterson, B. L. (1998). Religiosity and remission of depression in medically ill older patients. *American Journal of Psychiatry, 155,* 536–542.

Koenig, H. G., & Kuchibhatla, M. (1998). Use of health services by hospitalized medically ill depressed elderly patients. *American Journal of Psychiatry, 155,* 871–877.

Koivumaa-Honkanen, H., Honkanen, R., Viinamaki, H., Heikkila, K., Kaprio, J., & Koskenvuo, M. (2001). Life satisfaction and suicide: A 20-year follow-up study. *American Journal of Psychiatry, 158,* 433–439.

Kolko, D. J., Brent, D. A., Baugher, M., Bridge, J., & Birmaher, B. (2000). Cognitive and family therapies for adolescent depression: Treatment specificity, mediation, and moderation. *Journal of Consulting and Clinical Psychology, 68,* 603–614.

Koocher, G. P., & Keith-Spiegel, P. (1998). *Ethics in psychology: Professional standards and cases* (2nd ed.). New York: Oxford University Press.

Kopper, B. A., & Epperson, D. L. (1996). The experience and expression of anger: Relationships with gender, gender role socialization, depression, and mental health functioning. *Journal of Counseling Psychology, 43,* 158–165.

Kovacs, M. (1996). Presentation and course of Major Depressive Disorder during childhood and later years of the life span. *Journal of the American Academy of Child and Adolescent Psychiatry, 35,* 705–715.

Kovacs, M., Akiskal, H. S., Gatsonis, C., & Parrone, P. L. (1994). Childhood-onset Dysthymic Disorder: Clinical features and prospective naturalistic outcome. *Archives of General Psychiatry, 51,* 365–374.

Kovacs, M., Devlin, B., Pollock, M., Richards, C., & Mukerji, P. (1997). A controlled family history study of childhood-onset depressive disorder. *Archives of General Psychiatry, 54,* 613–623.

Kovacs, M., Feinberg, T. L., Crouse-Novak, M. A., Paulauskas, S. L., & Finkelstein, R. (1984). Depressive disorders in childhood: I. A longitudinal prospective study of characteristics and recovery. *Archives of General Psychiatry, 41,* 229–237.

Kovacs, M., Feinberg, T. L., Crouse-Novak, M. A., Paulauskas, S. L., Pollock, M., & Finkelstein, R. (1984). Depressive disorders in childhood: II. A longitudinal study of the risk for a subsequent major depression. *Archives of General Psychiatry, 41,* 643–649.

Krug, E. G., Kresnow, M. J., Peddicord, J. P., Dahlberg, L. L., Powell, K. E., Crosby, A. E., & Annest, J. L. (1998). Suicide after natural disasters. *New England Journal of Medicine, 338,* 373–378.

Kumanyika, S. K., Van Horn, L., Bowen, D., Perri, M. G., Rolls, B. J., Czajkowski, S. M., & Schron, E. (2000). Maintenance of dietary behavior change. *Health Psychology, 19* [#1, supplement], 42–56.

Kupfer, D. J. (1999). Research in affective disorders comes of age. *American Journal of Psychiatry, 156,* 165–167.

Kupfer, D. J., Frank, E., Perel, J. M., Cornes, C., Mallinger, A. G., Thase, M. E., McEachran, A. B., & Grochocinski, V. J. (1992). Five-year outcome for maintenance therapies in recurrent depression. *Archives of General Psychiatry, 49,* 769–773.

Kurpius, S. E. R., Nicpon, M. F., & Maresh, S. E. (2001). Mood, marriage, and menopause. *Journal of Counseling Psychology, 48,* 77–84.

Kuyken, W., Kurzer, N., DeRubeis, R. J., Beck, A. T., & Brown, G. K. (2001). Response to cognitive therapy in depression: The role of maladaptive beliefs and personality disorders. *Journal of Consulting and Clinical Psychology, 69,* 560–566.

Lambert, G., Johansson, M., Agren, H., & Friberg, P. (2000). Reduced brain norepinephrine and dopamine release in treatment-refractory depressive illness: Evidence in support of the catecholamine hypothesis of mood disorders. *Archives of General Psychiatry, 57,* 787–793.

Lantz, P. M., House, J. S., Lepkowski, J. M., Williams, D. R., Mero, R. P., & Chen, J. (1998). Socioeconomic factors, health behaviors, and mortality: Results from a nationally representative prospective study of U.S. adults. *Journal of the American Medical Association, 279,* 1703–1708.

Lara, M. E., Leader, J., & Klein, D. N. (1997). The association between social support and course of depression: Is it confounded with personality? *Journal of Abnormal Psychology, 106,* 478–482.

Larson, D. B., Swyers, J. P., & McCullough, M. E. (Eds.). (1998). *Scientific research on spirituality and health: A consensus report.* Rockville, MD: National Institute for Healthcare Research.

Lave, J. R., Frank, R. G., Schulberg, H. C., & Kamlet, M. S. (1998). Cost-effectiveness of treatments for major depression in primary care practice. *Archives of General Psychiatry, 55,* 645–651.

Leahy, R. L., & Holland, S. J. (2000). *Treatment plans and interventions for depression and anxiety disorders.* New York: Guilford.

Lebowitz, B. D. (1997). Depression in the nursing home: Developments and prospects. In R. L. Rubinstein & M. P. Lawton (Eds.), *Depression in long term and residential care: Advances in research and treatment* (pp. 223–233). New York: Springer.

Lefkowitz, M. M., & Tesiny, E. P. (1985). Depression in children: Prevalence and correlates. *Journal of Consulting and Clinical Psychology, 53,* 647–656.

Leon, A. C., Keller, M. B., Warshaw, M. G., Mueller, T. I., Solomon, D. A., Coryell, W., & Endicott, J. (1999). Prospective study of fluoxetine treatment and suicidal behavior in affectively ill subjects. *American Journal of Psychiatry, 156,* 195–201.

Leshner, A. I. (1999). Science is revolutionizing our view of addiction—and what to do about it. *American Journal of Psychiatry, 156,* 1–3.

Lewinsohn, P. M., Allen, N. B., Seeley, J. R., & Gotlib, I. H. (1999). First onset versus recurrence of depression: Differential processes of psychosocial risk. *Journal of Abnormal Psychology, 108,* 483–489.

Lewinsohn, P. M., Gotlib, I. H., & Seeley, J. R. (1997). Depression-related psychosocial variables: Are they specific to depression in adolescents? *Journal of Abnormal Psychology, 106,* 365–375.

Lewinsohn, P. M., Joiner, T. E., & Rohde, P. (2001). Evaluation of cognitive diathesis–stress models in predicting Major Depressive Disorder in adolescents. *Journal of Abnormal Psychology, 110,* 203–215.

Lewinsohn, P. M., Rohde, P., & Seeley, J. R. (1994). Psychosocial risk factors for future adolescent suicide attempts. *Journal of Consulting and Clinical Psychology, 62,* 297–305.

Lewinsohn, P. M., Rohde, P., & Seeley, J. R. (1996). Adolescent suicidal ideation and attempts: Prevalence, risk factors, and clinical implications. *Clinical Psychology: Science and Practice, 3,* 25–46.

Lewinsohn, P. M., Rohde, P., & Seeley, J. R. (1998). Major Depressive Disorder in older adolescents: Prevalence, risk factors, and clinical implications. *Clinical Psychology Review, 18,* 765–794.

Lewinsohn, P. M., Solomon, A., Seeley, J. R., & Zeiss, A. (2000). Clinical implications of "subthreshold" depressive symptoms. *Journal of Abnormal Psychology, 109,* 345–351.

Lin, E. H. B., Simon, G. E., Katon, W. J., Russo, J. E., Von Korff, M., Bush, T. M., Ludman, E. J., & Walker, E. A. (1999). Can enhanced acute-phase treatment of depression improve long-term outcomes? A report of randomized trials in primary care. *American Journal of Psychiatry, 156,* 643–645.

Linehan, M. M., Heard, H. L., & Armstrong, H. E. (1993). Naturalistic follow-up of a behavioral treatment for chronically parasuicidal borderline patients. *Archives of General Psychiatry, 50,* 971–974.

Little, J. T., Reynolds, C. F., Dew, M. A., Frank, E., Begley, A. E., Miller, M. D., Cornes, C., Mazumdar, S., Perel, J. M., & Kupfer, D. J. (1998). How common is resistance to treatment in recurrent, nonpsychotic geriatric depression? *American Journal of Psychiatry, 155,* 1035–1038.

Lydiard, R. B., Brawman-Mintzer, O., & Ballenger, J. C. (1996). Recent developments in the psychopharmacology of anxiety disorders. *Journal of Consulting and Clinical Psychology, 64,* 660–668.

Lyness, J. M., Duberstein, P. R., King, D. A., Cox, C., & Caine, E. D. (1998). Medical illness burden, trait neuroticism, and depression in older primary care patients. *American Journal of Psychiatry, 155,* 969–971.

Malone, R. P., Delaney, M. A., Luebbert, J. F., Cater, J., & Campbell, M. (2000). A double-blind placebo-controlled study of lithium in hospitalized aggressive children and adolescents with conduct disorder. *Archives of General Psychiatry, 57,* 649–654.

Mamdani, M. M., Parikh, S. V., Austin, P. C., & Upshur, R. E. G. (2000). Use of antidepressants among elderly subjects: Trends and contributing factors. *American Journal of Psychiatry, 157,* 360–367.

Mann, J. J., Huang, Y. Y., Underwood, M. D., Kassir, S. A., Oppenheim, S., Kelly, T. M., Dwork, A. J., & Arango, V. (2000). A serotonin transporter gene promoter polymorphism (5–HTTLPR) and prefrontal cortical binding in major depression and suicide. *Archives of General Psychiatry, 57,* 729–738.

Maris, R. W., Berman, A. L., & Silverman, M. M. (2000). *Comprehensive textbook of suicidology.* New York: Guilford.

Markowitz, J. C. (1998). *Interpersonal psychotherapy for Dysthymic Disorder.* Washington, DC: American Psychiatric Press.

Markowitz, J. C., Kocsis, J. H., Fishman, B., Spielman, L. A., Jacobsberg, L. B., Frances, A. J., Klerman, G. L., & Perry, S. W. (1998). Treatment of depressive symptoms in human immunodeficiency virus–positive patients. *Archives of General Psychiatry, 55,* 452–457.

Martin, D. J., Garske, J. P., & Davis, M. K. (2000). Relation of the therapeutic alliance with outcome and other variables: A meta-analytic review. *Journal of Consulting and Clinical Psychology, 68,* 438–450.

Marx, E. M., Williams, J. M. G., & Claridge, G. C. (1992). Depression and social problem solving. *Journal of Abnormal Psychology, 101,* 78–86.

Massie, M. J., & Popkin, M. K. (1998). Depressive disorders. In J. C. Holland (Ed.), *Psycho-Oncology* (pp. 518–540). New York: Oxford University Press.

Mazure, C. M. (1998). Life stressors as risk factors in depression. *Clinical Psychology: Science and Practice, 5,* 291–313.

McCrady, B. S., & Ziedonis, D. (2001). American Psychiatric Association Practice Guideline for substance use disorders. *Behavior Therapy, 32*, 309–336.

McCullough, J. P. (2000). *Treatment for chronic depression: Cognitive behavioral analysis system of psychotherapy.* New York: Guilford.

McCullough, M. E. (1999). Research on religion-accommodative counseling: Review and meta-analysis. *Journal of Counseling Psychology, 46*, 92–98.

McDaniel, D. M., & Richards, S. (1990). Coping with dysphoria: Gender differences in college students. *Journal of Clinical Psychology, 46*, 896–899.

McGrath, P. J., Stewart, J. W., Janal, M. N., Petkova, E., Quitkin, F. M., & Klein, D. F. (2000). A placebo-controlled study of fluoxetine versus imipramine in the acute treatment of Atypical Depression. *American Journal of Psychiatry, 157*, 344–350.

McGuffin, P., Katz, R., Watkins, S., & Rutherford, J. (1996). A hospital-based twin register of the heritability of *DSM-IV* unipolar depression. *Archives of General Psychiatry, 53*, 129–136.

McKenna, M. C., Zevon, M. A., Corn, B., & Rounds, J. (1999). Psychosocial factors and the development of breast cancer: A meta-analysis. *Health Psychology, 18*, 520–531.

McLean, P. D., Woody, S., Taylor, S., & Koch, W. J. (1998). Comorbid Panic Disorder and major depression: Implications for cognitive-behavioral therapy. *Journal of Consulting and Clinical Psychology, 66*, 240–247.

Meier, S. T., & Davis, S. R. (1997). *The elements of counseling* (3rd ed.). Pacific Grove, CA: Brooks/Cole.

Merluzzi, T. V., & Sanchez, M. A. M. (1997). Assessment of self-efficacy and coping with cancer: Development and validation of the Cancer Behavior Inventory. *Health Psychology, 16*, 163–170.

Meston, C. M., & Frohlich, P. F. (2000). The neurobiology of sexual function. *Archives of General Psychiatry, 57*, 1012–1030.

Meyer, J. H., Kapur, S., Eisfeld, B., Brown, G. M., Houle, S., DaSilva, J., Wilson, A. A., Rafi-Tari, S., Mayberg, H. S., & Kennedy, S. H. (2001). The effect of paroxetine on 5-HT2A receptors in depression: An [18F] setoperone PET imaging study. *American Journal of Psychiatry, 158*, 78–85.

Meyerowitz, B. E., Richardson, J., Hudson, S., & Leedham, B. (1998). Ethnicity and cancer outcomes: Behavioral and psychosocial considerations. *Psychological Bulletin, 123*, 47–70.

Miller, G. E., & Cohen, S. (2001). Psychological interventions and the immune system: A meta-analytic review and critique. *Health Psychology, 20*, 47–63.

Mineka, S., Watson, D., & Clark, L. A. (1998). Comorbidity of anxiety and unipolar mood disorders. *Annual Review of Psychology, 49*, 377–412.

Moeller, D. M., Richards, S., Hooker, K. A., & Ursino, A. A. D. (1992). Gender differences in the effectiveness of coping with dysphoria: A longitudinal study. *Counselling Psychology Quarterly, 5*, 349–358.

Moncrieff, J., Wessely, S., & Hardy, R. (1998). Meta-analysis of trials comparing antidepressants with active placebos. *British Journal of Psychiatry, 172*, 227–231.

Monroe, S. M., Rhode, P., Seeley, J. R., & Lewinsohn, P. M. (1999). Life events and depression in adolescence: Relationship loss as a prospective risk factor for first onset of Major Depressive Disorder. *Journal of Abnormal Psychology, 108,* 606–614.

Moos, R. H., Cronkite, R. C., & Moos, B. S. (1998). Family and extrafamily resources and the 10-year course of treated depression. *Journal of Abnormal Psychology, 107,* 450–460.

Morin, C. M., Colecchi, C., Stone, J., Sood, R., & Brink, D. (1999). Behavioral and pharmacological therapies for late-life insomnia: A randomized controlled trial. *Journal of the American Medical Association, 281,* 991–999.

Mort, J. R., & Aparasu, R. R. (2000). Prescribing potentially inappropriate psychotropic medications to the ambulatory elderly. *Archives of Internal Medicine, 160,* 2825–2831.

Muehrer, P. (2000). Research on adherence, behavior change, and mental health: A workshop overview. *Health Psychology, 19,* 304–307.

Mueller, T. I., Leon, A. C., Keller, M. B., Solomon, D. A., Endicott, J., Coryell, W., Warshaw, M., & Maser, J. D. (1999). Recurrence after recovery from Major Depressive Disorder during 15 years of observational follow-up. *American Journal of Psychiatry, 156,* 1000–1006.

Mufson, L., & Moreau, D. (1998). Interpersonal psychotherapy for adolescent depression. In J. C. Markowitz (Ed.), *Interpersonal psychotherapy* (pp. 35–66). Washington, DC: American Psychiatric Press.

Mufson, L., Weissman, M. M., Moreau, D., & Garfinkel, R. (1999). Efficacy of interpersonal psychotherapy for depressed adolescents. *Archives of General Psychiatry, 56,* 573–579.

Murphy, J. M., Laird, N. M., Monson, R. R., Sobol, A. M., & Leighton, A. H. (2000). A 40-year perspective on the prevalence of depression: The Stirling County Study. *Archives of General Psychiatry, 57,* 209–215.

Murphy, J. M., Monson, R. R., Laird, N. M., Sobol, A. M., & Leighton, A. H. (2000). A comparison of diagnostic interviews for depression in the Stirling County Study: Challenges for psychiatric epidemiology. *Archives of General Psychiatry, 57,* 230–236.

Musselman, D. L., Evans, D. L., & Nemeroff, C. B. (1998). The relationship of depression to cardiovascular disease: Epidemiology, biology, and treatment. *Archives of General Psychiatry, 55,* 580–592.

Nathan, P. E. (1998). Practice guidelines: Not yet ideal. *American Psychologist, 53,* 290–299.

Nathan, P. E., Stuart, S. P., & Dolan, S. L. (2000). Research on psychotherapy efficacy and effectiveness: Between Scylla and Charybdis? *Psychological Bulletin, 126,* 964–981.

National Institute of Child Health and Human Development (NICHHD), Early Child Care Research Network. (1999). Chronicity of maternal depressive symptoms, maternal sensitivity, and child functioning at 36 months. *Developmental Psychology, 35,* 1297–1310.

National Institutes of Health (NIH), Consensus Development Panel on Depression in Late Life. (1992). Diagnosis and treatment of depression in late life. *Journal of the American Medical Association, 268,* 1018–1024.

Nelson, C. B., Heath, A. C., & Kessler, R. C. (1998). Temporal progression of alcohol dependence symptoms in the U.S. household population: Results from the National Comorbidity Survey. *Journal of Consulting and Clinical Psychology, 66,* 474–483.

Nelson, J. C., Kennedy, J. S., Pollock, B. G., Laghrissi-Thode, F., Narayan, M., Nobler, M. S., Robin, D. W., Gergel, I., McCafferty, J., & Roose, S. (1999). Treatment of major depression with nortriptyline and paroxetine in patients with ischemic heart disease. *American Journal of Psychiatry, 156,* 1024–1028.

Nemeroff, C. B., & Schatzberg, A. F. (1998). Pharmacological treatment of unipolar depression. In P. E. Nathan & J. M. Gorman (Eds.), *A guide to treatments that work* (pp. 212–225). New York: Oxford University Press.

Nesse, R. M. (2000). Is depression an adaptation? *Archives of General Psychiatry, 57,* 14–20.

Newman, D. L., Moffitt, T. E., Caspi, A., & Silva, P. A. (1998). Comorbid mental disorders: Implications for treatment and sample selection. *Journal of Abnormal Psychology, 107,* 305–311.

Nezlek, J. B., Hamptom, C. P., & Shean, G. D. (2000). Clinical depression and day-to-day social interaction in a community sample. *Journal of Abnormal Psychology, 109,* 11–19.

Nezu, A. M., Nezu, C. M., Friedman, S. H., Faddis, S., & Houts, P. S. (1998). *Helping cancer patients cope: A problem-solving approach.* Washington, DC: American Psychological Association.

Nezu, A. M., Nezu, C. M., & Perri, M. G. (1989). *Problem-solving therapy for depression: Theory, research, and clinical guidelines.* New York: John Wiley.

Nezu, A. M., Ronan, G. F., Meadows, E. A., & McClure, K. S. (Eds.). (2000). *Practitioner's guide to empirically based measures of depression.* Norwell, MA: Kluwer/Plenum.

Nicassio, P. M., & Smith, T. W. (Eds.). (1995). *Managing chronic illness: A biopsychosocial perspective.* Washington, DC: American Psychological Association.

Nicklin, J. L. (2000, June 9). Arrests at colleges surge for alcohol and drug violations. *Chronicle of Higher Education,* pp. A48–A50.

Niederehe, G., & Schneider, L. S. (1998). Treatments for depression and anxiety in the aged. In P. E. Nathan & J. M. Gorman (Eds.), *A guide to treatments that work* (pp. 270–287). New York: Oxford University Press.

Nolen-Hoeksema, S. (1987). Sex differences in unipolar depression: Evidence and theory. *Psychological Bulletin, 101,* 259–282.

Nolen-Hoeksema, S., & Girgus, J. S. (1994). The emergence of gender differences in depression during adolescence. *Psychological Bulletin, 115,* 424–443.

Nolen-Hoeksema, S., Girgus, J. S., & Seligman, M. E. P. (1992). Predictors and consequences of childhood depressive symptoms: A 5-year longitudinal study. *Journal of Abnormal Psychology, 101,* 405–422.

Nolen-Hoeksema, S., Wolfson, A., Mumme, D., & Guskin, K. (1995). Helplessness in children of depressed and non-depressed mothers. *Developmental Psychology, 31,* 377–387.

O'Connor, T. G., McGuire, S., Reiss, D., Hetherington, E. M., & Plomin, R. (1998). Co-occurrence of depressive symptoms and antisocial behavior in adolescence: A common genetic liability. *Journal of Abnormal Psychology, 107,* 27–37.

O'Hara, M. W., Stuart, S., Gorman, L. L., & Wenzel, A. (2000). Efficacy of interpersonal psychotherapy for Postpartum Depression. *Archives of General Psychiatry, 57,* 1039–1045.

Olfson, M., Kessler, R. C., Berglund, P. A., & Lin, E. (1998). Psychiatric disorder onset and first treatment contact in the United States and Ontario. *American Journal of Psychiatry, 155,* 1415–1422.

Olfson, M., Marcus, S. C., & Pincus, H. A. (1999). Trends in office-based psychiatric practice. *American Journal of Psychiatry, 156,* 451–457.

Olfson, M., Marcus, S. C., Pincus, H. A., Zito, J. M., Thompson, J. W., & Zarin, D. A. (1998). Antidepressant prescribing practices of outpatient psychiatrists. *Archives of General Psychiatry, 55,* 310–316.

Orbach, I., Mikulincer, M., Stein, D., & Cohen, O. (1998). Self-representation of suicidal adolescents. *Journal of Abnormal Psychology, 107,* 435–439.

Ormel, J. (2000). Synchrony of change in depression and disability: What next? *Archives of General Psychiatry, 57,* 381–382.

Ormel, J., Oldehinkel, A. J., & Brilman, E. I. (2001). The interplay and etiological continuity of neuroticism, difficulties, and life events in the etiology of major and subsyndromal first and recurrent depressive episodes in later life. *American Journal of Psychiatry, 158,* 885–891.

Othmer, E., & Othmer, S. C. (1994). *The clinical interview using DSM-IV: Vol. 1. Fundamentals.* Washington, DC: American Psychiatric Press.

Parker, G., Brown, L., & Blignault, I. (1986). Coping behaviors as predictors of the course of clinical depression. *Archives of General Psychiatry, 43,* 561–565.

Paykel, E. S., Scott, J., Teasdale, J. D., Johnson, A. L., Garland, A., Moore, R., Jenaway, A., Cornwall, P. L., Hayhurst, H., Abbott, R., & Pope, M. (1999). Prevention of relapse in residual depression by cognitive therapy: A controlled trial. *Archives of General Psychiatry, 56,* 829–835.

Peirce, R. S., Frone, M. R., Russell, M., Cooper, M. L., & Mudar, P. (2000). A longitudinal model of social contact, social support, depression, and alcohol use. *Health Psychology, 19,* 28–38.

Penninx, B. W. J. H., Beekman, A. T. F., Honig, A., Deeg, D. J. H., Schoevers, R. A., Van Eijk, J. T. M., & Van Tilburg, W. (2001). Depression and cardiac mortality: Results from a community-based longitudinal study. *Archives of General Psychiatry, 58,* 221–227.

Penninx, B. W. J. H., Geerlings, S. W., Deeg, D. J. H., Van Eijk, J. T. M., Van Tilburg, W., & Beekman, A. T. F. (1999). Minor and major depression and the risk of death in older persons. *Archives of General Psychiatry, 56,* 889–895.

Penninx, B. W. J. H., Van Tilburg, W., Boeke, A. J. P., Deeg, D. J. H., Kriegsman, D. M. W., & Van Eijk, J. T. M. (1998). Effects of social support and personal coping resources on depressive symptoms: Different for various chronic diseases? *Health Psychology,* *17,* 551–558.

Perri, M. G. (1998). The maintenance of treatment effects in the long-term management of obesity. *Clinical Psychology: Science and Practice, 5,* 526–543.

Persons, J. B. (1989). *Cognitive therapy in practice: A case formulation approach.* New York: Norton.

Persons, J. B., Davidson, J., & Tompkins, M. A. (2001). *Essential components of cognitive-behavior therapy for depression.* Washington, DC: American Psychological Association.

Physicians' Desk Reference (54th ed.). (2000). Montvale, NJ: Medical Economics Company.

Piccinelli, M., Rucci, P., Ustun, B., & Simon, G. (1999). Typologies of anxiety, depression and somatization symptoms among primary care attenders with no formal mental disorder. *Psychological Medicine, 29,* 677–688.

Piccinelli, M., & Wilkinson, G. (2000). Gender differences in depression: Critical review. *British Journal of Psychiatry, 177,* 486–492.

Pilowsky, D. J., Wu, L. T., & Anthony, J. C. (1999). Panic attacks and suicide attempts in mid-adolescence. *American Journal of Psychiatry, 156,* 1545–1549.

Pincus, H. A., Zarin, D. A., Tanielian, T. L., Johnson, J. L., West, J. C., Pettit, A. R., Marcus, S. C., Kessler, R. C., & McIntyre, J. S. (1999). Psychiatric patients and treatments in 1997: Findings from the American Psychiatric Practice Research Network. *Archives of General Psychiatry, 56,* 441–449.

Pine, D. S., Cohen, E., Cohen, P., & Brook, J. (1999). Adolescent depressive symptoms as predictors of adult depression: Moodiness or mood disorder? *American Journal of Psychiatry, 156,* 133–135.

Pine, D. S., Cohen, P., Gurley, D., Brook, J., & Ma, Y. (1998). The risk for early-adulthood anxiety and depressive disorders in adolescents with anxiety and depressive disorders. *Archives of General Psychiatry, 55,* 56–64.

Pope, K. S., & Vasquez, M. J. T. (1998). *Ethics in psychotherapy and counseling: A practical guide* (2nd ed.). San Francisco: Jossey-Bass.

Posener, J. A., DeBattista, C., Williams, G. H., Kraemer, H. C., Kalehzan, B. M., & Schatzberg, A. F. (2000). 24-Hour monitoring of cortisol and corticotropin secretion in psychotic and nonpsychotic major depression. *Archives of General Psychiatry, 57,* 755–760.

Prince, M. J., Harwood, R. H., Thomas, A., & Mann, A. H. (1998). A prospective population-based cohort study of the effects of disablement and social *milieu* on the onset and maintenance of late-life depression: The Gospel Oak Project VII. *Psychological Medicine, 28,* 337–350.

Prince, S. E., & Jacobson, N. S. (1995). Couple and family therapy for depression. In E. E. Beckham & W. R. Leber (Eds.), *Handbook of depression* (2nd ed., pp. 404–424). New York: Guilford.

Quindlen, A. (1999, November 29). The C word in the hallways. *Newsweek,* p. 112.

Quindlen, A. (2001, July 2). Playing God on no sleep. *Newsweek*, p. 64.

Quitkin, F. M., Rabkin, J. G., Gerald, J., Davis, J. M., & Klein, D. F. (2000). Validity of clinical trials of antidepressants. *American Journal of Psychiatry, 157*, 327–337.

Radloff, L. S. (1977). The CES-D Scale: A self-report depression scale for research in the general population. *Applied Psychological Measurement, 1*, 385–401.

Radloff, L. S., & Locke, B. Z. (1986). The Community Mental Health Survey and the CES-D Scale. In M. M. Weissman, J. Meyers, & C. Ross (Eds.), *Community surveys for psychiatric disorders* (pp. 177–189). New Brunswick, NJ: Rutgers University Press.

Rankin, E. A. (Ed.). (2000). *Quick reference for psychopharmacology*. Stamford, CT: Thomson Learning.

Rauch, S. L., & Jenike, M. A. (1998). Pharmacological treatment of Obsessive-Compulsive Disorder. In P. E. Nathan & J. M. Gorman (Eds.), *A guide to treatments that work* (pp. 358–376). New York: Oxford University Press.

Ravindran, A. V., Anisman, H., Merali, Z., Charbonneau, Y., Telner, J., Bialik, R. J., Wiens, A., Ellis, J., & Griffiths, J. (1999). Treatment of primary dysthymia with group cognitive therapy and pharmacotherapy: Clinical symptoms and functional impairments. *American Journal of Psychiatry, 156*, 1608–1617.

Regier, D. A., Boyd, J. H., Burke, J. D., Rae, D. S., Myers, J. K., Kramer, M., Robins, L. N., George, L. K., Karno, M., & Locke, B. Z. (1988). One-month prevalence of mental disorders in the United States: Based on five epidemiologic catchment area sites. *Archives of General Psychiatry, 45*, 977–986.

Regier, D. A., Rae, D. S., Narrow, W. E., Kaelber, C. T., & Schatzberg, A. F. (1998). Prevalence of anxiety disorders and their comorbidity with mood and addictive disorders. *British Journal of Psychiatry, 173*, 24–28.

Rehm, L. P. (1977). A self-control model of depression. *Behavior Therapy, 8*, 787–804.

Reinecke, M. A., Ryan, N. E., & DuBois, D. L. (1998). Cognitive-behavioral therapy of depression and depressive symptoms during adolescence: A review and meta-analysis. *Journal of the American Academy of Child and Adolescent Psychiatry, 37*, 26–34.

Reinherz, H. Z., Giaconia, R. M., Hauf, A. M. C., Wasserman, M. S., & Silverman, A. B. (1999). Major depression in the transition to adulthood: Risks and impairments. *Journal of Abnormal Psychology, 108*, 500–510.

Reisberg, L. (2000, January 28). Student stress is rising, especially among women. *Chronicle of Higher Education*, pp. A49–A51.

Reynolds, C. F., Frank, E., Perel, J. M., Imber, S. D., Cornes, C., Miller, M. D., Mazumdar, S., Houck, P. R., Dew, M. A., Stack, J. A., Pollock, B. G., & Kupfer, D. J. (1999). Nortriptyline and interpersonal psychotherapy as maintenance therapies for recurrent major depression: A randomized controlled trial in patients older than 59 years. *Journal of the American Medical Association, 281*, 39–45.

Reynolds, C. F., Miller, M. D., Mulsant, B. H., Dew, M. A., & Pollock, B. G. (2000). Pharmacotherapy of geriatric depression: Taking the long view. In G. M. Williamson, D. R. Shaffer, & P. A. Parmelee (Eds.), *Physical illness and depression in older adults: A handbook of theory, research, and practice* (pp. 277–294). New York: Kluwer/Plenum.

Richards, S. (1999, Fall). Depression and relapse. *Outlook* (Society of Behavioral Medicine), pp. 5–6.

Richards, S., & Perri, M. G. (1978). Do self-control treatments last? An evaluation of behavioral problem solving and faded counselor contact as treatment maintenance strategies. *Journal of Counseling Psychology, 25,* 376–383.

Richards, S., & Perri, M. G. (1999). Depression and chronic health problems. *Annals of Behavioral Medicine, 21,* S209.

Richards, S., & Perri, M. G. (2000). The comorbidity of depression with cancer and cardiovascular disease. *Annals of Behavioral Medicine, 22,* S219.

Richards, S., & Perri, M. G. (2001, Summer). Depression and suicide in general health care patients. *Outlook* (Society of Behavioral Medicine), pp. 4–5.

Roberts, A. R. (Ed.). (2000). *Crisis intervention handbook: Assessment, treatment, and research* (2nd ed.). New York: Oxford University Press.

Roberts, R. E., Attkisson, C. C., & Rosenblatt, A. (1998). Prevalence of psychopathology among children and adolescents. *American Journal of Psychiatry, 155,* 715–725.

Roberts, R. E., Shema, S. J., Kaplan, G. A., & Strawbridge, W. J. (2000). Sleep complaints and depression in an aging cohort: A prospective perspective. *American Journal of Psychiatry, 157,* 81–88.

Robinson, R. G., Schultz, S. K., Castillo, C., Kopel, T., Kosier, J. T., Newman, R. M., Curdue, K., Petracca, G., & Starkstein, S. E. (2000). Nortriptyline versus fluoxetine in the treatment of depression and short-term recovery after stroke: A placebo-controlled, double-blind study. *American Journal of Psychiatry, 157,* 351–359.

Roose, S. P., Laghrissi-Thode, F., Kennedy, J. S., Nelson, J. C., Bigger, J. T., Pollock, B. G., Gaffney, A., Narayan, M., Finkel, M. S., McCafferty, J., & Gergel, I. (1998). Comparison of paroxetine and nortriptyline in depressed patients with ischemic heart disease. *Journal of the American Medical Association, 279,* 287–291.

Rosen, C. S. (2000). Is the sequencing of change processes by stage consistent across health problems? A meta-analysis. *Health Psychology, 19,* 593–604.

Rossello, J., & Bernal, G. (1999). The efficacy of cognitive-behavioral and interpersonal treatments for depression in Puerto Rican adolescents. *Journal of Consulting and Clinical Psychology, 67,* 734–745.

Rost, K., Zhang, M., Fortney, J., Smith, J., & Smith, G. R. (1998). Expenditures for the treatment of major depression. *American Journal of Psychiatry, 155,* 883–888.

Rotheram-Borus, M. J., Piacentini, J., Cantwell, C., Belin, T. R., & Song, J. (2000). The 18-month impact of an emergency room intervention for adolescent female suicide attempters. *Journal of Consulting and Clinical Psychology, 68,* 1081–1093.

Roy-Byrne, P. P., & Cowley, D. S. (1998). Pharmacological treatment of Panic, Generalized Anxiety, and Phobic Disorders. In P. E. Nathan & J. M. Gorman (Eds.), *A guide to treatments that work* (pp. 319–338). New York: Oxford University Press.

Rozanski, A., Blumenthal, J. A., & Kaplan, J. (1999). Impact of psychological factors on the pathogenesis of cardiovascular disease and implications for therapy. *Circulation, 99,* 2192–2217.

Rudd, M. D., & Joiner, T. (1998). The assessment, management, and treatment of suicidality: Toward clinically informed and balanced standards of care. *Clinical Psychology: Science and Practice, 5,* 135–150.

Rudd, M. D., Rajab, M. H., Orman, D. T., Stulman, D. A., Joiner, T., & Dixon, W. (1996). Effectiveness of an outpatient intervention targeting suicidal young adults: Preliminary results. *Journal of Consulting and Clinical Psychology, 64,* 179–190.

Rueter, M. A., Scaramella, L., Wallace, L. E., & Conger, R. D. (1999). First onset of depressive or anxiety disorders predicted by the longitudinal course of internalizing symptoms and parent-adolescent disagreements. *Archives of General Psychiatry, 56,* 726–732.

Sacco, W. P., & Beck, A. T. (1995). Cognitive theory and therapy. In E. E. Beckham & W. R. Leber (Eds.), *Handbook of depression* (2nd ed., pp. 329–351). New York: Guilford.

Sackeim, H. A., Haskett, R. F., Mulsant, B. H., Thase, M. E., Mann, J. J., Pettinati, H. M., Greenberg, R. M., Crowe, R. R., Cooper, T. B., & Prudic, J. (2001). Continuation pharmacotherapy in the prevention of relapse following electroconvulsive therapy: A randomized controlled trial. *Journal of the American Medical Association, 285,* 1299–1307.

Sadowski, H., Ugarte, B., Kolvin, I., Kaplan, C., & Barnes, J. (1999). Early life family disadvantages and major depression in adulthood. *British Journal of Psychiatry, 174,* 112–120.

Safran, J. D. (1998). *Widening the scope of cognitive therapy: The therapeutic relationship, emotion, and the process of change.* Northvale, CA: Jossey-Bass.

Safran, J. D., & Segal, Z. V. (1990). *Interpersonal process in cognitive therapy.* New York: Basic Books.

Salovey, P., Bedell, B. T., Detweiler, J. B., & Mayer, J. D. (1999). Coping intelligently: Emotional intelligence and the coping process. In C. R. Snyder (Ed.), *Coping: The psychology of what works* (pp. 141–164). New York: Oxford University Press.

Salzman, C. (1999a). Not all psychiatric research is bad! *American Journal of Psychiatry, 156,* 987–988.

Salzman, C. (1999b). Treatment of the suicidal patient with psychotropic drugs and ECT. In D. G. Jacobs (Ed.), *The Harvard Medical School guide to suicide assessment and intervention* (pp. 372–382). San Francisco: Jossey-Bass.

Sanders, M. R., & McFarland, M. (2000). Treatment of depressed mothers with disruptive children: A controlled evaluation of cognitive behavioral family intervention. *Behavior Therapy, 31,* 89–112.

Sanderson, W. C., Beck, A. T., & Beck, J. (1990). Syndrome comorbidity in patients with major depression or dysthymia: Prevalence and temporal relationships. *American Journal of Psychiatry, 147,* 1025–1028.

Santor, D. A., & Coyne, J. C. (2001). Evaluating the continuity of symptomatology between depressed and nondepressed individuals. *Journal of Abnormal Psychology, 110,* 216–225.

Sargent, P. A., Kjaer, K. H., Bench, C. J., Rabiner, E. A., Messa, C., Meyer, J., Gunn, R. N., Grasby, P. M., & Cowen, P. J. (2000). Brain serotonin 1A receptor binding measured by positron emission tomography with [11C] WAY-100635: Effects of depression and antidepressant treatment. *Archives of General Psychiatry, 57,* 174–180.

Schatzberg, A. F. (2000). Pros and cons of Prozac and its relatives. *American Journal of Psychiatry, 157,* 323–325.

Schatzberg, A. F., & Nemeroff, C. B. (Eds.). (1998). *Textbook of psychopharmacology* (2nd ed.). Washington, DC: American Psychiatric Press.

Schulberg, H. C., Katon, W., Simon, G. E., & Rush, A. J. (1998). Treating major depression in primary care practice: An update of the Agency for Health Care Policy and Research Practice Guidelines. *Archives of General Psychiatry, 55,* 1121–1127.

Schutte, K. K., Hearst, J., & Moos, R. H. (1997). Gender differences in the relations between depressive symptoms and drinking behavior among problem drinkers: A three-wave study. *Journal of Consulting and Clinical Psychology, 65,* 392–404.

Schwartz, J. A. J., Gladstone, T. R. G., & Kaslow, N. J. (1998). Depressive disorders. In T. H. Ollendick & M. Hersen (Eds.), *Handbook of child psychopathology* (3rd ed., pp. 269–289). New York: Plenum.

Scogin, F., Floyd, M., Jamison, C., Ackerson, J., Landreville, P., & Bissonnette, L. (1996). Negative outcomes: What is the evidence on self-administered treatments? *Journal of Consulting and Clinical Psychology, 64,* 1086–1089.

Scogin, F., & McElreath, L. (1994). Efficacy of psychosocial treatments for geriatric depression: A quantitative review. *Journal of Consulting and Clinical Psychology, 62,* 69–74.

Seligman, M. E. P. (1975). *Helplessness: On depression, development and death.* San Francisco: Freeman.

Seligman, M. E. P. (1991). *Learned optimism.* New York: Knopf.

Seligman, M. E. P., & Csikszentmihalyi, M. (Eds.). (2000). Special issue on happiness, excellence, and optimal human functioning. *American Psychologist, 55,* 5–183.

Seroczynski, A. D., Cole, D. A., & Maxwell, S. E. (1997). Cumulative and compensatory effects of competence and incompetence on depressive symptoms in children. *Journal of Abnormal Psychology, 106,* 586–597.

Shaw, B. F., Elkin, I., Yamaguchi, J., Olmsted, M., Vallis, T. M., Dobson, K. S., Lowery, A., Sotsky, S. M., Watkins, J. T., & Imber, S. D. (1999). Therapist competence ratings in relation to clinical outcome in cognitive therapy of depression. *Journal of Consulting and Clinical Psychology, 67,* 837–846.

Shea, C. (1995, June 16). Suicide signals: Harvard tragedy raises issue of when and how campus officials might intervene. *Chronicle of Higher Education,* pp. A35–A36.

Shea, C. (1998, January 30). Why depression strikes more women than men: "Ruminative coping" may provide answers. *Chronicle of Higher Education,* p. A14.

Shea, M. T., Elkin, I., Imber, S. D., Sotsky, S. M., Watkins, J. T., Collins, J. F., Pilkonis, P. A., Beckham, E., Glass, D. R., Dolan, R. T., & Parloff, M. B. (1992). Course of depressive symptoms over follow-up: Findings from the National Institute of Mental Health Treatment of Depression Collaborative Research Program. *Archives of General Psychiatry, 49,* 782–787.

Sherbourne, C. D., Hays, R. D., & Wells, K. B. (1995). Personal and psychosocial risk factors for physical and mental health outcomes and course of depression among depressed patients. *Journal of Consulting and Clinical Psychology, 63*, 345–355.

Sherbourne, C. D., Wells, K. B., Duan, N., Miranda, J., Unutzer, J., Jaycox, L., Schoenbaum, M., Meredith, L. S., & Rubenstein, L. V. (2001). Long-term effectiveness of disseminating quality improvement for depression in primary care. *Archives of General Psychiatry, 58*, 696–703.

Silberg, J., Pickles, A., Rutter, M., Hewitt, J., Simonoff, E., Maes, H., Carbonneau, R., Murrelle, L., Foley, D., & Eaves, L. (1999). The influence of genetic factors and life stress on depression among adolescent girls. *Archives of General Psychiatry, 56*, 225–232.

Simon, G. E., Manning W. G., Katzelnick, D. J., Pearson, S. D., Henk, H. J., & Helstad, C. P. (2001). Cost-effectiveness of systematic depression treatment for high utilizers of general medical care. *Archives of General Psychiatry, 58*, 181–187.

Simpson, H. B., Nee, J. C., & Endicott, J. (1997). First-episode major depression: Few sex differences in course. *Archives of General Psychiatry, 54*, 633–639.

Sloan, R. P., Bagiella, E., & Powell, T. (1999, February 20). Religion, spirituality, and medicine. *Lancet, 353*, 664–667.

Small, G. W., Rabins, P. V., Barry, P. P., Buckholtz, N. S., DeKosky, S. T., Ferris, S. H., Finkel, S. I., Gwyther, L. P., Khachaturian, Z. S., Lebowitz, B. D., McRae, T. D., Morris, J. C., Oakley, F., Schneider, L. S., Streim, J. E., Sunderland, T., Teri, L. A., & Tune, L. E. (1997). Diagnosis and treatment of Alzheimer disease and related disorders. *Journal of the American Medical Association, 278*, 1363–1371.

Snyder, C. R. (Ed.). (1999). *Coping: The psychology of what works.* New York: Oxford University Press.

Solomon, D. A., Keller, M. B., Leon, A. C., Mueller, T. I., Lavori, P. W., Shea, M. T., Coryell, W., Warshaw, M., Turvey, C., Maser, J. D., & Endicott, J. (2000). Multiple recurrences of Major Depressive Disorder. *American Journal of Psychiatry, 157*, 229–233.

Solomon, D. A., Keller, M. B., Leon, A. C., Mueller, T. I., Shea, M. T., Warshaw, M., Maser, J. D., Coryell, W., & Endicott, J. (1997). Recovery from major depression: A 10-year prospective follow-up across multiple episodes. *Archives of General Psychiatry, 54*, 1001–1006.

Sommers-Flanagan, J., & Sommers-Flanagan, R. (1995). Intake interviewing with suicidal patients: A systematic approach. *Professional Psychology: Research and Practice, 26*, 41–47.

Spanier, C., & Frank, E. (1998). Maintenance interpersonal psychotherapy: A preventive treatment for depression. In J. C. Markowitz (Ed.), *Interpersonal psychotherapy* (pp. 67–97). Washington, DC: American Psychiatric Press.

Special to reveal Wallace's "dark days." (1998, January 6). *Lubbock Avalanche-Journal,* p. B5.

Speier, P. L., Sherak, D. L., Hirsch, S., & Cantwell, D. P. (1995). Depression in children and adolescents. In E. E. Beckham & W. R. Leber (Eds.), *Handbook of depression* (2nd ed., pp. 467–493). New York: Guilford.

Spiegel, D., Bloom, J. R., Kraemer, H. C., & Gottheil, E. (1989, October 14). Effect of psychosocial treatment on survival of patients with metastatic breast cancer. *Lancet, 2*, 888–891.

Spitzer, R. L., Gibbon, M., Skodol, A. E., Williams, J. B. W., & First, M. B. (Eds.). (1994). *DSM-IV casebook*. Washington, DC: American Psychiatric Press.

Statham, D. J., Heath, A. C., Madden, P. A. F., Bucholz, K. K., Bierut, L., Dinwiddie, S. H., Slutske, W. S., Dunne, M. P., & Martin, N. G. (1998). Suicidal behaviour: An epidemiological and genetic study. *Psychological Medicine, 28*, 839–855.

Steffens, D. C., Skoog, I., Norton, M. C., Hart, A. D., Tschanz, J. T., Plassman, B. L., Wyse, B. W., Welsh-Bohmer, K. A., & Breitner, J. C. S. (2000). Prevalence of depression and its treatment in an elderly population: The Cache County Study. *Archives of General Psychiatry, 57*, 601–607.

Stevens, D. E., Merikangas, K. R., & Merikangas, J. R. (1995). Comorbidity of depression and other medical conditions. In E. E. Beckham & W. R. Leber (Eds.), *Handbook of depression* (2nd ed., pp. 147–199). New York: Guilford.

Strakowski, S. M., Keck, P. E., McElroy, S. L., West, S. A., Sax, K. W., Hawkins, J. M., Kmetz, G. F., Upadhyaya, V. H., Tugrul, K. C., & Bourne, M. L. (1998). Twelve-month outcome after a first hospitalization for affective psychosis. *Archives of General Psychiatry, 55*, 49–55.

Summers, P., Forehand, R., Armistead, L., & Tannenbaum, L. (1998). Parental divorce during early adolescence in Caucasian families: The role of family process variables in predicting the long-term consequences for early adult psychosocial adjustment. *Journal of Consulting and Clinical Psychology, 66*, 327–336.

Swindle, R., Heller, K., Pescosolido, B., & Kikuzawa, S. (2000). Responses to nervous breakdowns in America over a 40-year period: Mental health policy implications. *American Psychologist, 55*, 740–749.

Tang, T. Z., & DeRubeis, R. J. (1999). Sudden gains and critical sessions in cognitive-behavioral therapy for depression. *Journal of Consulting and Clinical Psychology, 67*, 894–904.

Task Force on Education and Training of the Section on Clinical Emergencies and Crises, Division of Clinical Psychology, American Psychological Association. (2000, July). Report on education and training in behavioral emergencies. *Association of Psychology Postdoctoral and Internship Centers (APPIC) Newsletter, 35*(1), 10, 33–38.

Taylor, C. B., Carney, R. M., Burg, M. M., Saab, P., Thoresen, C. E., Skala, J. A., & Czajkowski, S. M. (2000). The Enhancing Recovery in Coronary Heart Disease (ENRICHD) patients trial: Challenges and successes in recruiting, treating and following a diverse population. *Annals of Behavioral Medicine, 22*, S028.

Taylor, S. E., Klein, L. C., Lewis, B. P., Gruenewald, T. L., Gurung, R. A. R., & Updegraff, J. A. (2000). Biobehavioral responses to stress in females: Tend-and-befriend, not fight-or-flight. *Psychological Review, 107*, 411–429.

Teasdale, J. D., Scott, J., Moore, R. G., Hayhurst, H., Pope, M., & Paykel, E. S. (2001). How does cognitive therapy prevent relapse in residual depression? Evidence from a controlled trial. *Journal of Consulting and Clinical Psychology, 69,* 347–357.

Teasdale, J. D., Segal, Z. V., Williams, J. M. G., Ridgeway, V. A., Soulsby, J. M., & Lau, M. A. (2000). Prevention of relapse/recurrence in major depression by mindfulness-based cognitive therapy. *Journal of Consulting and Clinical Psychology, 68,* 615–623.

Thase, M. E., Fasiczka, A. L., Berman, S. R., Simons, A. D., & Reynolds, C. F. (1998). Electroencephalographic sleep profiles before and after cognitive behavior therapy of depression. *Archives of General Psychiatry, 55,* 138–144.

Thase, M. E., Greenhouse, J. B., Frank, E., Reynolds, C. F., Pilkonis, P. A., Hurley, K., Grochocinski, V., & Kupfer, D. J. (1997). Treatment of major depression with psychotherapy or psychotherapy-pharmacotherapy combinations. *Archives of General Psychiatry, 54,* 1009–1015.

Thase, M. E., & Kupfer, D. J. (1996). Recent developments in the pharmacotherapy of mood disorders. *Journal of Consulting and Clinical Psychology, 64,* 646–659.

Thompson, C., Peveler, R. C., Stephenson, D., & McKendrick, J. (2000). Compliance with antidepressant medication in the treatment of Major Depressive Disorder in primary care: A randomized comparison of fluoxetine and a tricyclic antidepressant. *American Journal of Psychiatry, 157,* 338–343.

Tram, J. M., & Cole, D. A. (2000). Self-perceived competence and the relation between life events and depressive symptoms in adolescence: Mediator or moderator? *Journal of Abnormal Psychology, 109,* 753–760.

Turvey, C. L., Carney, C., Arndt, S., Wallace, R. B., & Herzog, R. (1999). Conjugal loss and syndromal depression in a sample of elders aged 70 years or older. *American Journal of Psychiatry, 156,* 1596–1601.

U.S. Public Health Service. (1999). *The Surgeon General's call to action to prevent suicide.* Washington, DC: Government Printing Office.

U.S. Surgeon General. (1999, December 13). Mental health: A report of the Surgeon General. <www.Surgeongeneral.gov/library/mentalhealth/>.

Vaillant, G. E. (1998). Natural history of male psychological health, XIV: Relationship of mood disorder vulnerability to physical health. *American Journal of Psychiatry, 155,* 184–191.

Vaillant, G. E., & Mukamal, K. (2001). Successful aging. *American Journal of Psychiatry, 158,* 839–847.

Van Gorp, W. G., Altshuler, L., Theberge, D. C., Wilkins, J., & Dixon, W. (1998). Cognitive impairment in euthymic bipolar patients with and without prior alcohol dependence: A preliminary study. *Archives of General Psychiatry, 55,* 41–46.

Walters, S. T., & Bennett, M. E. (2000, April). Assessing clients' spirituality and religious behavior: Recommendations for research and practice in mental health settings. *Behavior Therapist, 23*(4), 79–90.

Watson, D., Clark, L. A., Weber, K., Assenheimer, J. S., Strauss, M. E., & McCormick, R. A. (1995). Testing a tripartite model: II. Exploring the symptom structure of anxiety and depression in student, adult, and patient samples. *Journal of Abnormal Psychology, 104*, 15–25.

Weiss, B., Weisz, J. R., Politano, M., Carey, M., Nelson, W. M., & Finch, A. J. (1992). Relations among self-reported depressive symptoms in clinic-referred children versus adolescents. *Journal of Abnormal Psychology, 101*, 391–397.

Weissman, M. M., Bland, R. C., Canico, G. J., Faravelli, C., Greenwald, S., Hwu, H. G., Joyce, P. R., Karam, E. G., Lee, C. K., Lellouch, J., Lepine, J. P., Newman, S. C., Rubio-Stipec, M., Wells, J. E., Wickramaratne, P. J., Wittchen, H. U., & Yeh, E. K. (1996). Cross-national epidemiology of major depression and Bipolar Disorder. *Journal of the American Medical Association, 276*, 293–299.

Weissman, M. M., & Markowitz, J. C. (1998). An overview of interpersonal psychotherapy. In J. C. Markowitz (Ed.), *Interpersonal psychotherapy* (pp. 1–33). Washington, DC: American Psychiatric Press.

Weissman, M. M., & Olfson, M. (1995). Depression in women: Implications for health care research. *Science, 269*, 799–801.

Weissman, M. M., Warner, V., Wickramaratne, P., Moreau, D., & Olfson, M. (1997). Offspring of depressed parents: 10 years later. *Archives of General Psychiatry, 54*, 932–940.

Weissman, M. M., Wickramaratne, P., Adams, P. B., Lish, J. D., Horwath, E., Charney, D., Woods, S. W., Leeman, E., & Frosch, E. (1993). The relationship between Panic Disorder and major depression: A new family study. *Archives of General Psychiatry, 50*, 767–780.

Weissman, M. M., Wickramaratne, P., Adams, P., Wolk, S., Verdeli, H., & Olfson, M. (2000). Brief screening for family psychiatric history: The Family History Screen. *Archives of General Psychiatry, 57*, 675–682.

Weissman, M. M., Wolk, S., Wickramaratne, P., Goldstein, R. B., Adams, P., Greenwald, S., Ryan, N. D., Dahl, R. E., & Steinberg, D. (1999). Children with prepubertal-onset Major Depressive Disorder and anxiety group up. *Archives of General Psychiatry, 56*, 794–801.

Weisz, J. R., Thurber, C. A., Sweeney, L., Proffitt, V. D., & LaGagnoux, G. L. (1997). Brief treatment of mild-to-moderate child depression using primary and secondary control enhancement training. *Journal of Consulting and Clinical Psychology, 65*, 703–707.

Weisz, J. R., Weiss, B., Han, S. S., Granger, D. A., & Morton, T. (1995). Effects of psychotherapy with children and adolescents revisited: A meta-analysis of treatment outcome studies. *Psychological Bulletin, 117*, 450–468.

Wells, K. B., & Sherbourne, C. D. (1999). Functioning and utility for current health of patients with depression or chronic medical conditions in managed, primary care practices. *Archives of General Psychiatry, 56*, 897–904.

Westefeld, J. S., Range, L. M., Rogers, J. R., Maples, M. R., Bromley, J. L., & Alcorn, J. (2000). Suicide: An overview. *Counseling Psychologist, 28*, 445–510.

Whisman, M. A. (1999). Marital dissatisfaction and psychiatric disorders: Results from the National Comorbidity Survey. *Journal of Abnormal Psychology, 108*, 701–706.

Whisman, M. A. (2001). Marital adjustment and outcome following treatments for depression. *Journal of Consulting and Clinical Psychology, 69*, 125–129.

Whisman, M. A., & Bruce, M. L. (1999). Marital dissatisfaction and incidence of Major Depressive Episode in a community sample. *Journal of Abnormal Psychology, 108*, 674–678.

Whisman, M. A., Sheldon, C. T., & Goering, P. (2000). Psychiatric disorders and dissatisfaction with social relationships: Does type of relationship matter? *Journal of Abnormal Psychology, 109*, 803–808.

Wichstrom, L. (1999). The emergence of gender difference in depressed mood during adolescence: The role of intensified gender socialization. *Developmental Psychology, 35*, 232–245.

Williams, R. B., Barefoot, J. C., Califf, R. M., Haney, T. L., Saunders, W. B., Pryor, D. B., Hlatky, M. A., Siegler, I. C., & Mark, D. B. (1992). Prognostic importance of social and economic resources among medically treated patients with angiographically documented coronary artery disease. *Journal of the American Medical Association, 267*, 520–524.

Wilson, G. T., & Agras, W. S. (2001). Practice guidelines for eating disorders. *Behavior Therapy, 32*, 219–234.

Wing, R. R., Voorhees, C. C., & Hill, D. R. (Eds.). (2000). Maintenance of behavior change in cardiorespiratory risk reduction [Special issue]. *Health Psychology, 19*(Suppl.), 1–90.

Wong, A. H. C., Smith, M., & Boon, H. S. (1998). Herbal remedies in psychiatric practice. *Archives of General Psychiatry, 55*, 1033–1044.

Wulsin, L. R., Vaillant, G. E., & Wells, V. E. (1999). A systematic review of the mortality of depression. *Psychosomatic Medicine, 61*, 6–17.

Yaffe, K., Blackwell, T., Gore, R., Sands, L., Reus, V., & Browner, W. S. (1999). Depressive symptoms and cognitive decline in nondemented elderly women: A prospective study. *Archives of General Psychiatry, 56*, 425–430.

Yatham, L. N., Liddle, P. F., Dennie, J., Shiah, I. S., Adam, M. J., Lane, C. J., Lam, R. W., & Ruth, T. J. (1999). Decrease in brain serotonin 2 receptor binding in patients with major depression following desipramine treatment: A positron emission tomography study with fluorine-18–labeled setoperone. *Archives of General Psychiatry, 56*, 705–711.

Yatham, L. N., Liddle, P. F., Shiah, I. S., Scarrow, G., Lam, R. W., Adam, M. J., Zis, A. P., & Ruth, T. J. (2000). Brain serotonin 2 receptors in major depression: A positron emission tomography study. *Archives of General Psychiatry, 57*, 850–858.

Yehuda, R., Marshall, R., & Giller, E. L. (1998). Psychopharmacological treatment of Post-Traumatic Stress Disorder. In P. E. Nathan & J. M. Gorman (Eds.), *A guide to treatments that work* (pp. 377–397). New York: Oxford University Press.

Young, A. S., Klap, R., Sherbourne, C. D, & Wells, K. B. (2001). The quality of care for depressive and anxiety disorders in the United States. *Archives of General Psychiatry, 58*, 55–61.

Young, E. A., Midgley, A. R., Carlson, N. E., & Brown, M. B. (2000). Alteration in the hypothalamic-pituitary-ovarian axis in depressed women. *Archives of General Psychiatry, 57,* 1157–1162.

Young, J. E., Beck, A. T., & Weinberger, A. (1993). Depression. In D. H. Barlow (Ed.), *Clinical handbook of psychological disorders: A step-by-step treatment manual* (2nd ed., pp. 240–277). New York: Guilford.

Young, M. A., Fogg, L. F., Scheftner, W., Fawcett, J., Akiskal, H., & Maser, J. (1996). Stable trait components of hopelessness: Baseline and sensitivity to depression. *Journal of Abnormal Psychology, 105,* 155–165.

Zimmerman, M., & Coryell, W. (1994). Screening for Major Depressive Disorder in the community: A comparison of measures. *Psychological Assessment, 6,* 71–74.

Zito, J. M., Safer, D. J., DosReis, S., Gardner, J. F., Boles, M., & Lynch, F. (2000). Trends in the prescribing of psychotropic medications to preschoolers. *Journal of the American Medical Association, 283,* 1025–1030.

Zlotnick, C., Warshaw, M., Shea, M. T., & Keller, M. B. (1997). Trauma and chronic depression among patients with anxiety disorders. *Journal of Consulting and Clinical Psychology, 65,* 333–336.

Zonderman, A. B., Herbst, J. H., Schmidt, C., Costa, P. T., & McCrae, R. R. (1993). Depressive symptoms as a nonspecific, graded risk for psychiatric diagnoses. *Journal of Abnormal Psychology, 102,* 544–552.

Zuroff, D. C., Blatt, S. J., Sanislow, C. A., Bondi, C. M., & Pilkonis, P. A. (1999). Vulnerability to depression: Reexamining state dependence and relative stability. *Journal of Abnormal Psychology, 108,* 76–89.

Zuroff, D. C., Blatt, S. J., Sotsky, S. M., Krupnick, J. L., Martin, D. J., Sanislow, C. A., & Simmens, S. (2000). Relation of therapeutic alliance and perfectionism to outcome in brief outpatient treatment of depression. *Journal of Consulting and Clinical Psychology, 68,* 114–124.

Author Index

Abbott, R., xi, 7, 77, 78, 193, 209, 213
Abramson, L. Y., 36, 53, 59, 64, 204
Achat, H., 88
Achenbach, T. M., 54, 55, 56
Ackerson, J., 58, 212
Adam, M. J., 26
Adams, P., 37, 41, 45, 56, 57, 102, 103
Addis, M. E., 22, 172
Agras, W. S., 61
Agren, H., 26
Akiskal, H. S., 10, 13, 45, 69, 141, 202,
    203, 204, 209
Albano, A. M., 10, 37, 55
Alcorn, J., 56, 60, 139, 142, 144, 145, 146,
    148, 151, 154, 185
Alexander, J. F., 173
Alexopoulos, G. S., 88, 90, 94, 97, 131, 144
Alferi, S. M., 128
Allen, N. B., 18, 20, 55
Allumbaugh, D. L., 87, 95
Altham, P. M. E., 26, 29
Altshuler, L., 203
Amos, T., 143
Andersen, P. K., 13, 202
Anderson, J. C., 36
Anderson, P., 109, 111
Andrews, B., 204
Andrews, J., 58, 171
ands, L., 131
Angell, K. E., 36, 53, 59, 64, 204
Angold, A., 37, 102
Anisman, H., 193
Annest, J. L., 143
Anthony, J. C., 13, 69, 141
Antoni, M. H., 128
Aparasu, R. R., 91, 121, 184, 198
Appelbaum, M., 122
Appelbaum, P. S., 80, 149

Appleby, L., 143
Arango, V., 26
Arean, P. A., 74, 92, 98, 171
Arena, P. L., 128
Armenian, H. K., 194
Armistead, L., 56
Armstrong, H. E., 141
Arndt, S., 95
Arnow, B., 75, 79, 80, 84, 147, 148, 149, 162,
    179, 192, 198, 204, 207
Aro, H. M., 107, 140, 141
Aronson, T. A., 79
Ashton, J. E., 11
Assenheimer, J. S., 102
Attkisson, C. C., 36, 56
Austin, P. C., 43, 91

Babyak, M. A., 122
Bach, P. B., 121
Backman, L., 88
Bagiella, E., 94
Baldessarini, R. J., 43
Ballenger, J. C., 105
Barber, J., 148
Barefoot, J. C., 124
Barkham, M., 173, 174
Barlow, D. H., 10, 37, 55, 103, 105, 115
Barnes, J., 23
Barnett, P. A., 22, 109, 111, 114
Barraclough, B., 140, 141
Barrios, L. C., 1, 107, 140, 141, 155
Barry, P. P., 89, 90, 94, 130, 131
Bartels, S. J., 90, 97, 131, 144
Basco, M. R., 70, 77, 78, 203, 209
Bassuk, S. S., 89, 131
Baucom, D. H., 41, 61, 109, 111, 114, 172, 173
Baugher, M., 22, 29, 57, 58, 61, 64, 173
Baumeister, R. F., 142, 151

261

Beach, S. R. H., 22, 61, 76, 109, 111, 114, 143, 172
Beardslee, W. R., 43, 59
Beck, A. T., 10, 11, 12, 20, 21, 22, 27, 28, 72, 74,
    83, 103, 107, 141, 142, 143, 155, 162, 163,
    164, 172, 177, 178, 185, 200, 204, 206,
    208, 211, 221
Beck, J., 10, 107
Beck, S. J., 37
Beckham, E. E., 14, 110, 150, 179, 200, 203
Bedell, B. T., 207
Beekman, A. T. F., 10, 88, 94, 102, 103,
    115, 122, 136
Beers, M. H., 106, 182
Begg, C. B., 121
Begley, A. E., 92
Belin, T. R., 60, 65, 148
Bellavance, F., 88, 209
Bello, L. R., 108
Belluardo, P., 77, 78, 193, 212
Bench, C. J., 26
Bennett, M. E., 94
Berger, A. K., 88
Berglund, P. A., 78, 80, 104
Bergman, U., 185
Berhow, R., 106
Berkman, L. F., 89, 131
Berkow, R., 182
Berman, A. L., 60, 139, 141, 142, 143, 144, 145,
    149, 150, 154, 185, 204
Berman, S. R., 204
Bernal, G., 23, 24, 30, 58, 110, 111, 168, 179
Bersoff, D. N., 46, 150
Bialik, R. J., 193
Bierhals, A. J., 88, 144
Bierut, L. J., 54, 141, 143
Bigger, J. T., 91, 123, 184
Bingham, R. C., 131
Birmaher, B., 22, 29, 30, 37, 39, 40, 42, 45, 49,
    53, 57, 58, 59, 61, 64, 106, 173
Bishop, D. S., 77
Bissonnette, L., 212
Blackburn, I. M., 203
Black, D. W., 188
Blackwell, T., 131
Blalock, J., 109
Bland, R. C., 8, 9, 18, 69
Blatt, S. J., 20, 21
Blazer, D. G., 8, 9, 10, 11, 17, 53, 68, 107, 121, 126
Blignault, I., 207
Bloch, S., 150, 183

Block, J. H., 37, 55
Bloom, J. R., 127
Blow, F. C., 131
Blumenthal, J. A., 122, 124, 135
Boeke, A. J. P., 95
Boes, M., 94, 185
Boles, M., 44, 50, 182
Bollini, P., 182, 197
Bolwig, T. G., 13, 202
Bondi, C. M., 20, 21
Boney-McCoy, S., 37
Bongar, B., 139, 143, 144, 146, 147,
    149, 151, 154
Borges, G., 115, 155
Bostwick, J. M., 144
Bourassa, M. G., 10, 95, 121, 122, 123
Bourne, M. L., 203
Bovasso, G. B., 194
Bowen, D., 208
Bowers, C. A., 108, 115
Boyd, J. H., 8, 11, 102, 103, 116
Boyers, A. E., 128
Bradford, W. D., 124, 136
Brawman-Mintzer, O., 105
Breitner, J. C. S., 88, 103, 104, 131, 185,
    199, 206, 211
Brener, N. D., 107, 140, 141, 155
Brennan, P. A., 9, 23, 55, 56, 110
Brent, D. A., 22, 29, 36, 37, 39, 40, 42, 45, 49, 53,
    57, 58, 59, 61, 64, 106, 173
Bridge, J., 22, 29, 57, 58, 61, 64, 173
Brilman, E. I., 94
Brimaher, B., 36
Brink, D., 91, 98, 129
Bromley, J. L., 56, 60, 139, 142, 144, 145, 146,
    148, 151, 154, 185
Brook, J., 59, 64, 71, 203
Brook, J. S., 56
Brown, G. K., 12, 72, 107, 141, 142, 143, 155,
    164, 185
Brown, G. M., 26, 188
Brown, G. W., 92, 124, 204
Brown, L., 207
Brown, M. B., 26, 54
Brown, R. A., 108
Brown, W. A., 146, 149, 182, 183
Browners, W. S., 131
Bruce, M. L., 10, 22, 79, 84, 88, 110, 172
Bucholz, K. K., 54, 141, 143
Buchwald, A. M., 9

Buckholtz, N. S., 89, 90, 94, 130, 131
Bulzebruck, H., 207
Burge, D., 10, 22, 23, 55, 56, 110, 204, 205
Burgess, E. S., 108
Burg, M. M., 123
Burke, J. D., 8, 11, 102, 103, 116
Burns, D. D., 10, 20, 21, 29, 79, 103, 110, 163, 164
Bush, T. M., xi, 77, 78, 84, 184, 209, 213
Butler, L. D., 127
Butzlaff, R. L., 76, 77, 109, 204
Buysse, D. J., 9, 91, 104, 131
Byford, S., 42, 60, 148

Cai, G., 11, 13, 69, 121
Caine, E. D., 88, 94, 132, 140
Califf, R. M., 124
Campbell, M., 44
Campbell, S. B., 41
Canico, G. J., 8, 9, 18, 69
Cantwell, C., 60, 65, 148
Cantwell, D. P., 37, 54
Carbonneau, R., 26, 54
Carey, M., 37
Carlson, N. E., 26, 54
Carlson, R. W., 127
Carmody, T., 44, 59, 182
Carney, C., 95
Carney, R. M., 123
Carrere, S., 76, 110
Carver, C. S., 128
Caspi, A., 10, 18, 50, 104
Castillo, C., 123
Catalan, J., 148
Catanzaro, S. J., 37
Cater, J., 44
Chang, P. P., 76, 122, 136
Chapman, D., 188
Charbonneau, Y., 193
Charney, D., 102, 103
Chassin, L., 107
Chen, C., 23
Chen, J., 53, 69
Chen, J. H., 88, 144
Chen, L., 13, 69
Chen, L. S., 11, 121
Chen, P., 131, 135
Chevron, E. S., 23, 24, 28, 74, 83, 222
Chodoff, P., 183
Chorpita, B. F., 10, 37, 55

Christensen, H., 103
Christopher, F., 74, 92, 98, 171
Cicchetti, D., 37, 39, 43, 45, 53, 54, 59, 206
Claridge, G. C., 10
Clark, D. A., 10, 20, 21, 22, 27, 74, 103, 162, 172, 178, 200, 204, 206, 208, 211
Clark, D. C., 142, 146
Clark, L. A., 10, 17, 60, 88, 102, 103, 115, 141
Clarke, G., 58, 171
Clary, C., 188
Classen, C., 127
Coan, J., 76, 110
Cohen, E., 59, 64, 203
Cohen, O., 55
Cohen, P., 56, 59, 64, 71, 203
Cohen, R. D., 121
Cohen, S., 127, 128, 129, 136
Cohn, J. F., 41
Colecchi, C., 91, 98, 129
Cole, D. A., 37, 39, 40, 55, 204
Coleman, R. E., 122
Cole, M. G., 88
Collins, J. F., 110, 179, 203
Compas, B. E., 53, 54, 55, 56, 126, 128, 129
Conger, R. D., 56
Connor, J. K., 54, 56
Conti, S., 77, 78, 193, 209, 212
Conwell, Y., 140
Cook, A., 10
Cooper, J., 143
Cooper, M. L., 108, 116
Cooper, T. B., 75, 92, 148
Cooper-Patrick, L., 12, 72, 76, 90, 120, 122, 136, 141, 142
Copeland, J. R. M., 88
Copeland, L. A., 131
Corn, B., 127, 129
Cornes, C., xi, 23, 24, 77, 78, 92, 93, 110, 168, 186, 193, 203, 207, 208, 209, 212, 213
Cornwall, P. L., xi, 77, 78, 193, 209, 213
Coryell, W., 10, 11, 12, 13, 18, 69, 72, 146, 202, 203, 204, 209
Costa, P. T., 204
Costello, E. J., 37, 102
Courneya, K. S., 128
Cowen, P. J., 26
Cowley, D. S., 105
Cox, C., 88, 94, 140
Coyne, J. C., 10, 22, 41, 45, 57, 76, 109, 111, 114, 172, 179

Craighead, L. W., 22, 25, 74, 79, 83, 162, 168, 171, 173, 194, 208
Craighead, W. E., 21, 22, 25, 74, 79, 83, 162, 168, 171, 173, 194, 208
Cramer, L. D., 121
Craske, M. G., 60, 104, 105, 106, 112, 114
Crits-Christoph, P., 22, 74, 79, 105, 162, 168, 171, 173, 174
Cronkite, R. C., 10, 76, 84, 95, 110, 143, 172, 173, 203
Crosby, A. E., 143
Crouse-Novak, M. A., 45
Crowe, R. R., 75, 92, 148
Crum, R. M., 12, 72, 90, 120, 141, 142
Csikszentmihalyi, M., vii, 74
Cudar, P., 108
Culver, J. L., 128
Cummings, E. M., 109
Cummings, J. L., 90, 97, 131, 144
Cunn, M. E., 108
Curdue, K., 123
Currier, G. W., 132
Cyranowski, J. M., 8, 9, 26, 36, 54, 63, 69, 109, 111, 205
Czajkowski, S. M., 123

Dahlberg, L. L., 143
Dahl, R. E., 36, 37, 39, 45, 49, 53, 56, 59, 107
Daiuto, A. D., 41, 61, 109, 111, 114, 172, 173
Daley, S. E., 10, 22, 23, 55, 56, 110, 204, 205
Dancu, C. V., 104
DaSilva, J., 26, 188
Davidson, J., 162, 177, 208, 222
Davidson, K., 148
Davies, P. T., 109
Davila, J., 10, 22, 23, 55, 56, 110, 204, 205
Davis, J. M., 183
Davis, M. C., 54, 109
Davis, M. K., 163
Davis, R. B., 93
Davis, S. R., 72, 73, 163, 164
Davison, G. C., 21, 28, 162, 163, 164, 177
Davison, K. P., 126, 128, 129
DeBattista, C., 26
De Beurs, E., 102, 103, 115
Deeg, D. J. H., 10, 94, 95, 102, 103, 115, 122, 136
DeKosky, S. T., 89, 90, 94, 130, 131, 135
Delaney, M. A., 44
De Lima, M. S., 43, 90, 184, 197
DeLucia, C., 107

DeMolles, D. A., 88
Dennie, J., 26
Dent, J., 148
DeRubeis, R. J., 22, 43, 74, 75, 79, 83, 105, 148, 162, 163, 164, 168, 171, 173, 179, 194, 197, 203, 208
Detweiler, J. B., 207
Devlin, B., 45, 57
Dew, M. A., xi, 9, 23, 24, 77, 78, 91, 92, 93, 104, 110, 123, 131, 168, 184, 193, 198, 207, 208, 209, 213
Dewey, M. E., 88
Dickerson, S. S., 126, 128, 129
DiMartini, A., 123
DiMiceli, S., 127
Dinwiddie, S. H., 54, 141, 143
Dixon, W., 75, 148, 149, 203
Dobson, K. S., 20, 21, 22, 84, 163, 172, 179, 203
Doerfler, L. A., 78, 207
Dolan, R. T., 110, 179, 203
Dolan, S. L., 22, 178
Dong, Q., 23
DosReis, S., 44, 50, 182
Downey, G., 41, 45
Doyle, J., xi, 70, 78, 172, 208, 209, 213
Dozois, D. J. A., 20
Drezner, K., 43, 59
Drings, P., 207
Druid, H., 185
Drumm, K., 150
Druss, B. G., 124, 136
Duan, N., 192, 194, 198, 209
Duberstein, P. R., 88, 94, 140
DuBois, D. L., 57
Dunn, M. E., 115
Dunne, M. P., 54, 141, 143
Dunner, D. L., 19, 75, 79, 80, 84, 147, 148, 149, 162, 192, 198, 204, 207
Dusseldorp, E., 122, 124, 134
Dwork, A. J., 26
Dyer, E., 42, 60, 148
Dzajkowski, S. M., 208
D'Zurilla, T. J., 21, 25, 74, 92, 135, 148, 149, 168, 171, 205, 207, 208, 212

Eaton, W. W., 11, 13, 69, 121, 194
Eaves, G. G., xi, 70, 78, 172, 208, 209, 213
Eaves, L., 26, 54
Eidelson, R. J., 103
Eisenberg, D. M., 93

Eisfeld, B., 26, 188
Eist, H. I., 121
Elashoff, R., 127
Elderen, T. V., 122, 124, 134
Elkin, I., 21, 84, 110, 163, 179, 203
Elliot, C., 149
Ellis, J., 193
Emery, B. L., 37, 74, 164, 178
Emery, G., 20, 21, 22, 28, 83, 162, 221
Emmanuel, J., 76, 104, 114
Emslie, G. J., 44, 59, 182
Endicott, J., 8, 10, 13, 18, 69, 146, 202,
    203, 204, 209
Epperson, D. L., 10, 69
Epstein, N. B., 77
Ernst, E., 93, 97, 105
Eshleman, S., 53, 69, 76, 78, 79
Esler, J. L., 105
Estrada, R., 56
Evans, D. L., 91, 120, 121, 124, 184, 185, 203
Evans, D. M., 108
Evans, K., 148
Evans, M. D., 203
Evans, M. O., 155
Everson, S. A., 121
Ey, S., 53, 54, 55, 56

Faddis, S., 126, 129, 135
Fahey, J. L., 127
Faller, h., 207
Faragher, B., 143
Faravelli, C., 8, 9, 18, 69
Fasiczka, A. L., 204
Fava, G. A., 77, 78, 193, 207, 209, 212
Fava, M., 75, 91, 147
Fawcett, J., 141, 142, 204
Fawzy, F. I., 127, 129
Fawzy, N. W., 127, 129
Feinberg, T. L., 45
Ferguson, C. P., 184, 186
Ferketich, A. K., 10, 76, 88, 122, 136
Ferris, R., 88, 89, 90, 91
Ferris, S. H., 89, 90, 94, 130, 131
Ferro, T., 41, 45, 50, 56, 79
Fichter, M., 88
Field, T. M., 93
Finch, A. J., 37
Finkel, M. S., 91, 123, 184
Finkel, S. I., 89, 90, 94, 130, 131
Finkelhor, D., 37

Finkelstein, R., 45
Finney, J. W., 108
First, M. B., 5, 11, 17
Fishman, B., 23, 168
Fletcher, A. J., 106, 182
Flett, G. L., 9, 10, 179
Flint, A. J., 203
Floyd, M., 212
Foa, E. B., 104, 105
Fobair, P., 127
Fogg, L. F., 141, 204
Foley, D., 26, 54
Fombonne, E., 107
Forbes, N. T., 140
Ford, D. E., 12, 72, 76, 90, 120, 122, 136,
    141, 142
Forehand, R., 45, 56, 57
Forsell, Y., 88
Fortney, J., 74
Foster, B. M., xi, 70, 78, 172, 208, 209, 213
Foster, D. F., 93
Foster, T., 111
Fowler, R. C., 107
Frances, A. J., 23, 168
Frank, E., xi, 8, 9, 23, 24, 26, 28, 36, 54, 63, 69,
    75, 77, 78, 91, 92, 93, 104, 109, 110, 111,
    131, 147, 148, 149, 168, 186, 192, 193,
    197, 203, 205, 207, 208, 209, 212, 213
Franklin, M. E., 105
Frank, R. G., 74
Frasure-Smith, N., 10, 95, 121, 122, 123
Friberg, P., 26
Frid, D. J., 10, 76, 88, 122, 136
Friedenreich, C. M., 128
Friedman, R. A., 79, 209
Friedman, S. H., 126, 129, 135
Fristad, M. A., 37
Frohlich, P. F., 187
Frone, M. R., 108, 116
Frosch, E., 102, 103
Funder, D. C., 103
Futterman, A., 88, 89, 90, 91

Gaffney, A., 91, 123, 184
Gallagher-Thompson, D., 88, 89, 90, 91, 92
Gallo, J. J., 13, 69, 90, 97, 131, 144
Ganguli, M., 131, 135
Garber, R. A., 123
Garbin, M. G., 12
Gardner, C. O., 10, 69, 203

Gardner, J. F., 44, 50, 182
Garfinkel, R., 23, 24, 58, 110, 168, 179
Garland, A. F., xi, 77, 78, 151, 193, 209, 213
Garske, J. P., 163
Garvey, M. J., 203
Gaston, L., 174
Gatsonis, C., 45
Geerlings, S. W., 94
Gelenberg, A. J., 75, 79, 80, 84, 147, 148, 149,
        162, 179, 192, 198, 204, 207
Gelfand, L. A., 22, 43, 75, 79, 83, 148, 162,
        179, 194, 197, 208
Gemar, M. C., 20
George, L. K., 8, 11, 90, 94, 102, 103, 116
Gerald, J., 183
Gergel, I., 91, 123, 184
Gerhardt, C. A., 54, 56
Ghaemi, S. N., 7
Giaconia, R. M., 37, 45, 55, 56
Gibbon, M., 5, 11, 17
Gibbons, R. D., 142
Giese-Davis, J., 127
Gilbert, P., 21, 23, 28, 110, 111, 148, 166,
        168, 177, 178, 200, 208, 221
Giles, D. E., 9, 142
Gill, J., 42, 60, 148
Giller, E. L., 105
Gillespie, K., 111
Gillham, J. E., 43, 45, 50, 59, 173
Girgus, J. S., 8, 9, 36, 45, 53, 54, 55, 69, 205
Gjerde, P. F., 37, 55
Gladstone, T. R. G., 25, 36, 37, 39, 40, 43,
        49, 56, 59
Glass, D. R., 110, 179, 203
Glassman, A. H., 94, 121, 142, 184, 186
Glick, I., 178, 192
Gniwesch, L., 79, 209
Goering, P., 110, 115, 203
Goldberg, D. E., 121
Goldfried, M. R., 21, 28, 162, 163, 164, 177
Goldstein, R. B., 37, 45, 56
Gollan, J. K., 22, 172, 203
Goodwin, F. K., 7
Goodyer, I. M., 26, 29
Gore, R., 131
Gorman, L. L., 23, 24, 30, 110, 111, 168, 179, 205
Gortner, E. T., 22, 172, 203
Gose, B., 56, 107, 150
Gotlib, I. H., 18, 20, 22, 53, 55, 109, 111, 114, 205
Gottheil, E., 127

Gottlieb, G. L., 90, 97, 131, 144
Gottman, J. M., 76, 110
Goycoolea, J. M., 123
Graham, P., 43, 46
Grandi, S., 77, 78, 193, 209, 212
Granger, D. A., 39
Grant, K. E., 53, 54, 55, 56
Grasby, P. M., 26
Gravel, G., 10, 95, 121, 122
Green, S. A., 183
Greenberg, R. M., 75, 92, 148
Greenberger, E., 23
Greenfield, S. F., 108, 194
Greenhouse, J. B., 75, 147, 148, 149, 192,
        197, 207
Greenwald, S., 8, 9, 18, 37, 45, 56, 69
Greist, J. H., 188
Griffiths, J., 193
Grisham, J. R., 107, 141, 142, 143, 155, 185
Grisso, T., 80, 149
Grochocinski, V. J., 75, 77, 110, 147, 148, 149,
        168, 186, 192, 197, 203, 207, 209, 212
Grove, W. M., 203
Gruenwald, T. L., 9, 54, 69, 205
Grundy, C. T., 11
Gunnell, D. J., 155
Gunn, R. N., 26
Gurley, D., 71
Gurung, R. A. R., 9, 54, 69, 205
Guskin, K., 41
Guthrie, D., 127
Gwyther, L. P., 89, 90, 94, 130, 131

Haaga, D. A. F., 126, 128, 129
Halbreich, U., x, 25, 26, 29, 59, 75, 77, 90, 105,
        106, 123, 146, 181, 182, 183, 184, 186,
        187, 188, 189, 190, 191, 192,
        194, 196, 209
Haley, J., 35, 80, 164
Hall, M., 9, 91, 104, 131
Halpain, M. C., 90, 97, 131, 144
Hammen, C. L., 9, 10, 11, 12, 14, 21, 22, 23,
        25, 37, 39, 45, 54, 55, 56, 57, 75, 107, 109,
        110, 147, 150, 162, 200, 204, 205, 206
Hamptom, C. P., 110
Haney, T. L., 124
Hankin, B. L., 36, 53, 59, 64, 204
Hanson, M., 122
Han, S. S., 39
Hardwood, R. H., 88

Hardy, G. E., 173, 174
Hardy, R., 183
Harkness, K. L., 109, 110
Harrington, R., 39, 40, 42, 43, 49, 57, 60, 148
Harrington, V., 42, 60, 148
Harris, E. A., 144, 149, 154
Harris, E. C., 140, 141
Harrison, W., 188
Harris, S. D., 128
Harris, T., 92, 124
Hart, A. D., 88, 103, 104, 185, 199, 206, 211
Harwood, R. H., 94, 95, 98
Haskett, R. F., 75, 92, 148
Hassan, S. S., 107, 140, 141, 155
Hauf, A. M. C., 37, 45, 55, 56
Hawkins, J. M., 203
Hawton, K., 143
Hayes, A. M., 21
Hayhurst, H., xi, 7, 77, 78, 172, 179, 193, 208, 209, 211, 213
Hays, R. D., 204
Hayward, A., 155
Heard, H. L., 141
Hearst, J., 108
Heath, A. C., 54, 107, 141, 143
Heikkila, K., 155
Heikkinen, M. E., 107, 140, 141
Helgeson, V. S., 128, 129, 136
Heller, K., 22
Helstad, C. P., 121, 131, 136, 185
Hembree, E. A., 104
Henderson, A. S., 103
Hendrick, C., 109, 114
Hendrick, S. S., 22, 109, 111, 114
Henk, H. J., 121, 131, 136, 185
Henriksson, M. M., 107, 140, 141
Henry, R., 23
Henry, W. P., 174
Heppner, P. P., 178, 183
Herbst, J. H., 204
Herrmann, J. H., 140
Herzberg, D. S., 10, 22, 56, 110
Herzog, R., 95
Hetherington, E. M., 55
Heun, R., 131
Hewitt, J., 26, 54
Heyd, D., 150
Hill, D. R., 124, 128, 135, 206, 208
Hinden, B. R., 54, 55, 56
Hirsch, S., 37

Hirschfeld, R. M. A., 87, 90, 139, 140, 141, 143, 145, 154, 204, 206
Hlatky, M. A., 124
Hoehn-Saric, R., 188
Hohkanen, R., 155
Holahan, C. J., 10, 95, 110, 172, 203
Holahan, C. K., 10, 95, 110, 172, 203
Holder, D., 58, 61, 64, 173
Holland, S. J., 23, 25, 28, 126, 127, 128, 129, 148, 162, 177
Hollon, S. D., 11, 12, 21, 22, 23, 28, 57, 74, 75, 79, 83, 91, 104, 154, 162, 168, 171, 172, 177, 192, 194, 196, 200, 203, 206, 208, 209, 221
Holtzworth-Munroe, A., 173
Homgren, P., 185
Honig, A., 10, 122, 136
Hooker, K. A., 207
Hooley, J. M., 76, 77, 109, 204
Hops, H., 58, 171
Horwath, E., 102, 103
Hotoph, M., 43, 90, 184, 197
Houck, P. R., xi, 9, 23, 24, 77, 78, 91, 92, 93, 104, 110, 131, 168, 193, 207, 208, 209, 213
Houle, S., 26, 188
House, J. S., 53, 69
Houston, K., 143
Houts, P. S., 126, 129, 135
Howell, D. C., 55
Hoyt, W. T., 87, 95
Huang, Y. Y., 26
Hudson, S., 128
Hughes, C. W., 44, 59, 182
Hughes, M., 53, 69, 76, 78, 79
Hull, J., 88
Hurley, K., 75, 147, 148, 149, 192, 197, 207
Hurry, J., 56
Hwu, H. G., 8, 9, 18, 69
Hyun, C. S., 127

Ilardi, S. S., 21, 22, 25, 74, 79, 83, 162, 168, 171, 173, 194, 208
Imber, S. D., xi, 21, 23, 24, 77, 78, 84, 92, 93, 110, 163, 168, 179, 193, 203, 207, 208, 209, 213
Ingram, R. E., 11, 12, 20, 22, 204, 211
Inskip, H. M., 140, 141
Irvin, J. E., 108, 115
Isacsson, G., 185

Isometsa, E. T., 107, 140, 141, 142, 143
Iyengar, S., 58, 61, 64, 173

Jacob, T., 110, 115
Jacobs, D. G., 60, 90, 139, 142, 144, 145, 149,
        150, 154, 185, 194, 204, 222
Jacobs, S., 88, 144
Jacobsberg, L. B., 23, 168
Jacobson, N. S., 22, 172, 173, 203
Jacomb, P. A., 103
Jamison, C., 212
Jamison, K. R., 7, 45, 60, 77, 111, 139, 140, 141,
        142, 143, 149, 151, 155, 185, 204, 209, 222
Janal, M. N., 188
Jarrett, D. B., 110, 168, 186, 203, 207, 209, 212
Jarrett, R. B., xi, 70, 75, 77, 78, 172, 189, 192,
        198, 203, 208, 209, 213
Jaycox, L. H., 43, 45, 50, 59, 104, 173, 192, 194,
        198, 209
Jenaway, A., xi, 77, 78, 193, 209, 213
Jenike, M. A., 105
Jessen, F., 131
Jeste, D. V., 90, 97, 131, 144
Jiang, W., 122
Jobes, D. A., 60, 139, 145
Johansson, M., 26
Johnson, A. L., xi, 77, 78, 193, 209, 213
Johnson, J. G., 56
Johnson, J. L., 43, 103
Johnson, S. L., 110, 115
Joiner, T. E., 20, 22, 37, 55, 57, 75, 76, 109,
        111, 114, 142, 143, 146, 148, 149, 172
Jones, D. A., 123
Jones, D. J., 45, 57
Jordan, A., 88
Jorm, A. F., 8, 88, 103, 115
Joseph, T. X., 74, 92, 98, 171
Joyce, P. R., 8, 9, 18, 69
Judd, L. L., 10, 13, 69, 202, 203, 209
Juneau, M., 10, 95, 121, 122, 123

Kaelber, C. T., 10, 76
Kaiser, A. S., 11, 12
Kakuma, T., 88
Kalayam, B., 88
Kalehzan, B. M., 26
Kales, H. C., 131
Kamlet, M. S., 74
Kammerer, E. E., 131
Kaplan, C., 23

Kaplan, G. A., 9, 88, 98, 121, 129
Kaplan, J., 122, 124, 135
Kaprio, J., 155
Kapur, S., 26, 188
Karam, E. G., 8, 9, 18, 69
Karno, M., 8, 11, 102, 103, 116
Kasch, K. L., 79
Kasen, S., 56
Kaslow, N. J., 25, 36, 37, 39, 40, 49, 56, 109, 111
Kasl, S. V., 88, 144
Kassir, S. A., 26
Katon, W., xi, 77, 78, 84, 89, 90, 184, 209, 213
Katzelnick, D. J., 121, 131, 136, 185
Katz, I. R., 89
Katz, R., 10, 11, 12
Kaufman, J., 36, 37, 39, 40, 42, 45, 49, 53, 59, 106
Kawachi, I., 88
Kazdin, A. E., 22, 25, 39, 40, 42, 43, 49, 54, 57,
        59, 63, 64, 162, 173, 178, 183
Keane, T. M., 105
Keck, P. E., 203
Keefe, F. J., 126, 128, 129
Keith-Spiegel, P., 46, 61, 150, 183, 222
Keitner, G. I., 77
Keller, M. B., 10, 13, 18, 69, 75, 79, 80, 84,
        102, 104, 146, 147, 148, 149, 162,
        179, 192, 198, 202, 203, 204, 207, 209
Kelly, J. F., 108
Kelly, T. M., 26
Kendall, P. C., 11, 12, 54
Kendler, K. S., 10, 53, 69, 76, 78, 79, 203
Kennedy, J. S., 91, 123, 184
Kennedy, S. H., 26, 188
Kennedy, S. J., 20
Kerfoot, M., 42, 60, 148
Kessing, L. V., 13, 89, 202
Kessler, R. C., 8, 9, 10, 11, 17, 43, 53, 68, 69,
        76, 78, 79, 80, 93, 103, 104, 107, 115,
        121, 126, 155, 205
Khachaturian, Z. S., 89, 90, 94, 130, 131
Khan, A., 146, 149, 182, 183
Kikuzawa, S., 22
Kilbourn, K. M., 128
Kim, S. Y. H., 132
Kind, D. A., 94
King, D. A., 88
Kivlighan, D. M., 178, 183
Kjaer, K. H., 26
Klag, M. J., 76, 122, 136
Klap, R., 179, 185, 199, 206, 212

Klein, D. F., 183, 188
Klein, D. N., 10, 55, 75, 79, 80, 84, 147, 148, 149,
    162, 179, 192, 198, 204, 205, 207
Klein, L. C., 9, 54, 69, 205
Klein, L. M., 79
Klerman, G. L., 23, 24, 28, 74, 83, 168, 178,
    192, 222
Kmetz, G. F., 203
Koch, W. J., 104, 115
Kocsis, J. H., 23, 79, 168, 209
Koenig, H. G., 90, 94
Koerner, K., 22, 172
Kohn, R., 77
Koivumaa-Honkanen, H., 155
Kolko, D. J., 22, 29, 57, 58, 61, 64, 173
Kolvin, I., 23
Koocher, G. P., 46, 61, 150, 183, 222
Koopman, C., 127
Kopans, B., 194
Kopel, T., 123
Kopper, B. A., 10, 69
Korten, A. E., 103
Kosier, J. T., 123
Koskenvuo, M., 155
Kovacs, M., 36, 37, 42, 45, 57
Kowatch, R. A., 44, 59, 182
Kozloff, R. C., 194
Kraaij, V., 122, 124, 134
Kraemer, H. C., 26, 127
Kraft, D., xi, 70, 75, 77, 78, 172, 189, 198,
    203, 208, 209, 213
Kramer, M., 8, 11, 102, 103, 116
Krames, L., 9, 10, 179
Krantz, D. S., 122
Kresnow, M. J., 143
Kriegsman, D. M. W., 95
Krug, E. G., 143
Krumholz, H. M., 124, 136
Kuchibhatla, M., 90
Kufman, J., 36
Kumanyika, S. K., 208
Kunovac, J. L., 10, 13, 69, 202, 203, 209
Kuoppasalmi, K. I., 107, 140, 141
Kupelnick, B., 182, 197
Kupfer, D. J., xi, 9, 23, 24, 25, 59, 75, 77, 78,
    80, 90, 91, 92, 93, 104, 110, 123, 131, 142,
    146, 147, 148, 149, 168, 180, 181, 182, 184,
    186, 187, 189, 190, 192, 193, 197, 203,
    207, 208, 209, 212, 213
Kurpius, S. E. R., 110, 115

Kurzer, N., 164
Kuyken, W., 164

LaGagnoux, G. L., 42, 50, 173
Laghrissi-Thode, F., 91, 123, 184
Laird, N. M., 8, 11, 18, 68, 121, 126
Lambert, G., 26
Lambert, M. J., 11
Lam, R. W., 26
Landreville, P., 212
Lane, C. J., 26
Lang, H., 207
Lantz, P. M., 53, 69
Lara, M. E., 205
Larson, D. B., 94
Lau, M. A., 172, 179, 193, 211
Laurent, J., 37
Lave, J. R., 74
Lavori, P. W., 18, 203
Lawlor, B. A., 88
Leader, J. B., 79, 205
Leahy, R. L., 23, 25, 28, 148, 162, 177
Leber, W. R., 14, 150, 200
Lebowitz, B. D., 89, 90, 92, 94, 95, 97,
    130, 131, 144
Lee, C. K., 8, 9, 18, 69
Leedham, B., 128
Leeman, E., 102, 103
Lefkowitz, M. M., 36
Lehman, J. M., 128
Leibovici, A., 132
Leighton, A. H., 8, 11, 18, 68, 121, 126
Leitenberg, H., 126, 128, 129
Lellouch, J., 8, 9, 18, 69
Leon, A. C., 10, 13, 18, 69, 79, 146, 202,
    203, 204, 209
Lepine, J. P., 8, 9, 18, 69
Lepkowski, J. M., 53, 69
Leshner, A. I., 108
Lesperance, F., 10, 95, 121, 122, 123
Lewinsohn, P. M., 8, 9, 10, 18, 20, 23, 25, 28,
    53, 55, 56, 57, 58, 59, 60, 64, 69, 73,
    102, 107, 111, 148, 171, 178, 204, 205, 206
Lewis, B. P., 9, 54, 69, 205
Liddle, P. F., 26
Lin, E. H. B., xi, 77, 78, 80, 84, 104, 109, 184, 213
Lindberg, N., 10, 22, 56, 110
Linden, M., 88
Lineham, M. M., 141
Lish, J. D., 102, 103

Little, J. T., 92
Lobo, A., 88
Locke, B. Z., 8, 11, 12, 102, 103, 116
Lonnqvist, J. K., 107, 140, 141, 142, 143
Lowery, A., 21, 84, 163, 179
Ludman, E. J., xi, 77, 78, 84, 184, 209, 213
Luebbert, J. F., 44
Lunnen, K. M., 11
Lydiard, B., 188
Lydiard, R. B., 105
Lyman, R. D., 58
Lynch, F., 44, 50, 182
Lyness, J. M., 88, 94

MacKinnon, A. J., 103
Madden, P. A. F., 54, 141, 143
Maes, H., 26, 54
Maes, S., 122, 124, 134
Magee, W. J., 205
Magnusson, H., 88
Maier, W., 131
Mallinger, A. G., 77, 110, 168, 186, 203,
    207, 209, 212
Malone, R. P., 44
Mamdani, M. M., 43, 91
Maneson, P. B., 173
Mann, A. H., 88, 94, 95, 98
Mann, J. J., 26, 75, 92, 148
Manning, W. G., 121, 131, 136, 185
Mansour, A., 88
Maples, M. R., 56, 60, 139, 142, 144, 145,
    146, 148, 151, 154, 185
Marcus, S. C., 43, 75, 103, 146, 182
Maresh, S. E., 110, 115
Maris, R. W., 60, 139, 141, 142, 143, 144, 145,
    149, 150, 154, 185, 204
Mark, D. B., 124
Markowitz, J. C., 23, 24, 28, 74, 75, 79, 80, 83,
    84, 111, 147, 148, 149, 162, 168, 178,
    179, 192, 198, 200, 204, 206, 207,
    208, 209, 222
Marshall, R., 105
Martin, C. E., 60, 139, 145
Martin, D. J., 163
Martin, J. M., 37, 204
Martin, N. G., 54, 141, 143
Marttunen, M. J., 107, 140, 141
Marwill, M., 70, 77, 78, 203, 209
Marx, E. M., 10
Maser, J. D., 10, 13, 18, 69, 141, 202, 203, 204, 209
Mason, B., 178, 192

Massie, M. J., 120
Masson, A., 10, 95, 121, 122
Matthews, K. A., 54, 109
Maxwell, S. E., 39, 40
Ma, Y., 71
Mayberg, H. S., 26, 188
Mayer, J. D., 207
Mazumdar, S., xi, 23, 24, 77, 78, 92, 93, 110,
    168, 193, 207, 208, 209, 213
Mazure, C. M., 88, 109, 119, 144
McCafferty, J., 91, 123, 184
McClelland, R., 111
McClure, K. S., 12
McCormick, R. A., 103
McCrady, B. S., 61, 108, 115, 206
McCrae, R. R., 204
McCullough, J. P., 75, 79, 80, 84, 147, 148,
    149, 162, 179, 192, 198, 204, 206, 207, 222
McCullough, M. E., 94
McDaniel, D. M., 207
McDermott, V., 94, 185
McEachran, A. B., 77, 110, 168, 186, 203, 207,
    209, 212
McElreath, L., 91, 131
McElroy, S., 188
McElroy, S. L., 203
McFarland, M., 111, 172
McGee, R., 36, 53, 59, 64, 204
McGonagle, K. A., 8, 9, 10, 11, 17, 53, 68, 69,
    76, 78, 79, 107, 121, 126
McGrath, P. J., 188
McGregor, B. A., 128
McGuffin, P., 10
McGuire, S., 55
McIntire, D., 75, 103, 189, 198
McIntyre, J. S., 43
McKendree-Smith, N., 58
McKendrick, J., 188
McKenna, M. C., 127, 129
McLean, P. D., 104, 115
McNiven, F., 42, 60m148
McRae, T. D., 89, 90, 94, 130, 131
Mead, L. A., 76, 122, 136
Meadows, E. A., 12, 104
Meier, S. T., 72, 73, 163, 164
Mellow, A. M., 131
Merali, Z., 193
Meredith, L. S., 192, 194, 198, 209
Merikangas, J. R., 91, 94, 121, 126
Merikangas, K. R., 91, 94, 121, 126
Merluzzi, T. V., 128

Mero, R. P., 53, 69
Messa, C., 26
Meston, C. M., 187
Meulman, J., 122, 124, 134
Meyer, J., 26
Meyer, J. H., 26, 188
Meyerowitz, B. E., 128
Meyers, B. S., 88
Meyers, T., 41
Micheal, J., 108
Midgley, A. R., 26, 54
Mikulincer, M., 55
Miller, E., 127
Miller, G. E., 127, 129
Miller, I. W., 77, 108
Miller, M. D., xi, 23, 24, 77, 78, 91, 92, 93, 110,
    168, 184, 193, 198, 207, 208, 209, 213
Miller, N. L., 79, 209
Mineka, S., 10, 17, 60, 88, 102, 103, 115, 141
Miranda, J., 20, 22, 192, 194, 198, 204, 209, 211
Moeller, D. M., 207
Moeschberger, M. L., 10, 76, 88, 122, 136
Moffitt, T. E., 10, 18, 36, 50, 53, 59, 64, 104, 204
Moncrieff, J., 183
Monroe, S. M., 23, 55, 109, 110
Monson, R. R., 8, 11, 18, 68, 121, 126
Montgomery, S. A., x, 25, 26, 29, 59, 75, 77,
    90, 105, 106, 123, 146, 181, 182, 183,
    184, 186, 187, 188, 189, 190, 191, 192,
    194, 196, 209
Moore, R. G., xi, 77, 78, 172, 179, 193, 203,
    208, 209, 211, 213
Moos, B. S., 76, 84, 110, 143
Moos, R. H., 10, 76, 84, 95, 108, 110, 143,
    172, 173, 203
Moras, K., 10, 79, 110
Moreau, D., 10, 23, 24, 41, 45, 56, 57, 58, 107,
    110, 168, 179, 204
Morgan, H. G., 155
Morin, C. M., 91, 98, 129
Morris, J. C., 13, 89, 90, 94, 131
Morris, J. J., 122
Mort, J. R., 91, 121, 184, 198
Mortensen, P. B., 13, 202
Morton, D. L., 127
Morton, T., 39
Mount, J. H., 205
Mudar, P., 116
Muehrer, P., 206, 208
Mueller, T. I., 10, 13, 18, 69, 108, 146, 202,
    203, 204, 209

Muenz, L. R., 108, 194
Mueser, K. T., 41, 61, 109, 111, 114, 172, 173
Mufson, L., 23, 24, 58, 110, 168, 179
Mukamal, K., 95, 98, 108
Mukerji, P., 45, 57
Mulsant, B. H., 75, 91, 92, 131, 135, 148, 184,
    198, 209
Mumme, D., 41
Munizza, C., 182, 197
Murphy, J. M., 8, 11, 18, 68, 121, 126
Murrelle, L., 26, 54
Musselman, D. L., 91, 120, 121, 124, 184,
    186, 203
Myers, J. K., 8, 11, 102, 103, 116

Narayan, M., 91, 123, 184
Narrow, W. E., 10, 76
Nathan, P. E., 22, 74, 178
Neary, E. M., 45, 57
Nee, J. C., 8, 69
Nelson, B., 36, 37, 39, 45, 49, 53, 59, 107
Nelson, C. B., 53, 69, 76, 78, 79, 107
Nelson, J. C., 91, 123, 184
Nelson, W. M., 37
Nemeroff, C. B., 25, 29, 43, 59, 75, 77, 79, 80,
    84, 90, 91, 120, 121, 123, 124, 146, 147,
    148, 149, 162, 179, 180, 181, 182, 183,
    184, 185, 186, 187, 188, 189, 190, 191,
    192, 197, 198, 203, 204, 207
Nesse, R. M., 151
Neufeld, K., 11, 121
Newman, D. L., 10, 18, 104
Newman, R. M., 123
Newman, S. C., 8, 9, 18, 69
Nezlek, J. B., 110
Nezu, A. M., 12, 21, 25, 74, 92, 98, 126, 129,
    135, 148, 168, 171, 205, 206, 207,
    208, 212
Nezu, C. M., 21, 25, 74, 126, 129, 135, 148, 168,
    171, 205, 206, 208, 212
Nicassio, P. M., 120
Nicklin, J. L., 107
Nicpon, M. F., 110, 115
Niederehe, G., 43, 59, 90, 92, 93, 97, 105, 124,
    131, 144, 184, 192
Ninan, P., 188
Nobler, M. S., 123
Nolen-Hoeksema, S., 8, 9, 21, 36, 41, 45,
    53, 54, 55, 69, 164, 205
Norden, K. A., 79
Norton, M. C., 88, 103, 104, 185, 199, 206, 211

Oakley, F., 89, 90, 94, 130, 131
O'Connor, C., 122
O'Connor, T. G., 55
O'Donnell, S., 80, 149
O'Hara, M. W., 23, 24, 30, 110, 111, 168, 179, 205
Oldehinkel, A. J., 94
Oldham, J. M., 56
Olfson, M., 9, 10, 41, 43, 45, 54, 56, 57, 69, 75, 78, 80, 104, 107, 146, 182, 204
Olmsted, M., 21, 84, 163, 179
Oppedisano, G., 54, 56
Oppenheim, S., 26
Orbach, I., 55
Orman, D. T., 75, 148, 149
Ormel, J., 94, 203, 209
Othmer, E., 7, 14, 72, 164
Othmer, S. C., 7, 14, 72, 164

Packman, W. L., 144, 149, 154
Paley, B., 10, 22, 23, 55, 56, 110, 204, 205
Palmer, B. W., 90, 97, 131, 144
Pampallona, S., 182, 197
Pankratz, V. S., 144
Papassotiropoulos, A., 131
Parides, M., 79, 209
Parikh, S. V., 43, 91
Parker, G., 207
Parloff, M. B., 110, 179, 203
Parmelee, P. A., 89
Parrone, P. L., 45
Patterson, C., 111
Patterson, T. L., 90, 97, 131, 144
Paulauskas, S. L., 45
Paulus, M., 10, 13, 69, 202, 203, 209
Paykel, E. S., xi, 77, 78, 172, 179, 193, 208, 209, 211, 213
Pearson, S. D., 121, 131, 136, 185
Peddicord, J. P., 143
Peeke, L. G., 37
Peirce, R. S., 108, 116
Pennebaker, J. W., 126, 128, 129
Penninx, B. W. J. H., 10, 94, 95, 122, 136
Perel, J. M., xi, 23, 24, 36, 37, 39, 45, 49, 53, 59, 77, 78, 92, 93, 107, 110, 168, 186, 193, 203, 207, 208, 209, 212, 213
Perri, M. G., xi, 21, 25, 74, 77, 78, 87, 88, 92, 94, 98, 123, 124, 126, 129, 144, 148, 149, 150, 154, 168, 171, 203, 205, 206, 208, 212

Perry, S. W., 23, 168
Persons, J. B., 21, 28, 83, 162, 163, 164, 166, 177, 208, 222
Pescosolido, B., 22
Peterson, B. I., 90, 94
Petkova, E., 188
Petracca, G., 123
Pettinati, H. M., 75, 92, 148
Pettit, A. R., 43, 103
Peveler, R. C., 188
Piacentini, J., 60, 65, 148
Piasecki, J. M., 203
Piccinelli, M., 54, 103
Pickles, A., 26, 54
Pierre, F., 41, 45, 50, 56
Pigott, T. A., 184, 186
Pilkonis, P. A., 20, 21, 75, 110, 147, 148, 149, 179, 192, 197, 203, 207
Pilowsky, D. J., 141
Pincus, H. A., 43, 75, 103, 146, 182
Pine, D. S., 59, 64, 71, 203
Pitts, S. C., 107
Plassman, B. L., 88, 103, 104, 185, 199, 206, 211
Plomin, R., 55
Politano, M., 37
Pollock, B. G., xi, 23, 24, 57, 77, 78, 91, 92, 93, 110, 123, 168, 184, 193, 198, 207, 208, 209, 213
Pollock, M., 45
Pope, K. S., 46, 61, 150
Pope, M., xi, 77, 78, 172, 179, 193, 208, 209, 211, 213
Popkin, M. K., 120
Posener, J. A., 26
Powell, K. E., 143
Powell, T., 94
Powers, B., 204
Price, A. A., 128
Prigerson, H. G., 88, 144
Prince, M. J., 88, 94, 95, 98
Prince, R. H., 123
Prince, S. E., 22, 172, 173
Proffitt, V. D., 42, 50, 173
Prudic, J., 75, 92, 148
Pryor, D. B., 124
Pukkala, E., 121

Quindlen, A., 45, 59, 77, 111, 205
Quitkin, F. M., 183, 188

Rabiner, E. A., 26
Rabins, P. V., 89, 90, 94, 130, 131
Rabkin, J. G., 183
Radford, M. J., 124, 136
Radloff, L. S., 12
Rae, D. S., 8, 10, 11, 76, 102, 103, 116
Rafanelli, C., 77, 78, 193, 209, 212
Rafi-Tari, S., 26, 188
Rajab, M. H., 75, 148, 149
Ramanan, J., 70, 77, 78, 203, 209
Rand, J. I., 93, 97, 105
Range, L. M., 56, 60, 139, 142, 144, 145, 146,
    148, 151, 154, 185
Rankin, E. A., 25, 26, 29, 75, 77, 78, 91, 105,
    106, 146, 181, 183, 184, 186, 187,
    189, 197, 209
Rauch, s. L., 105
Ravindran, A. V., 193
Rees, A., 173, 174
Regier, D. A., 8, 10, 11, 76, 102, 103, 116
Rehm, L. P., 25
Reinecke, M. A., 57
Reinherz, H. Z., 37, 45, 55, 56
Reisberg, L., 54
Reiss, D., 55
Reivich, K. J., 43, 45, 50, 59, 173
Reizes, J. M., 194
Reus, V., 131
Reynolds, C. F., xi, 9, 23, 24, 75, 77, 78, 90, 91,
    92, 93, 97, 104, 110, 131, 144, 147, 148,
    149, 168, 184, 192, 193, 197, 198, 204,
    207, 208, 209, 213
Rhode, P., 9, 110
Rice, J. P., 10, 13, 69, 202, 203, 209
Richards, C., 45, 57
Richards, S., xi, 77, 78, 87, 88, 94, 124, 126, 129,
    144, 149, 150, 154, 203, 207, 209
Richardson, J., 128
Rich, C. L., 107
Ridgeway, V. A., 172, 179, 193, 211
Rifat, S. L., 203
Rintelmann, J., 44, 59, 182
Risser, R. C., 70, 75, 77, 78, 189, 198, 203, 209
Roberts, R. E., 9, 36, 56, 88, 98, 129, 155
Robin, D. W., 123
Robins, L. N., 8, 11, 102, 103, 116
Robinson, R., 92, 124
Robinson, R. G., 123
Rodgers, B., 103
Roffwarg, H. P., 9, 142

Rogers, J. R., 56, 60, 139, 142, 144, 145, 148, 151,
    154, 185
Rohde, P., 8, 10, 18, 20, 23, 25, 28, 53, 55, 56,
    57, 58, 59, 60, 64, 73, 102, 107, 148, 171,
    204, 205, 206
Rolls, B. J., 208
Romanoski, A., 13, 69
Ronan, G. F., 12
Roose, S. P., 91, 123, 184
Rosen, C. S., 124, 135, 206
Rosenbaum, J. F., 75, 91, 147
Rosenblatt, A., 36, 56
Rosenheck, R. A., 124, 136
Rossello, J., 23, 24, 30, 58, 110, 111, 168, 179
Rost, K., 74
Rothberg, P. C., 43, 59
Rotheram-Borus, M. J., 60, 65, 148
Roth, l. H., 123
Rounds, J., 127, 129
Rounsaville, B. J., 23, 24, 28, 74, 83, 222
Roy-Burne, P. P., 103
Roy-Byrne, P. P., 105
Rozanski, A., 122, 124, 135
Rubenstein, L. V., 192, 194, 198, 209
Rubio-Stipec, M., 8, 9, 18, 69
Rucci, P., 103
Rudd, M. D., 75, 142, 143, 146, 148, 149
Rudick-Davis, D., 9
Rueter, M. A., 56
Rush, A. J., 9, 20, 21, 22, 28, 44, 59, 70, 74,
    77, 78, 83, 90, 142, 162, 164, 178,
    182, 203, 209, 221
Russell, J. M., 75, 79, 80, 84, 87, 90, 139, 140,
    141, 143, 145, 147, 148, 149, 154, 162,
    179, 192, 198, 204, 206, 207, 209
Russell, M., 108, 116
Russo, J., 184
Rutherford, J., 10
Ruth, T. J., 26
Rutter, C., xi, 54, 77, 78, 84, 209, 213
Rutter, M., 26
Ryan, C. E., 77
Ryan, J. M., 132
Ryan, N. D., 36, 37, 39, 40, 42, 45, 49, 53,
    56, 59, 106
Ryan, N. E., 57

Saab, P., 123
Sacco, W. P., 162, 163
Sackeim, H. A., 75, 92, 148

Sadowski, H., 23
Safer, D. J., 44, 50, 182
Safran, J. D., 21, 164, 166, 177
Sagrati, S., 20
Salonen, J. T., 121
Salovey, P., 207
Salt, P., 43, 59
Salzman, C., 149, 185, 198
Sanchez, M. A. M., 128
Sanders, M. R., 111, 172
Sanderson, W. C., 10, 107
Sanislow, C. A., 20, 21
Santor, D. A., 10, 179
Sargent, P. A., 26
Saunders, W. B., 124
Sax, K. W., 203
Sayers, S. L., 10, 79, 110
Saz, P., 88
Scaramella, L., 56
Scarrow, G., 26
Schacht, T. E., 174
Schaffer, M., 75, 189, 198
Schatzberg, A. F., 10, 25, 26, 29, 43, 59, 76, 77, 90,
       91, 123, 131, 146, 180, 181, 182, 183, 184,
       185, 186, 187, 188, 189, 190, 191, 192,
       197, 209
Scheftner, W. A., 141, 142, 204
Schein, R. L., 74, 92, 98, 171
Schmidt, C., 204
Schmidt, U., 148
Schneider, L. S., 43, 59, 89, 90, 92, 93, 94, 97,
       105, 124, 130, 131, 144, 184, 192
Schoenbaum, M., 192, 194, 198, 209
Schoevers, R. A., 10, 122, 136
Schron, E., 208
Schulberg, H. C., 74, 90
Schultz, S. K., 123
Schulz, R., 128, 136
Schutte, K. K., 108
Schwartz, J. A. J., 25, 36, 37, 39, 40, 49, 56
Schwartz, J. E., 79
Schwartzbaum, J. A., 10, 76, 88, 122, 136
Scogin, F., 58, 91, 131, 212
Scott, J., xi, 77, 78, 172, 179, 193, 208, 209,
       211, 213
Seeley, J. R., 8, 9, 10, 18, 20, 23, 25, 28, 53, 55,
       56, 57, 58, 59, 60, 64, 69, 73, 102, 107,
       110, 111, 148, 171, 178, 204, 205, 206
Segal, Z. V., 20, 21, 22, 164, 166, 172, 177,
       179, 193, 204, 211

Seligman, M. E. P., vii, 43, 45, 50, 59, 74, 173
Seroczynski, A. D., 37, 39, 40
Shapiro, D. A., 173, 179
Shapiro, P. A., 94, 121, 124, 184, 186
Shaw, B. F., 11, 12, 20, 21, 22, 28, 74, 83, 84,
       162, 163, 164, 178, 179, 221
Shea, C., 9, 54, 144, 150, 205
Shea, M. T., 10, 13, 18, 69, 102, 104, 110, 179, 203
Shean, G. D., 110
Shear, M. K., 8, 9, 26, 36, 54, 63, 69, 109, 111,
       178, 192, 205
Sheldon, C. T., 110, 115, 203
Shelton, R. C., 21, 22, 23, 28, 57, 74, 75, 79, 83, 91,
       104, 154, 162, 168, 171, 172, 177, 192,
       194, 196, 200, 206, 208, 209, 221
Shema, S. J., 9, 88, 98, 129
Shepperd, R., 143
Sherak, D. L., 37
Sherbourne, C. D., 122, 179, 185, 192, 194,
       198, 199, 204, 206, 209, 212
Shiah, I. S., 26
Shoebridge, P., 39, 40, 43, 49, 57, 148
Shoham, V., 41, 61, 109, 111, 114, 172, 173
Siegler, I. C., 124
Silberg, J., 26, 54
Silva, P. A., 10, 18, 36, 50, 53, 59, 64, 104, 204
Silver, P. C., xi, 70, 78, 172, 208, 209, 213
Silverman, A. B., 37, 45, 55, 56
Silverman, M. M., 60, 139, 141, 142, 143, 144,
       145, 149, 150, 154, 185, 204
Simmonds, S., 76, 104, 114
Simmons, A. D., 75, 179
Simmons, R. G., 123
Simon, G. E., xi, 77, 78, 84, 90, 103, 121, 131,
       136, 184, 185, 209, 213
Simonoff, E, 26, 54
Simons, A. D., 22, 43, 79, 83, 109, 110, 148, 162,
       194, 197, 204, 208
Simpson, H. B., 8, 69
Sirey, J. A., 88
Skala, J. A., 123
Skodol, A. E., 5, 17, 56
Skoog, I., 88, 103, 104, 185, 199, 206, 211
Sloan, R. P., 94
Slutske, W. S., 141, 143
Small, B. J., 88
Small, G. W., 89, 90, 94, 130, 131
Smith, G. R., 74
Smith, J., 74
Smith, T. W., 120

Snow, D., 10
Snyder, C. R., 173
Sobol, A. M., 8, 11, 18, 68, 121, 126
Solomon, A., 9, 55, 69, 178
Solomon, D. A., 13, 18, 69, 146, 203, 204
Sommers-Flanagan, J., 139, 144
Sommers-Flanagan, R., 139, 144
Song, J., 60, 65, 148
Sood, R., 91, 98, 129
Sotsky, S. M., 21, 84, 110, 163, 179, 203
Soukup, J., 93
Soulsby, J. M., 172, 179, 193, 211
Spangler, D. L., 20, 21, 29, 163
Spanier, C., 23, 28, 168, 207
Sparrow, D., 88
Speier, P. L., 37
Spiegel, D., 127
Spielman, L. A., 23, 168
Spiro, A., 88
Spitzer, R. L., 5, 11, 17
Stack, J. A., xi, 23, 24, 77, 78, 92, 93, 110, 168, 193, 207, 208, 209, 213
Stahl, S., 188
Stang, P. E., 103
Starkstein, S. E., 123
Statham, D. J., 54, 141, 143
Steer, R. A., 12, 72, 107, 141, 142, 143, 155, 185
Steffen, A. M., 92
Steffens, D. C., 88, 103, 104, 185, 199, 206, 211
Steinberg, D., 37, 45, 56
Stein, D., 55
Stephenson, D., 188
Stevens, D. E., 91, 94, 121, 126
Stevinson, C., 93, 97, 105
Stewart, J. W., 188
Stickle, T. R., 41, 61, 109, 114, 172, 173
Stone, J., 91, 98, 129
Storey, P. A., 56
Strakowski, S. M., 203
Strauss, J. L., 21
Strauss, M. E., 103
Strawbridge, W. J., 9, 88, 98, 129
Street, G. P., 104
Streim, J. E., 89, 90, 94, 130, 131
Strupp, H. H., 174
Stuart, S. P., 22, 23, 24, 30, 110, 111, 168, 179, 205
Stukas, A. A., 123
Stulman, D. A., 75, 148, 149
Sullivan, M. D., 89

Summers, P., 56
Sunderland, T., 89, 90, 94, 130, 131
Swanson, C., 76, 110
Swartz, M. S., 8, 9, 10, 11, 17, 53, 68, 107, 121, 126
Sweeney, L., 42, 50, 173
Swindle, R., 22
Switzer, G. E., 123
Swyers, J. P., 94

Talagic, M., 10, 95
Talajic, M., 121, 122
Tally, S. R., 23
Tamplin, A., 26, 29
Tang, T. Z., 22, 43, 75, 79, 83, 148, 162, 163, 179, 194, 197, 208
Tanielian, T. L., 43, 103
Tannenbaum, L., 56
Tata, P., 148
Taylor, C. B., 123, 205
Taylor, S., 104, 115
Taylor, S. E., 9, 54, 69
Teasdale, J. D., xi, 77, 78, 172, 179, 193, 208, 209, 211, 213
Telner, J., 193
Teri, L. A., 89, 90, 94, 130, 131
Tesiny, E. P., 36
Thase, M. E., 25, 59, 75, 77, 79, 80, 84, 90, 92, 109, 110, 123, 146, 147, 148, 149, 162, 168, 179, 180, 181, 182, 184, 186, 187, 189, 190, 192, 197, 198, 203, 204, 207, 209, 212
Theberge, D. C., 203
Thomas, A., 88, 94, 95, 98
Thompson, C., 188
Thompson, J. W., 43, 75, 146, 182
Thompson, L., 88, 89, 90, 91
Thompson, S., 148
Thorensen, C. E., 123
Thornton, S., 148
Thurber, C. A., 42, 50, 173
Tibaldi, G., 182, 197
Tien, A., 13, 69
Todd, M., 107
Tompkins, M. A., 28, 162, 177, 208, 222
Tondo, L., 43
Torgerson, D., 148
Toth, S. L., 37, 39, 43, 45, 53, 54, 59, 206
Tovey, D. R., 11
Tram, J. M., 55

Trivedi, M. H., 75, 79, 80, 84, 147, 148, 149, 162,
    179, 192, 198, 204, 207
Truax, P. A., 22, 172
Truglio, R., 37, 204
Truvey, C. L., 95
Tschanz, J. T., 88, 103, 104, 185, 199, 206, 211
Tuason, V. B., 203
Tugrul, K. C., 203
Tune, L. E., 89, 90, 94, 130, 131
Tuomilehto, J., 121
Turrina, C., 88
Turvey, C., 18, 203
Twamley, E. W., 54, 109
Tyrer, P., 76, 104, 114, 148

Ugarte, B., 23
Ulloa, R. E., 58, 61, 64, 173
Underwood, M. D., 26
Unutzer, J., xi, 77, 78, 84, 184, 192, 194, 198,
    209, 213
Upadhyaya, V. H., 203
Updegraff, J. A., 9, 54, 69, 205
Upshur, R. E. G., 43, 91
Ursino, A. A. D., 207
Ustun, B., 103

Vagge, L. M., 108
Vaillant, G. E., 95, 98, 108, 121
Vallis, M., 11, 12
Vallis, T. M., 21, 84, 163, 179
Van Balkom, A. J. L. M., 102, 103, 115
Van Dyck, R., 102, 103, 115
Van Eijk, J. T. M., 10, 94, 95, 122, 136
Van Gorp, W. G., 203
Van Horn, L., 208
Van Rompay, M. I., 93
Van Tilburg, W., 10, 94, 95, 102, 103,
    115, 122, 136
Vasquez, M. J. T., 46, 61, 150
Verdeli, H., 41, 45, 50, 56, 57
Verrier, P., 123
Versage, E. M., 43, 59
Viinamaki, H., 155
Vitali, A. E., 105
Von Korff, M., xi, 77, 78, 84, 184, 209, 213
Voorhees, C. C., 124, 128, 135, 206, 208
Vredenburg, K., 9, 10, 179

Walker, E. A., xi, 77, 78, 84, 184, 209, 213
Wallace, L. E., 56

Wallace, M., 12
Wallace, P. M., 205
Wallace, R. B., 95
Walters, E. E., 103, 115, 155
Walters, S. T., 94
Wampold, B. E., 178, 183
Wang, M. C., 108, 115
Wang, N. Y., 76, 122, 136
Warner, H. A., 146, 149, 182, 183
Warner, V., 10, 41, 45, 56, 57, 107, 204
Warren, J. L., 121
Warshaw, M. G., 10, 13, 18, 69, 102, 104,
    146, 203, 204
Wasserman, M. S., 37, 45, 55, 56
Watkins, J. T., 21, 84, 110, 163, 179, 203
Watkins, S., 10
Watson, D., 10, 17, 60, 88, 102, 103, 115, 141
Waugh, R., 122
Weber, K., 103
Weinberg, W. A., 44, 59, 182
Weinberger, A., 28, 162, 164, 177
Weiss, B., 37, 39
Weissman, M. M., 8, 9, 10, 18, 23, 24, 28, 37,
    41, 45, 50, 54, 56, 57, 58, 69, 74, 83,
    102, 103, 107, 110, 168, 178, 179, 192,
    204, 222
Weiss, R. D., 108
Weisz, J. R., 25, 37, 39, 40, 42, 43, 49, 50, 57,
    59, 64, 173
Wells, J. E., 8, 9, 18, 69
Wells, K. B., 122, 179, 185, 192, 194, 198, 199,
    204, 206, 209, 212
Wells, V. E., 121
Welsh-Bohmer, K. A., 88, 103, 104, 185,
    199, 206, 211
Wenzel, A., 23, 24, 30, 110, 111, 168, 179, 205
Wessely, S., 43, 90, 183, 184, 197
West, J. C., 43, 103
West, R. R., 123
West, S. A., 203
Westefeld, J. S., 56, 60, 139, 142, 144, 145,
    146, 148, 151, 154, 185
Whiffen, v. E., 205
Whisman, M. A., 10, 22, 79, 84, 110, 111,
    115, 172, 203
Whittaker, J., 39, 40, 43, 49, 57, 148
Wichstrom, L., 36, 53, 59, 64, 204
Wickramaratne, P. J., 8, 9, 10, 18, 37, 41, 45,
    56, 57, 69, 102, 103, 107, 204
Wiens, A., 193

Wilkey, S. A., 93
Wilkins, J., 203
Wilkinson, G., 54
Williams, D. A., 126, 128, 129
Williams, D. R., 53, 69
Williams, G. H., 26
Williams, J., 58, 171
Williams, J. B. W., 5, 11, 17
Williams, J. M. G., 10, 172, 179, 193, 211
Williams, R. B., 124
Williams, S., 36
Williamson, D. E., 36, 37, 39, 40, 42, 45, 49, 53, 59, 106
Wilner, P. J., 178, 192
Wilson, A. A., 26, 188
Wilson, G. T., 61
Wilson, K. C. M., 88
Winblad, B., 88
Wing, R. R., 124, 128, 135, 206, 208
Winokur, G., 13, 69
Witt-Browder, A., 75, 189, 198
Wittchen, H. U., 8, 9, 18, 53, 69, 76, 78, 79, 103
Wolfson, A., 41
Wolfson, C., 123
Wolk, S., 37, 41, 45, 56, 57
Woodham, A., 42, 60, 148
Woods, S. W., 102, 103
Woody, S., 104, 115
Wright, E. J., 43, 59
Wulsin, L. R., 121
Wu, l. T., 141
Wypij, D., 89, 131
Wyse, B. W., 88, 103, 104, 185, 199, 206, 211

Yaffe, K., 131
Yamaguchi, J., 21, 84, 163, 179
Yasko, J., 128, 136
Yatham, L. N., 26
Yeh, E. K., 8, 9, 18, 69
Yehuda, R., 105
Young, A. S., 179, 185, 199, 206, 212
Young, D., 107
Young, E. A., 8, 9, 26, 36, 54, 63, 69, 109, 111, 205
Young, J. E., 28, 162, 164, 177
Young, M. A., 141, 204
Young, R. C., 88
Yount, S. E., 128

Zajecka, J., 75, 79, 80, 84, 147, 148, 149, 162, 179, 188, 192, 198, 204, 207
Zarin, D. A., 43, 75, 103, 146, 182
Zeiss, A., 9, 55, 69, 178
Zeller, P. J., 10, 13, 69, 202, 203, 209
Zevon, M. A., 127, 129
Zhang, M., 74
Zhao, S., 53, 69, 76, 78, 79
Ziedonis, D., 61, 108, 115, 206
Zigler, E., 151
Zimmerman, M., 11, 12, 72
Zis, A. P., 26
Zito, J. B., 44, 146
Zito, J. M., 43, 50, 75, 182
Zlotnick, C., 10, 69, 102, 104
Zonderman, A. B., 204
Zucker, B. G., 60, 104, 105, 106, 112, 114
Zuroff, D. C., 20, 21

Subject Index

Acetylcholine, 25
Adjustment disorder, 7
Adolescent depression, 8
  assessment of, 54-55
  case study, 51-53
  clinical guidelines, 61-62
  comorbid conditions, 60-61
  family therapy and, 61
  gender and, 53-54
  genetic factors and, 9-10
  interpersonal relationships and, 56-57
  parental depression and, 57
  pharmacotherapy and, 59, 182
  prevalence of, 53
  prevention of, 59
  readings on, 63-65
  skill-training intervention, 57-58
  suicide risk and, 60, 63, 140
  symptoms of, 55-56
  treatment for, 57-59, 63
Adult depression:
  assessment of, 70-72
  case study, 66-68
  chronic, dysthymic disorder, 79-80
  clinical guidelines, 81-82
  combination therapies, 74-75
  comorbid conditions, 69, 76-77
  course of, 69-70
  double depression and, 71
  electro-convulsive therapy, 75-76
  ethical/practical issues, 80
  interpersonal relationships and, 76-77
  interview outline, 71, 72-73
  pharmacotherapy and, 75, 82
  prevalence of, 68-69
  psychotherapies and, 73-74, 75
  readings on, 83-84
  relapse in, 77-78, 82-83

  rule-out criteria, 71
  self-coping and, 78, 206-207
  suicide risk and, 75
  symptoms, 73
  treatment for, 73-78, 80
  See also Older adult depression
Alcohol abuse, 10
  adolescents/young adults and, 107
  depression and, 106-107, 113
  parental influence and, 107
  readings on, 115, 116
  relapse in, 108
  suicide risk and, 107, 141
  treatment for, 108
Alzheimer's disease, 130-131, 134
Anafranil, 185
Anger, 10
Anhedonia, 142
Antidepressant medications, 180, 182, 183
  dopamine-norepinephrine reuptake
      inhibitors, 190
  monoamine oxidase inhibitors, 188-190
  norephinephrine-serotonin modulators, 192
  selective serotonin reuptake inhibitors,
      186-188
  serotonin modulators, 191-192
  serotonin-norepinephrine reuptake
      inhibitors, 190-191
  tetracyclics, 190
  tricyclics, 185-186
Anxiety disorders, 10, 76
  case study, 102
  cognitive behavior therapy and, 104-105
  comorbidities, sequencing of, 103-104
  depression and, 102-103
  multiple disorders, treatment of, 104
  neuroticism and, 103
  panic disorder, 103, 141

pharmacotherapy and, 105-106, 113
   readings on, 114, 115, 116
   treatment rates, 104
Arbitrary inference, 21
Ascendin, 190
Assessment, 11-13
   adolescent depression, 54-55
   childhood depression, 35, 37-39
   interpersonal relationships, 111
   interview outline, 14-16
   suicide risk, 144-146, 178
Atypical depression, 189-190
Aventyl, 185

Beck Depression Inventory (BDI), 12, 13, 71
Behavior therapy, 171-172
   marital therapies and, 172
   readings on, 28
   theoretical basis for, 25
   See also Cognitive behavior therapy
Bipolar disorder, 7
Booster sessions, 193, 209-210
Borderline personality disorder, 141
Bulimia nervosa, 10, 184

Cancer, 126, 133-134
   educational-based interventions, 128
   pharmacotherapy and, 126
   psychological intervention, 126, 127-129
   readings on, 135, 136
   survival extension, 127
   See also Chronic health problems
Cardiovascular disease, 10, 76, 88, 133
   caregiver coping strategies, 123
   clinical guidelines, 124-125
   depression incidence and, 121-122
   health-promoting behaviors and, 123-124
   interpersonal relationships and, 124
   monoamine oxidase inhibitors and, 188-189
   pharmacotherapy and, 123
   psychological treatment, 122-123
   psychosocial treatment, 123, 124
   readings on, 134-135, 136
   tricyclic antidepressants and, 186
   See also Chronic health problems
Case studies:
   adolescent depression, 51-53
   adult depression, 66-68
   alcohol abuse, 106
   anxiety disorders, 102

childhood depression, 33-35
chronic health problems, 117-119
interpersonal relationships, 109
major depressive disorder, 3-7
older adult depression, 85-87
psychotherapy outcome, 214-217
psychotherapeutic intervention, 159-161
readings on, 17
relapse prevention, 200-203
suicide, 137-139
Celexa, 187
Center for Epidemiologic Studies-Depression
      Scale (CES-D), 12, 13, 72
Childhood depression:
   assessment of, 35, 37-39
   case study, 33-35
   child abuse and, 46
   clinical guidelines, 46-47
   comorbid conditions, 37, 38
   ethical issues and, 46
   parental depression and, 45
   parent reports and, 38-39
   pharmacotherapy and, 43-45
   prevalence of, 36
   readings on, 49-50
   skill-training interventions, 39-43
   social stigma of, 45
   symptoms of, 35, 36-38
   treatment for, 39-45, 46
Chronic health problems, 88, 89, 94-95, 97
   assessment and, 119-121
   cancer, 126-130
   cardiovascular disease, 121-125
   case study, 117-119
   dementia, 130-133
   readings on, 134-136
   symptoms in, 120, 121
Clinical practice. See Practice guidelines
Close relationships. See Interpersonal
      relationships
Cognitive behavior therapy, 162-163
   anxiety disorders and, 104-105, 115-116
   collaborative therapeutic relationship,
      164-167
   dysfunctional thinking and, 20-21, 164-166
   dysthymic disorder and, 79-80
   nonspecific factors in, 21, 22
   pharmacotherapy and, 192-193, 197
   readings on, 27-28, 49, 83, 115-116, 177-178
   relapse prevention and, 77-78, 208

structuring in, 164
theoretical basis for, 19-22
therapeutic relationship in, 163-164,
166-167
See also Behavior therapy
Combined therapies, 93, 97, 105, 192-194,
197, 209
Comorbid conditions, 10
adolescent depression and, 60-61
adult depression and, 69, 76-77
childhood depression and, 37
multiple disorders, treatment of, 104
older adult depression and, 88
pharmacotherapy and, 184
readings on, 17
sequencing significance of, 103-104
skill-training intervention and, 41
See also Alcohol abuse; Anxiety disorders;
Interpersonal relationships
Continuous-care model, 77, 82-83, 108, 123,
208-209
Coping skills. *See* Relapse prevention;
Self-coping; Skill-training interventions
Coronary heart disease. *See* Cardiovascular
disease
Crisis intervention, 150-151, 154, 155

Dementia, 89, 130-131, 134
clinical guidelines, 131-133
depression and, 131
readings on, 134, 135
Depression. *See* Major depressive disorder
Desyrel, 191
Dopamine, 25
Double depression, 71
Dysfunctional thinking, 19-21
chronic health problems and, 120
scar hypothesis, 204
skills-training and, 40
See also Cognitive behavior therapy
Dysthymic disorder, 13, 70, 71, 197
cognitive behavior therapy and, 79-80
pharmacotherapy and, 79

Eating disorders, 10, 76
Elavil, 185
Elder population. *See* Older adult depression
Electro-convulsive therapy (ECT), 75-76, 91-92,
147-148
Environmental factors, 10

Epidemiologic Catchment Area Study,
102-103, 116
Ethical issues:
adult depression and, 80
childhood depression and, 46
suicide risk and, 149-150

Family therapy, 61, 172-173

Gender:
adolescent depression and, 53-54, 63
childhood depression and, 36
depression incidence and, 8-9
relapse risk and, 204, 205
suicide prevalence and, 139, 140, 143
Genetic links, 9-10, 57
Geriatric population. *See* Older adult depression
Grief, 23-24

Hopelessness, 141-142
Hospitalization, 75, 92, 145, 147, 148-149

Impulsivity, 7
Interpersonal psychotherapy, 167-168, 170-171
depression and, 58, 168
focus issues in, 23-24
manuals for, 168
pharmacotherapy and, 193
problem-solving focus of, 168-169
readings on, 28, 83, 178
relapse prevention and, 208
role dispute/transition, 169-170
theoretical basis for, 22-24
Interpersonal relationships, 10, 22
adolescents and, 56-57
adult depression and, 76-77
assessment of, 111
case study, 109
clinical guidelines for, 111-113
communication patterns and, 110
deficits in, 24
dysfunctional close relationships,
109-110, 114
dysthymic disorder and, 79
marital dissatisfaction, 110, 172
readings on, 114, 115
relapse risk and, 204
skill-training for, 40
social interactions and, 110-111
treatment of, 111

Interviewing:
    outlines for, 14-16, 72-73
    questionnaires and, 11-12, 72
    structured, 11

Learned helplessness, 43
Ludiomil, 190
Luvox, 187
Lyketsos, C., 13, 69

Magnification/minimization, 21
Major depressive disorder:
    anxiety disorders and, 76
    assessment of, 11-13, 14-15
    atypical depression, 189-190
    case study, 3-7
    clinical guidelines, 15-16
    course of, 13-14
    demographics of, 8-9
    dysfunctional thinking and, 19-21
    genetic factors in, 9-10
    interview outline, 14-16
    prevalence of, 8
    readings on, 17-18
    rule-out symptoms, 7, 71, 73
    suicide and, 140
    symptoms of, 6, 9, 73
    treatment rates in, 104
    See also Chronic health problems; Comorbid
        conditions
Manerex, 188
Manic-depressive disorder, 7
Marital dissatisfaction. See Interpersonal
        relationships
Marital therapies, 172
Medications. See Pharmacotherapy
Monoamine oxidase inhibitors (MAOIs), 188-190

Nardil, 188
National Comorbidity Survey, 115
Negative triad, 20
Neuroendocrine system, 26
Neurotransmitters, 25-26
Norepinephrine, 25
Norpramin, 185
No-suicide contract, 146, 147 (table)
Nursing home care, 95, 97

Older adult depression:
    assessment of, 90, 96
    case study, 85-87
    chronic health problems and, 88, 89, 94-95
    clinical guidelines, 95-96
    cognitive decline and, 89
    electro-convulsive therapy, 91-92
    pharmacotherapy and, 90-91
    prevalence of, 89
    psychotherapy and, 92, 93
    readings on, 97-98
    relapse in, 93
    religious beliefs and, 94
    supplemental therapies, 93
    symptoms of, 87-88, 96
    treatment of, 90-93
Optimistic thinking, 40, 43
Overgeneralization, 20

Panic disorder, 103, 141
Parnate, 188
Paxil, 187
Personality disorders, 76, 141
Pharmacotherapy, 7, 180-181
    adolescent depression and, 59, 182
    adult depression and, 75
    antidepressant medications, 180, 182, 183,
        185-192
    anxiety disorders and, 105-106
    cardiovascular diseases/depression and, 123
    childhood depression and, 43-45, 182
    clinical guidelines, 194-195
    comorbid conditions and, 184
    controlled trials and, 182-183
    dopamine-norepinephrine reuptake
        inhibitor, 190
    dysthymic disorder and, 79
    interpersonal psychotherapy and, 193
    literature reviews, 181-185, 196-197
    maintenance schedules for, 183-184
    monoamine oxidase inhibitors, 188-190
    norepinephrine-serotonin modulators, 192
    older adult depression and, 90-91
    practice guidelines, 181-182, 183
    psychotherapy and, 192-194
    readings on, 29, 84, 196-199
    relapse prevention and, 209
    selective serotonin reuptake inhibitors,
        186-188
    serotonin modulators, 191-192
    serotonin-norepinephrine reuptake inhibitor,
        190-191

suicide risk and, 146, 149, 185
  tetracyclics, 190
  theoretical basis for, 25-26
  tricyclics, 185-186
Positive reinforcement, 40-41
Post-partum depression, 23
Practice guidelines, 218-220
  adolescent depression, 61-62
  adult depression, 81-82
  cardiovascular disease/depression, 124-125
  childhood depression, 46-47
  dementia/depression, 131-133
  interpersonal psychotherapy, 168
  interpersonal relationships, dysfunctional,
    111-113
  major depressive disorder, 15-16
  older adult depression, 95-96
  pharmacotherapy, 181-182, 194-195, 196
  psychotherapy, 174-176, 177
  readings on, 221-222
  relapse prevention, 210
  suicide risk, 151-153, 154
Problem-solving therapy, 41, 110, 168-169, 208
Prozac, 187
Psychiatric disorders. *See* Comorbid conditions
Psychodynamic therapy, 173-174
Psychoeducational intervention, 58
Psychotherapeutic theory:
  behavior therapy, 25
  cognitive behavior therapy and, 19-22
  interpersonal psychotherapy, 22-24
  pharmacotherapy, 25-26
  readings on, 27-30
Psychotherapy:
  adolescent depression and, 63-64
  adult depression and, 73-75, 83
  anxiety disorders and, 104-105
  behavior therapy, 171-172
  cancer patients and, 126, 127-129
  cardiovascular disease and, 122-123
  case study, 159-161
  challenges in, 217-218
  clinical guidelines, 174-176, 218-220
  coping skills training, 173
  dysthymic disorder and, 79
  family/systems therapy, 172-173
  marital therapies, 172
  outcome case study, 214-217
  pharmacotherapy and, 192-194, 197
  problem-solving therapy, 171

psychodynamic therapy, 173-174
  readings on, 177-179, 221-222
  suicide risk and, 148-149
  supervision of, 178
  See also Cognitive behavior therapy;
    Interpersonal psychotherapy;
    Skill-training interventions

Questionnaires, 11-12, 72

Recovery, 14
Recurrence, 14
Relapse, 14, 20, 77
Relapse prevention, 13-14
  adult depression and, 69, 77-78, 80,
    82-83
  alcohol abuse and, 108
  booster sessions and, 209-210
  case study, 200-203
  chronic health problems and, 120
  clinical guidelines, 210
  combination therapies, 207
  coping strategies, active/passive, 205
  life-long adjustments, 208
  pharmacotherapy, long-term, 209
  readings on, 211-213
  relapse risk factors, 203-206
  scar hypothesis, 204
  self-coping and, 206-207
  skill-oriented psychotherapies, 208
Religious beliefs, 94, 97
Remeron, 192
Research studies:
  adolescent depression, 64-65
  adult depression, 84
  alcohol abuse, 116
  anxiety disorder, 115, 116
  cancer, 136
  cardiovascular disease, 136
  childhood depression, 50
  chronic health problems, 136
  dementia, 135
  interpersonal relationships, 115
  major depressive disorders, 17-18
  older adult depression, 98
  psychotherapeutic practice,
    178-179
  psychotherapeutic theory, 29-30
  relapse prevention, 212-213
  suicide risk, 155

Role disputes/transitions, 24, 169-170
Rule-out symptoms, 7, 71, 73

San Diego Suicide Study, 107
Scar hypothesis, 204
Schizoaffective disorder, 71, 141
Selective abstraction, 20-21
Selective serotonin reuptake inhibitors (SSRIs),
        186-188
Self-coping, 78, 206-207
Serotonin, 25
Serzone, 191
Sinequan, 185
Skill-training interventions, 39-40
    adolescent depression and, 57-58, 64
    childhood depression and, 39-43
    clinical application of, 42
    components of, 40-41
    group format in, 173
    prevention programs and, 42-43
    problem-solving therapy and, 173
    readings on, 49
    relapse prevention and, 208
    social skills training, 105
Sleep disturbance, 142
Social isolation, 95, 97, 108
Somatic symptoms, 9
Structured Clinical Interview for DSM-IV Axis I
        Disorders, Clinician Version
        (SCID-I), 11
Studies. See Research studies
Substance abuse, 10, 60, 76, 107, 141
Suicide risk:
    adolescents and, 60, 63
    alcoholism and, 107
    assessment of, 144-146, 178
    case study, 137-139
    clinical guidelines, 151-153
    combination therapy and, 146-147, 148
    crisis intervention, 150-151, 154, 155
    demographic factors in, 143-144

    dysfunctional relationships and, 110
    electro-convulsive therapy and, 147-148
    ethical issues and, 149-150
    ethnicity and, 140, 143
    gender and, 139, 140, 143
    hospitalization and, 145, 147, 148-149
    interventions for, 75
    interview, role of, 12-13
    no-suicide contract, 146, 147 (table)
    pharmacotherapy, 146, 149, 185, 198
    prevalence of, 139-140
    psychotherapy and, 148-149
    readings on, 154-155
    risk factors, 140-144, 153
    screening questionnaire for, 72
    treatments for, 146-149, 150-151
Supplemental therapies, 93, 97, 105
Surnotil, 185

Tetracyclic antidepressants, 190
Therapy. See Psychotherapeutic theory;
        Psychotherapy; Treatments
Thinking. See Dysfunctional thinking
Tofranil, 185
Treatments:
    anxiety disorders, 104-105
    challenges in, 217-218
    childhood depression, 39-45
    clinical guidelines, 218-220
    combined therapies, 93, 97, 105, 192-194, 197
    dysfunctional thinking and, 20
    See also Pharmacotherapy; Psychotherapeutic
        theory; Psychotherapy
Tricyclic antidepressants, 185-186

Vivactil, 185

Wellbutrin, 190

Zoloft, 187

About the Authors

Steven Richards is Professor of Psychology at Texas Tech University. He has also served as Department Chair, Counseling Program Director, Psychology Clinic Director, and Introductory Psychology Course Director at Texas Tech. Before his appointment at Texas Tech, he was on the faculty at Syracuse University and the University of Missouri-Columbia. He served as Director of the Clinical Psychology Program at Syracuse and as Associate Department Chair and Psychology Clinic Director at Missouri. His research interests include depression, health psychology, and stress and coping. He has authored approximately 50 publications on these topics and related areas. He has served as editor of the Society of Behavioral Medicine's newsletter Outlook, on the editorial boards of five journals, as an ad hoc reviewer for about 30 journals, and as a principal investigator on two grants from the National Institute of Mental Health. He earned his PhD in clinical psychology from the American Psychological Association (APA)-accredited program at the State University of New York-Stony Brook.

Michael G. Perri is Research Foundation Professor of Clinical and Health Psychology in the Health Science Center at the University of Florida. He has also served as Area Head for Health Psychology and as Director of the Psychology Internship Program at Florida. Before his appointment at Florida, he was on the faculty at Fairleigh Dickinson University, Indiana University, and the University of Rochester. His research interests include depression, obesity, and health psychology. He has authored more than 100 publications on these topics and related areas. He has served on the editorial boards of nine journals and national reporting groups, as an ad hoc reviewer for about 20 journals, and as a principal investigator or co-principal investigator on nine grants from the National Institutes of Health and other federal agencies. The American Board of Professional Psychology (ABPP) has certified him in clinical psychology. He earned his PhD in clinical psychology from the APA-accredited program at the University of Missouri-Columbia.